D1257776

MATH 5

A TEACHING TEXTBOOK

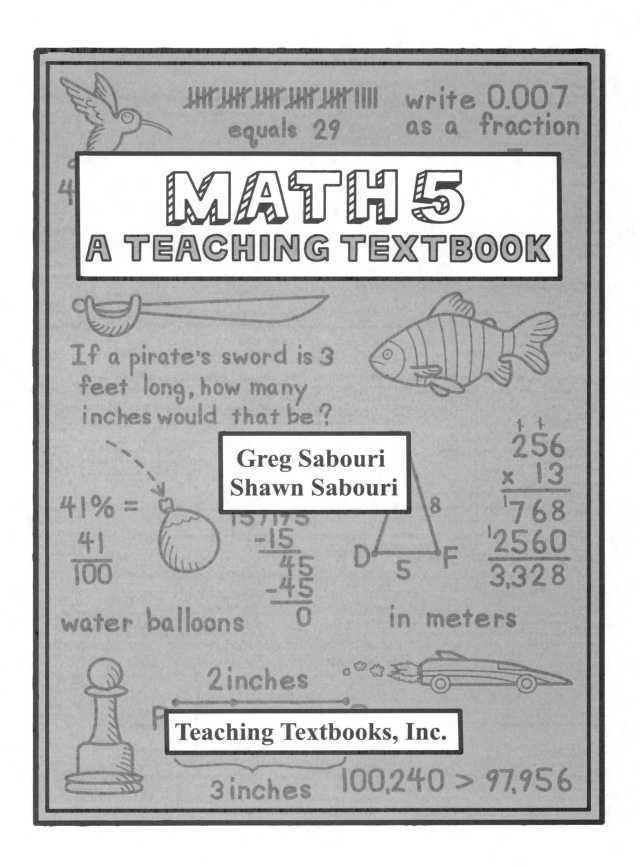

Math 5: A Teaching Textbook™
First Edition
Greg Sabouri and Shawn Sabouri

Copyright © 2007 by Teaching Textbooks, Inc.

All rights reserved.
No part of this publication may be reproduced,
stored in a retrieval system, or transmitted in any
form or by any means, electronic, mechanical,
photocopying, recording, or otherwise, without
the prior written permission of the publisher.

Printed in the United States of America.

ISBN: 978-0-9797265-4-5

Teaching Textbooks, Inc.
P. O. Box 60529
Oklahoma City, OK 73146
www.teachingtextbooks.com

Acknowledgements

The authors would like to thank the following individuals for their invaluable contributions to this product: Justin Briggs, Yen Soon Low, Eric Sandhop, Jared Weingartner, and Cacey Wells.

Table of Contents

A Letter to Homeschooling Parents

Dear Homeschooling Parents,

The Math 5 Teaching Textbook™ is a technologically-advanced, basic math curriculum designed specifically for homeschoolers. Let us tell you about it.

Textbook and Teacher Combined

Unlike traditional classroom textbooks, which are meant to be used only with the help of a teacher, the Math 5 Teaching Textbook™ is both a textbook and a teacher combined into one. Each lesson includes an engaging 5-10 minute interactive lecture (on CD) and a print summary of the lecture that reinforces the key concepts in a concise, easy-to-digest style.

Automated Grading and Audiovisual Solutions

In addition to the lectures and summaries, the CDs have a built-in, digital gradebook that grades every problem as soon as the student enters his or her answer. When students get a problem wrong, they can choose to watch a step-by-step audiovisual solution to that problem. Together, the gradebook and the step-by-step solutions free homeschool parents from some of their administrative and teaching responsibilities so they can spend more time with younger-age children who require direct assistance. For students, the instant feedback on each problem makes using the program feel just like working with a friendly, one-on-one tutor.

High-Tech but Easy-to-Use

The Math 5 CDs can be installed in three easy steps and registration is done automatically online (or with a toll-free number if you don't have internet access). There's no long, complicated instruction manual to wade through. Once installed, the CDs are as easy to use as a videotape. You just select the lecture or problem you want by clicking. Then you can control the presentation with simple play, pause, fast-forward, and rewind buttons on the bottom of the screen.

Fun and Friendly Presentation

Parents love the Math 5 Teaching Textbook™ primarily because it can be done by students independently, but if you ask students what makes the Math 5 special, they almost always say the same thing: *It's more fun*. Students love the easy-to-understand, interactive lectures, the clever animation and sound effects, and the often hilarious illustrations. They like the real-world examples too. These show students that the techniques they're learning have practical value. Finally, students appreciate the review method, which builds their confidence by helping them to retain what they learn.

Thank you for your purchase of the Math 5 Teaching Textbook™ and for the opportunity to serve you and your family's educational needs.

Greg Sabouri and Shawn Sabouri

Key Product Features

Practice Problems

The practice problems are not required. They are additional examples to help the student with the problem set. The gradebook indicates whether a student has done the practice problems and answered them correctly, but the student's performance on these problems does not affect their total score.

Each of the five practice problems is labeled with a letter (**a**, **b**, **c**, **d**, or **e**). The practice problems are similar to the problems in the graded assignment that are labeled with the same letters. So if a student is having trouble with number 16 and it is labeled **b**, he/she can see how a very similar problem was solved by referring to practice problem b. Usually, the hardest problems have a practice problem to match them. Therefore, the practice problems provide students with models for solving the toughest problems in each problem set.

Hints and Buddies

Some of the tougher problems also come with a short audio hint. The hints are delivered by one of the 18 different animated characters or "buddies" that sit atop the lesson box. The student can listen to a hint by just clicking on the hint sign that appears above the lesson box.

Buddies will even cheer the student on when he/she gives a correct answer, but the buddy sounds can be turned off at any time by clicking on the buddy sound button that appears in the lower left of the screen. Students may also change their buddy by clicking on it (whenever the buddy is not delivering a hint).

Second Chance Option

When students get a problem wrong they are asked if they would like to try again. If the student chooses not to enter a second answer, he/she will be shown the correct answer and the grade for that problem will be final. If the student tries the problem again and gets it right, his/her first answer will not be counted, but the gradebook will show that it took the student two times to get the correct answer. If the student chooses the second chance option but never enters a second answer, the gradebook will show that he/she has attempted the problem, but it will not assign a score for that problem until a second answer has been given.

Gradebook

The gradebook provides many benefits for parents. First, it automatically grades every answer the student enters, including all practice problems, assigned problems, and quiz problems. Second, it calculates the percentage that the student got right on each assignment and quiz. (Since practice problems are optional these are not included in the final percentage.) Third, it shows the number of attempts the student made on each problem. Fourth, it tells whether the student watched the step-by-step solution to a problem. This last measure is very important. Ideally, students should watch the step-by-step solution to every problem they miss.

Highlighted Text

The purpose of the highlighting in the workbook is to emphasize the most important points in a lesson. This improves reading comprehension and makes it easier for students to go back and review material that has already been covered. That can be particularly helpful with this book, since every problem set uses the review method. Also, students with vision and/or reading problems may want to read only the highlighted text (instead of the entire written summary) after they finish watching each lecture.

Suggestions on How to Use the Product

As a homeschooler, you already know the benefits of flexibility. That's why you should feel free to adapt this powerful and versatile product to the specific needs of your home school. However, many families have asked us to suggest the "best" way to use the Math 5 Teaching Textbook™. So here goes.

How to "Best" Use the Math 5 Teaching Textbook™

1) Watch the CD lecture.

2) Read the summary of the lecture in the consumable workbook.

3) Work each of the five practice problems in the workbook. Be sure to enter each answer in the computer immediately after finishing each problem. If the answer is incorrect, try it again. If the second answer is incorrect, watch the step-by-step solution.

4) Work each problem in the problem set in the workbook, entering each answer in the computer immediately after finishing a problem. If the answer is incorrect, try it again. If the second answer is incorrect, watch the step-by-step solution.

5) Review the score for that lesson in the gradebook (student and parent).

Lesson 1—Number Patterns

Math is all about numbers, some of which have special names. Here's an example.

1, 2, 3, …
Counting Numbers

These are called **counting numbers** because you count with them. The three dots at the end of the 3 are just a way to show that the numbers keep going. Numbers that have a pattern are called a **sequence**. The sequence of counting numbers goes up by 1 every time.

When we add the number 0 to the counting numbers, we get another sequence called the **whole numbers**.

0, 1, 2, 3, …
Whole Numbers

Some sequences actually skip certain numbers. For example, look at this sequence called the **even numbers**.

0, 2, 4, 6, 8, …
Even Numbers

The even numbers start at 0 and skip every other number. Fortunately, you can tell whether a number is even just by looking at the last digit—the ones digit. If the number has a ones digit of 0, 2, 4, 6, or 8, then the number has to be even. For instance, 3,276 is an even number because the number in the ones place is 6.

Another important sequence is the **odd numbers**. The odd numbers start at 1 and skip every other number.

1, 3, 5, 7, 9, …
Odd Numbers

You can tell if a number is odd by looking at the ones digit. If the ones digit is a 1, 3, 5, 7, or 9, the number has to be odd. Actually, every whole number is either even or odd. That means that if a whole number isn't even, then it has to be odd. Or if it isn't odd, then it has to be even.

There are lots of other sequences that we didn't talk about, and on some sequences, it can be hard to figure out the pattern. Here's an example.

0, 4, 8, 12, …

See, the pattern here is that each number increases by 4. That means the number after 12 is 16, because 16 is 4 greater than 12.

Practice 1

    a.   Tell whether 546 is an odd or even number. _____

    b.   Tell whether 287 is an odd or even number. _____

    c.   What is the next odd number after 17? _____

    d.   Give the next number in this sequence: 2, 6, 10… _____

    e.   Give the fifth number in this sequence: 5, 10, 15… _____

Problem Set 1

Tell whether each sentence below is True or False.

    1.   If a number has a ones digit of 1, 3, 5, 7, or 9 then it has to be even. _____

    2.   The sequence of whole numbers begins with zero. _____

Tell whether each number below is odd or even.

    3. 21 _____   **4.** 32 _____

    5. 48 _____   **(a) 6.** 194 _____

    7. 111 _____   **8.** 523 _____

    9. 452 _____   **(b) 10.** 119 _____

    11. 205 _____   **12.** 864 _____

Answer each question below.

(c) 13.   What is the next odd number after 11? _____

   14.   What is the next even number after 14? _____

   15.   What is the next odd number after 19? _____

   16.   What is the next even number after 18? _____

Give the next number in each of the sequences below.

   17.   1, 3, 5 … _____

(d) 18.   8, 11, 14… _____

Give the fifth number in each of the sequences below.

(e) 19.   3, 6, 9… _____

   20.   4, 7, 10… _____

Lesson 2—The Way Numbers Work

The symbols 0, 1, 2, 3, 4, 5, 6, 7, 8, and 9 are all called **digits**. We use these ten digits to write all of our numbers. Here's an example.

eight hundred thirty-six

836

The 8 stands for eight hundreds, the 3 stands for three tens, and the 6 stands for six ones.

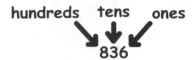

So 836 really means 8 hundreds + 3 tens + 6 ones. That's the way our number system works, and the technical name for it is the **place value system**, which just means that the value of a digit depends on its place. Here's another number.

six thousand, five hundred forty-two

6,542

This time we needed four digits. The 2 stands for ones because it's in the ones place. Four is in the tens place, so it stands for tens. The 5 has to stand for hundreds, since it's in the hundreds place, and the 6 is in the thousands place, so there have to be six thousands. Also, notice that there's a comma after the 6. That's because there's a rule that says you should put in a comma after every 3 digits starting from the right. Not everyone puts commas, but you *should* because it makes the number easier to read. Here's another example.

twenty-four thousand, seven hundred thirty-nine

24,739

Since the fifth digit always stands for ten thousands, the 2 is in the ten thousands place. If we were to put in one more digit to the left of the 2, it would be in the hundred thousands place. Here's what the number would look like then.

six hundred twenty-four thousand, seven hundred thirty-nine

624,739

Some numbers are hard to write. Here's one like that.

three hundred two

302

The 2 stands for ones and the 3 stands for hundreds, but since three hundred two doesn't have any tens, we had to put a zero in the tens place. We always use zero for the empty spots. Here's another example.

eighteen thousand, thirty-six

18,036

This time, we had to put a zero in the hundreds place since there are no hundreds, but the comma still goes after the third digit from the right because the 0 still counts as a digit.

Practice 2

a. Tell what the highlighted digit stands for in the number 64,875. _____

    A. ones   B. tens   C. hundreds
    D. thousands   E. ten thousands   F. hundred thousands

b. Tell which digit is in the hundred thousands place in 329,674. _____

c. Write the number four hundred fifteen thousand, two hundred fifty-seven using digits.
_____

d. Write the number 6 hundreds + 5 ones using digits. _____

e. Give the fifth number in this sequence: 3, 7, 11 … _____

Problem Set 2

Tell whether each sentence below is True or False.

1. The place value system means that the value of a digit depends on its place. _____

2. When writing numbers with digits, you're supposed to put a comma after every third digit, starting from the right. _____

Tell whether each number below is odd or even.

3. 7,634 _____

4. 8,439 _____

Answer each question below.

5. What is the next even number after 22? _____

6. What is the next odd number after 27? _____

Tell what each of the highlighted digits stands for in the numbers below.

7. 3,574

    A. ones   B. tens   C. hundreds
    D. thousands   E. ten thousands   F. hundred thousands

(a) 8. 28,643

    A. ones   B. tens   C. hundreds
    D. thousands   E. ten thousands   F. hundred thousands

Give the next number in each of the sequences below.

9. 5, 7, 9… _____

10. 6, 9, 12 … _____

11. 13, 15, 17 … _____

Answer each question below.

12. Which digit is in the tens place in 5,182? _____

(b) 13. Which digit is in the hundred thousands place in 796,104? _____

Put a comma where it belongs in each number below.

14. 42768 _____

15. 947012 _____

Write each number below using digits.

16.   8 hundreds + 3 tens + 2 ones _____

17.   three thousand, one hundred seventy-four _____

(c) 18.   six hundred eighteen thousand, six hundred thirty-five _____

(d) 19.   4 hundreds + 3 ones _____

Answer the question below.

(e) 20.   Give the fifth number in this sequence: 1, 5, 9 … _____

Lesson 3—Numbers and Words

There are rules for how to write a number in words. The first one is that you shouldn't use the word *and* when saying or writing a number. This means it's wrong to say two hundred *and* eighty-six; it should just be two hundred eighty-six.

Here's a number written in words and with symbols.

4,791
four thousand, seven hundred ninety-one

Notice that in both versions, the comma is between the thousands and hundreds places. That's because the second rule is that when a number is written in words, the commas go in the same places as when the number is written with digits. Here's an even tougher example.

387,465
three hundred eighty-seven thousand, four hundred sixty-five

Notice that here we wrote eighty-seven and sixty-five with hyphens in the middle. That's because the final rule says you should use hyphens in two-word numbers, even those that are a part of larger numbers. Here's one more example with hyphens.

48,273
forty-eight thousand, two hundred seventy-three

Again, we put a hyphen in forty-eight and seventy-three. It turns out that all of the hyphenated numbers are between 21 and 99. Smaller numbers like nineteen and twelve don't need hyphens because they're just a single word.

Practice 3

a. Which digit is in the ten thousands place in 925,347? _____

b. Write the number nine thousand, six hundred five using digits. _____

c. Give the next number in this sequence: 1, 7, 13 … _____

For each problem below, choose the group of words that belongs in the blank.

    d. 86,234   eighty-six thousand, _____

        A. thirty-four   B. two hundred thirty-four   C. two hundred thirty
        D. two hundred four   E. two hundred and thirty-four

    e. 216,198   _____, one hundred ninety-eight

        A. two hundred sixteen   B. two hundred sixteen thousand
        C. two hundred thousand   D. two hundred and sixteen thousand
        E. two hundred thousand sixteen

Problem Set 3

Tell whether each sentence below is True or False.

    1. The word "and" should never be used when writing a number, but it should be used when saying a number. _____

    2. When a number is written in words, you should put a comma in the same places that you do when writing the number with digits. _____

Tell what each of the highlighted digits stands for in the numbers below.

    3. 4,8**9**1

        A. ones   B. tens   C. hundreds
        D. thousands   E. ten thousands   F. hundred thousands

    4. 7**1**,452

        A. ones   B. tens   C. hundreds
        D. thousands   E. ten thousands   F. hundred thousands

Tell whether each number below is odd or even.

    5. 6,357 _____   **6.** 1,632 _____

Answer each question below.

(a) 7. Which digit is in the ten thousands place in 561,394? _____

8. Which digit is in the hundred thousands place in 258,437? _____

Put a comma in the proper place in each number below.

9. 9736 _____

10. 854901 _____

Write each number below using digits.

11. 8 thousands + 6 hundreds + 2 tens + 7 ones _____

12. fourteen thousand, one hundred seventeen _____

(b) 13. seven thousand, eight hundred two _____

Give the next number in each of the sequences below.

(c) 14. 7, 14, 21 … _____   **15.** 2, 11, 20 … _____

For each problem below, choose the group of words that belongs in the blank.

16. 4,268   four thousand, two hundred _____

      A. sixty-eight   B. sixty eight   C. sixty eight hundred
      D. and sixty eight   E. and sixty-eight

17. 53,216   fifty-three thousand, _____ sixteen

      A. and two hundred   B. two hundred   C. three thousand
      D. two thousand   E. twenty

18. 98,345 _____, three hundred forty-five

    A. ninety thousand   B. nine thousand   C. ninety eight thousand
    D. eight thousand   E. ninety-eight thousand

(d) 19. 47,326   forty-seven thousand, _____

    A. twenty-six   B. three hundred six   C. three hundred twenty-six
    D. three hundred twenty   E. three hundred and twenty-six

(e) 20. 275,164 _____, one hundred sixty-four

    A. seventy-five   B. two hundred seventy five
    C. two hundred thousand   D. two hundred seventy-five thousand
    E. two hundred and seventy-five thousand

Lesson 4—Millions

Numbers can be a lot bigger than hundred thousands. Here's an example

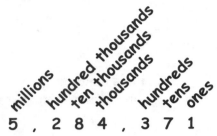

$$5 \, , \, 2 \; 8 \; 4 \, , \, 3 \; 7 \; 1$$

five million, two hundred eighty-four thousand, three hundred seventy-one

The digit 5 is in the *millions* place, and there are two commas since there has to be a comma after every third digit starting from the right. Also, notice that the commas separate hundreds from thousands and thousands from millions, and in the written version of the number, eighty-four and seventy-one have hyphens and the word *and* doesn't appear.

After the millions place comes the ten millions. Here's a number in the ten millions.

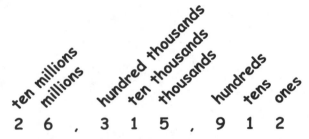

$$2 \; 6 \, , \, 3 \; 1 \; 5 \, , \, 9 \; 1 \; 2$$

twenty-six million, three hundred fifteen thousand, nine hundred twelve

This number also has a comma after every third digit from the right.

After ten millions comes hundred millions. Here's a number that goes all the way out to the hundred millions.

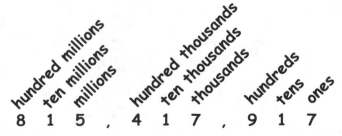

$$8 \; 1 \; 5 \, , \, 4 \; 1 \; 7 \, , \, 9 \; 1 \; 7$$

eight hundred fifteen million, four hundred seventeen thousand,
nine hundred seventeen

A number in the hundred millions actually has 9 digits, but that isn't enough to have to add a third comma. And notice, again, that the commas separate hundreds from thousands and thousands from millions in both the written version and the version with digits.

Practice 4

a. Give the next number in this sequence: 14, 22, 30 … _____

b. Write the number thirty-six million, two hundred fifteen thousand, thirty-seven using digits. _____

c. Write the number one hundred fourteen million, five hundred eighty-three thousand, four hundred seventy-six using digits. _____

For each problem below, choose the group of words that belongs in the blank.

d. 27,568,934   twenty-seven million, five hundred sixty-eight thousand, _____

    A. nine hundred thirty four   B. nine hundred and thirty-four
    C. nine hundred thirty-four   D. and nine hundred thirty-four
    E. and nine hundred thirty four

e. 361,579,842   _____, five hundred seventy-nine thousand, eight hundred forty-two

    A. three hundred sixty one million   B. three hundred and sixty one million
    C. three hundred and sixty-one million   D. and three hundred sixty-one million
    E. three hundred sixty-one million

Problem Set 4

Tell whether each sentence below is True or False.

1. The next place after the millions place is the ten millions place. _____

2. The next place after the ten millions place is the hundred millions place. _____

Give the next number in each of the sequences below.

    3. 9, 15, 21 … _____

(a) 4. 2, 7, 12 … _____

Tell what each of the highlighted digits stands for in the numbers below.

    5. 6,814,985

        A. ones   B. hundreds   C. thousands
        D. ten thousands   E. hundred thousands   F. millions

    6. 29,743,562

        A. thousands   B. ten thousands   C. hundred thousands
        D. millions   E. ten millions   F. hundred millions

Put a comma in the proper place in each number below.

    7. 589734 _____

    8. 8762154 _____

Answer each question below.

    9. Which digit is in the millions place in 893,641,257? _____

    10. Which digit is in the ten millions place in 127,034,185? _____

Tell whether each number below is odd or even.

    11. 56,978 _____   **12.** 86,147 _____

Write each number below using digits.

    13. two million, one hundred thirty-four thousand, six hundred fifty-eight _____

(b) 14. sixty-one million, seven hundred fourteen thousand, fifty-two _____

(c) 15. two hundred sixteen million, nine hundred forty-five thousand, six hundred thirty-eight

    _____

For each problem below, choose the group of words that belongs in the blank(s).

    16. 468,572   four hundred sixty-eight _____, five hundred _____ .

        A. thousand; and seventy-two   B. thousand; seventy-two
        C. thousand; and seventy two   D. thousand; seventy two
        E. million; seventy-two

    17. 75,438,619   _____, four hundred thirty-eight thousand, six hundred nineteen

        A. seventy five million   B. seventy-five thousand
        C. seventy-five million   D. seventy-five billion
        E. seven hundred five million

    18. 19,485,214   nineteen million, _____, two hundred fourteen

        A. four hundred eighty five thousand   B. four hundred eighty-five
        C. four hundred eighty-five thousand   D. four and eighty-five thousand
        E. four hundred and eighty-five thousand

(d) 19. 32,458,796   thirty-two million, four hundred fifty-eight thousand, _____

        A. seven hundred ninety-six   B. seven hundred ninety six
        C. and seven hundred ninety-six   D. and seven hundred ninety six
        E. seven hundred and ninety-six

(e) 20. 627,452,893 _____, four hundred fifty-two thousand, eight hundred ninety-three

    A. six hundred twenty seven million   B. six hundred and twenty-seven
    C. six hundred twenty-seven million   D. six and twenty-seven million
    E. six hundred and twenty-seven million

Lesson 5—Greater Than, Less Than

Mathematicians use special symbols to show that one number is bigger than another. For example, here's how to show that 15 is bigger than 12.

$$15 > 12$$

This means that 15 *is greater than* 12. The symbol in the middle is called an **inequality sign**. The pointed end of the sign is always towards the smaller number, and the open end is always towards the larger number, which means you can actually flip the sign around like this.

$$12 < 15$$

So when comparing two numbers, the numbers could be equal, which would mean you'd need to put an equals sign between them, or the numbers could be unequal, which would mean you'd need to put a < or > sign between them, depending on which number is bigger.

Comparing small numbers isn't too difficult, but comparing big numbers can be a lot harder. Here's an example.

$$101,111 > 99,999$$

It might seem like the number on the left is smaller because it just has 0s and 1s and the number on the right has all 9s. But actually, the only way to tell which number is bigger is to count the digits. Since the number on the left has 6 digits, and the one on the right has 5, the one on the left has to be greater. If the two numbers had the same number of digits, you'd have to start on the left and compare the digits one at a time. Here's an example.

$$3,521 > 3,496$$

The table below summarizes the rules for comparing two numbers.

To Compare Two Numbers

1.	Count the digits. The number with more digits is always greater.
2.	If the numbers have the same number of digits, compare each digit until you find one that's bigger than the other. The one with the bigger digit is the greater number.

Practice 5

a. Tell whether a <, >, or = should go between 523,417 _____ 532,417.

b. Rearrange the digits in the number 438,705 to make it as large as possible. _____

c. Write the following numbers in order from least to greatest: 958; 989; 948. _____

d. What is the biggest two digit number? _____

e. Choose the group of words that belongs in the blank.

342,279,384 _____, two hundred seventy-nine thousand, three hundred eighty-four

A. three hundred forty two million   B. three hundred forty two
C. three hundred forty-two million   D. three hundred and forty two
E. three hundred and forty-two million

Problem Set 5

Tell whether each sentence below is True or False.

1. With inequality signs, the open end should always open toward the smaller number. _____

2. With inequality signs, the pointed end should always point to the greater number. _____

Tell whether a <, >, or = should go between each pair of numbers below.

3. 93,939 _____ 9,393   **(a) 4.** 647,985 _____ 674,985

5. 47,931 _____ 47,913

Answer each question below.

6. Give the next number in this sequence: 11, 17, 23 … _____

7. Put commas where they belong in 83561704. _____

8. Tell whether 14,768 is odd or even. _____

Rearrange the digits in each number below to make the numbers as large as possible.

9. 4, 367 _____   **(b) 10.** 309,856 _____

Write the following numbers in order from least to greatest.

11. 956; 1,312; 965 _____

(c) 12. 602; 632; 613 _____

Answer each question below.

(d) 13. What is the biggest three digit number? _____

14. Which digit is in the ten thousands place in 23,907? _____

15. What does the highlighted digit in 84,561,607 stand for? _____

    A. hundreds   B. thousands   C. ten thousands
    D. hundred thousands   E. millions   F. ten millions

Write each number below using digits.

16. ninety-three million, six hundred five thousand, seven hundred eighteen _____

17. one hundred thirty-four million, eight hundred three thousand, five hundred seventeen
    _____

For each problem below, choose the group of words that belongs in the blank.

18. 9,274,358   nine million, _____, three hundred fifty-eight

   A. two hundred and seventy four thousand   B. two hundred seventy four
   C. and two hundred seventy-four thousand   D. two hundred seventy-four
   E. two hundred seventy-four thousand

19. 46,325,159   forty-six million, three hundred twenty-five thousand, _____

   A. one hundred and fifty-nine   B. and one hundred fifty nine
   C. and one hundred and fifty-nine   D. one hundred fifty-nine
   E. and one hundred fifty-nine

(e) 20. 271,345,867   _____, three hundred forty-five thousand, eight hundred sixty-seven

   A. two hundred seventy-one million   B. two hundred and seventy-one
   C. two hundred seventy million   D. two and seventy-one million
   E. two hundred and seventy-one million

Lesson 6—Addition Basics

Adding is probably the most basic thing you do in math, but there are a few technical details about addition that you may not know or may not remember. For example, numbers that are added are called **addends**.

$$4 \longleftarrow \text{The numbers being}$$
$$\underline{+\ 5} \longleftarrow \text{added are addends.}$$

So the addends are 4 and 5. The answer to an addition problem is called the **sum**, and since the answer to this problem is 9, we can say the sum of 4 plus 5 is 9.

$$
\begin{array}{r}
4 \\
+\ 5 \\
\hline
9
\end{array}
\Bigg\}
\begin{array}{l}
\text{The answer to an} \\
\text{addition problem is} \\
\text{called the sum.}
\end{array}
$$

Most people write addition problems vertically (up and down) like we did above, but they can be written horizontally too.

$$5 + 4 = 9$$

Another thing you should know is that two numbers can be added in any order. So $4+5$ is the same as $5+4$; both equal 9.

$$5 + 4 = 9 \qquad \text{Numbers can be}$$
$$4 + 5 = 9 \qquad \text{added in any order.}$$

The formal name for this is the **commutative property of addition**, and it just means we can add two numbers in any order and the answer will stay the same. Another important property is called the **identity property of addition**. This means that if we add zero to a number, the number doesn't change.

$$8 + 0 = 8 \qquad \text{Adding zero to a number}$$
$$0 + 6 = 6 \qquad \text{doesn't change its value.}$$

These rules are very important, but to use addition in real life, you need to know your addition facts, such as $6+7=13$. It's important to have facts like these memorized so you can add quickly.

$$7 + 6 = 13 \qquad \text{Memorize your addition}$$
$$2 + 6 = 8 \qquad \text{facts so you can add quickly.}$$

Practice 6

    a.   Tell whether a <, >, or = should go between 14,356 _____ 14,365.

    b.   Write the following numbers in order from least to greatest: 963; 1,120; 936. _____

    c.   What is the smallest two digit number? _____

    d.   Rearrange the digits in the number 19,837 to make it as large as possible. _____

    e.   Rearrange the digits in the number 134,625 to make it as small as possible. _____

Problem Set 6

Tell whether each sentence below is True or False.

    1.   Numbers that are added are called addends. _____

    2.   The answer to an addition problem is called a sum. _____

    3.   If we add zero to any number, the answer is zero. _____

Add each pair of numbers below.

    4. $\begin{array}{r} 8 \\ + 3 \\ \hline \end{array}$
        5. $\begin{array}{r} 7 \\ + 5 \\ \hline \end{array}$

    6. $\begin{array}{r} 9 \\ + 7 \\ \hline \end{array}$
        7. $\begin{array}{r} 9 \\ + 9 \\ \hline \end{array}$

Tell what the highlighted digit stands for in the number below.

8. 67,312,945

      A. hundreds   B. thousands   C. ten thousands
      D. hundred thousands   E. millions   F. ten millions

Tell whether a <, >, or = should go between each pair of numbers below.

9. 6,543 _____ 6,453   **(a) 10.** 78,997 _____ 78,979.

Answer each question below.

(b) 11. Write the following numbers in order from least to greatest: 943; 1,122; 934.
      _____

12. Which of the following numbers is not odd? 21,367   54,470   25,863 _____

(c) 13. What is the smallest three-digit number? _____

Write each number below using digits.

14. five million, one hundred four thousand, two hundred two _____

15. forty-six million, three hundred fifty thousand, eleven _____

For each problem below, choose the group of words that belongs in the blank.

16. 12,814,135   twelve million, eight hundred fourteen thousand, _____

      A. one hundred and thirty-five   B. one hundred thirty and five
      C. and one hundred thirty-five   D. one hundred thirty five
      E. one hundred thirty-five

17. 15,702,846   fifteen million, _____, eight hundred forty-six

      A. seven hundred and two   B. seven hundred thousand two
      C. seven hundred and two thousand   D. seven thousand and two
      E. seven hundred two thousand

Rearrange the digits in the numbers below to make them as large as possible.

(d) 18.   17,206 _____   **19.**   572,190 _____

(e) 20.   Rearrange the digits in 482,513 to make the number as small as possible. _____

Lesson 7—Subtraction Basics

Unlike addition, subtraction is taking something away. So subtracting 3 apples from 7 apples just means taking 3 apples away from the 7 apples, and we can write this either horizontally or vertically.

$$7-3 \qquad \begin{array}{r} 7 \\ -\ 3 \\ \hline \end{array} \qquad \text{Both of these mean to take 3 away from 7.}$$

The answer to a subtraction problem is called a **difference**, so if we subtract 3 from 7, the difference is 4.

$$\begin{array}{r} 7 \\ -\ 3 \\ \hline 4 \end{array} \qquad \text{The answer to a subtraction problem is called the difference.}$$

You should memorize the answers to simple subtraction problems like this because to use subtraction in real life, you need to be able to calculate really fast. But if you do happen to forget the answer to a subtraction problem, you can actually use the addition facts to figure it out. This works because addition is actually just like subtraction in reverse. For example, if you happen to forget what $9-6$ equals, you can just ask yourself what number added to 6 gives you 9. Since $3+6=9$, the answer has to be 3.

$$\begin{aligned} 9-6 &= ? \qquad \text{Use the addition facts} \\ 3+6 &= 9 \qquad \text{if you forget a subtraction} \\ 9-6 &= 3 \qquad \text{problem.} \end{aligned}$$

Also, since addition and subtraction are closely related, you can use addition to check the answer to a subtraction problem. This works if the subtraction is written horizontally or vertically.

$$\text{subtract} \Big\downarrow \begin{array}{r} 7 \\ -\ 5 \\ \hline 2 \end{array} \Big\uparrow \text{add} \qquad\qquad \begin{array}{c} \text{subtract} \rightarrow \\ 7-5=2 \\ \leftarrow \text{add} \end{array}$$

One more thing to keep in mind about subtraction is that, unlike addition, the order of the numbers matters. Remember, in addition $3+2$ is the same as $2+3$, but $3-2$ isn't the same as $2-3$.

$$3-2 \text{ is not equal to } 2-3 \qquad \begin{array}{l} \text{Order matters} \\ \text{when subtracting.} \end{array}$$

Practice 7

    a.   Tell whether a <, >, or = should go between 634,152 _____ 634,125.

    b.   Write the following numbers in order from least to greatest: 321; 312; 323..
         _____

    c.   Write ninety-four million, five hundred three thousand, one using digits. _____

    d.   Rearrange the digits in the number 367,105 to make it as large as possible. _____

    e.   Rearrange the digits in the number 569,147 to make it as small as possible. _____

Problem Set 7

Tell whether each sentence below is True or False.

    1.   The answer to a subtraction problem is called a sum. _____

    2.   You can use addition to check the answer to a subtraction problem. _____

    3.   You can't change the order of two numbers that are subtracted. _____

Add or subtract each pair of numbers below.

    4. $\begin{array}{r} 7 \\ + 6 \\ \hline \end{array}$
        5. $\begin{array}{r} 5 \\ - 3 \\ \hline \end{array}$

Do each problem below.

    6. Find the difference of 6 and 5.
        7. Find the sum of 8 and 7.

    $\begin{array}{r} - \\ \hline \end{array}$
               $\begin{array}{r} + \\ \hline \end{array}$

8. Find the sum of 8 and 8.   **9.** Find the difference of 9 and 6.

$$+ \underline{\hspace{1.5cm}}$$ $$- \underline{\hspace{1.5cm}}$$

Tell what the highlighted digit stands for in the number below.

10. 190,458,736

A. thousands	B. ten thousands	C. hundred thousands
D. millions	E. ten millions	F. hundred millions

Tell whether a <, >, or = should go between each pair of numbers below.

11. 82,752 _____ 82,152   **(a) 12.** 721,389 _____ 721,398

Answer each question below.

(b) 13. Write the following numbers in order from least to greatest: 825; 822; 831..
_____

(c) 14. Write the number twenty-three million, seven hundred forty thousand, eight using digits. _____

For each problem below, choose the group of words that belongs in the blank.

15. 11,793,142   eleven million, seven hundred ninety-three thousand, _____

A. one hundred and forty-two   B. one hundred forty-two
C. one thousand forty-two   D. and one hundred forty two
E. one hundred forty two

16. 19,874,926   nineteen million, _____, nine hundred twenty-six

A. eight hundred thousand   B. and eight hundred seventy four thousand
C. eight hundred seventy-four   D. eight hundred and seventy-four thousand
E. eight hundred seventy-four thousand

Rearrange the digits in the numbers below to make them as large as possible.

(d) 17.   17,536 _____

18.   142,587 _____

Rearrange the digits in the numbers below to make them as small as possible.

(e) 19.   27,893 _____

20.   496,857 _____

Quiz 1

Tell whether each sentence below is True or False.

1. When a number is written in words, you should put a comma in the same places that you do when writing the number with digits. _____

2. The answer to an addition problem is called a difference. _____

Tell whether each number below is odd or even.

3. 5,424 _____   4. 6,821 _____

Answer each question below.

5. What is the next odd number after 15? _____

6. Which digit is in the hundred thousands place in 610,214? _____

Tell what the highlighted digit stands for in the number below.

7. 120,803,271

    A. thousands   B. ten thousands   C. hundred thousands
    D. millions   E. ten millions   F. hundred millions

Give the next number in each of the sequences below.

8. 7, 9, 11 … _____

9. 4, 10, 16 … _____

Answer the question below.

10. Give the fifth number in this sequence: 3, 8, 13 … _____

Put a comma where it belongs in each number below.

11. 328479 _____

12. 1830264 _____

Write each number below using digits.

13. thirteen million, nine hundred sixty-four thousand, one hundred seventy-two

_____

14. six hundred fifty-seven thousand, five _____

For the problem below, choose the group of words that belongs in the blank.

15. 38,651,763   thirty-eight million, _____, seven hundred sixty-three

    A. six hundred fifty-one   B. six hundred and fifty one thousand
    C. six hundred fifty-one thousand   D. and six hundred and fifty-one thousand
    E. six hundred fifty-one million

Tell whether a <, >, or = should go between each pair of numbers below.

16. 7,560 _____ 7,460   **17.** 43,868 _____ 43,886

Do each problem below.

18. Find the sum of 6 and 9.   **19.** Find the difference of 7 and 3.

$$+ \underline{\quad\quad}$$

$$- \underline{\quad\quad}$$

20. Find the sum of 7 and 7.   **21.** Find the difference of 8 and 5.

$$+ \underline{\quad\quad}$$

$$- \underline{\quad\quad}$$

Answer each question below.

22. Write the following numbers in order from least to greatest: 976; 1,202; 967.

    _____

23. Rearrange the digits in 143,587 to make the number as large as possible. _____

24. Rearrange the digits in 913,284 to make the number as small as possible. _____

Lesson 8—Addition and Subtraction on Paper

To add 2 two-digit numbers on paper, all we have to do is line them up vertically and add the columns. Here's an example.

$$\begin{array}{r} 31 \\ +\ 26 \\ \hline 57 \end{array}$$

Line up the numbers vertically and add the columns.

Since the ones are over the ones and the tens are over the tens, we just added the columns. In the ones column, $1+6$ is 7, so we wrote a 7 underneath. Then in the tens column, $3+2$ is 5, which gave us an overall sum of 57. By the way, we could have also put the 26 on top of the 31 and then added, because we can add numbers in any order, remember?

Subtraction works nearly the same way, but this time we have to make sure that we put the larger number on top. Here's an example.

$$\begin{array}{r} 85 \\ -\ 42 \\ \hline 43 \end{array}$$

Put the larger number on top, line up the columns, and then just subtract.

After we lined up the columns, we just subtracted the columns starting with the ones. Since $5-2$ equals 3, we wrote a 3 underneath. In the tens column, $8-4$ is just 4, so we wrote a 4 on bottom, giving us an overall difference of 43. Here's one more subtraction example.

$$\begin{array}{r} 79 \\ -\ 6 \\ \hline 73 \end{array}$$

Treat the blank space as a zero.

As you can see, we lined up the columns vertically and then subtracted. However, there isn't a digit in the tens place in the bottom number. That's okay, though. All we have to do is treat the empty space like a zero. Since $7-0$ is just 7, we put a 7 underneath, giving us a final answer of 73.

The main thing to remember is that when adding or subtracting on paper, just be sure to put the ones over ones and tens over tens. If you do that, everything should work out fine.

Practice 8

a. Add $77 + 21$ **b.** Subtract $45 - 13$

$$+ \underline{\hspace{2cm}}$$ $$- \underline{\hspace{2cm}}$$

c. Write seventy million, twenty-one thousand, six using digits. _____

d. Write the following numbers in order from least to greatest: 801; 810; 811..
_____

e. Rearrange the digits in the number 517,852 to make it as small as possible. _____

Problem Set 8

Tell whether each sentence below is True or False.

1. When doing a subtraction on paper, we always put the smaller number over the larger number. _____

2. When adding or subtracting numbers on paper, the ones should go over the ones and the tens over the tens. _____

Tell what the highlighted digit stands for in the number below.

3. 254,716,489

     A. thousands   B. ten thousands   C. hundred thousands
     D. millions   E. ten millions   F. hundred millions

For the problem below, choose the group of words that belongs in the blank.

4. 146,129,135 _____, one hundred twenty-nine thousand, one hundred thirty-five

       A. one hundred forty-six   B. one hundred forty-six thousand
       C. forty-six million   D. one hundred forty-six million
       E. one hundred forty six million

Add or subtract each pair of numbers below.

5.
$$\begin{array}{r} 99 \\ -\ 24 \\ \hline \end{array}$$

(a) 6.
$$\begin{array}{r} 23 \\ +\ 36 \\ \hline \end{array}$$

7.
$$\begin{array}{r} 47 \\ -\ 16 \\ \hline \end{array}$$

(b) 8.
$$\begin{array}{r} 28 \\ -\ 12 \\ \hline \end{array}$$

Do each problem below.

9. Find the sum of 66 and 23.

       $$\begin{array}{r} + \quad\quad \\ \hline \end{array}$$

10. Find the difference of 72 and 51.

       $$\begin{array}{r} - \quad\quad \\ \hline \end{array}$$

Write each number below using digits.

11. twenty-four million, nine hundred sixty thousand, seven hundred thirteen _____

(c) 12. forty million, fifty-six thousand, three _____

Tell whether a <, >, or = should go between each pair of numbers below.

13. 3,321 ____ 3,231   14. 26,746 ____ 26,748

Write the following numbers in order from least to greatest.

15. 129; 1,131; 119 _____   **(d) 16.** 678; 687; 679 _____

Rearrange the digits in the numbers below to make them as large as possible.

17. 86,375 _____   **18.** 928,301 _____

19. 301,456 _____

Rearrange the digits in the numbers below to make them as small as possible.

20. 13,296 _____   **21.** 83,465 _____

(e) 22. 175,434 _____

Lesson 9—Surveys and Tally Marks

Adding is really just a fast way to count things. For example, if we knew that there were 14 cars on the first level of a parking garage and 12 on the second, we could find the number of cars on both levels by putting 14 over 12 and then adding the ones and tens columns.

$$\begin{array}{r} 12 \\ + 14 \\ \hline 26 \end{array}$$ Just add the columns.

Adding groups of cars on paper is definitely faster than counting the cars one-by-one, but sometimes we can't add totals on paper. For example, let's say we wanted to know people's opinions on a subject, and we had to ask them one at a time. This is called a **survey**, and when taking a survey, we ask a question and then write down the answer. Since we wouldn't be able to ask everyone in the world a question, the people we did ask would be called our **sample**, which just means part of a group. The group that we took our sample from would be called the **population**. The population could be anything larger than our sample, like the total number of people in a town, a state, a country, or even the world.

One of the best ways to keep track of the answers to a survey is to use **tally marks**. These are little vertical marks that each stand for one. Here are some tally marks, or tallies, as they're sometimes called, for the numbers 1 through 7.

	1 ‖‖‖ 5
	2 ‖‖‖	6
	3 ‖‖‖ || 7
	4

Notice that the number 5 has four vertical marks with a fifth diagonal mark through it. That's the way tallies work; every fifth number is shown with a diagonal, and *after* every fifth number, we start a new set of tallies.

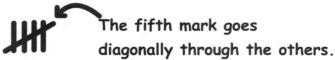

The fifth mark goes diagonally through the others.

Tallies are beneficial for surveys because they prevent us from having to erase a number and write a new one each time somebody answers the question. Also, it's really easy to add up the tallies because they're grouped in 5s. All we have to do is count by 5s and then count any additional tallies that aren't in a full group of five at the end.

Practice 9

    a.   Tell what number these tally marks represent. _____

    b.   Tell what number these tally marks represent. _____

    c.   Write twenty million, six thousand, eight using digits. _____

    d.   Write the following numbers in order from least to greatest: 347; 344; 343 _____

    e.   Rearrange the digits in the number 653,138 to make it as small as possible. _____

Problem Set 9

Tell whether each sentence below is True or False.

    1.   A sample is a group of people who participate in a survey. _____

    2.   With tally marks, every fifth number is shown with a diagonal. _____

    3.   Tally marks make it easy to add up the results of a survey. _____

Add or subtract each pair of numbers below.

    4. $73 - 42$ **5.** $53 + 36$ **6.** $65 - 13$

          − _____   + _____   − _____

For each problem below, tell what number the tally marks represent.

7. ||| **8.** |||| **(a) 9.**

_____   _____   _____

10. ~~||||~~ ||| **(b) 11.** ~~||||~~ ~~||||~~ |

_____   _____

12. ~~||||~~ ~~||||~~ ~~||||~~ ||

_____

Write each number below using digits.

13. one hundred fourteen million, eight hundred seventy thousand, five hundred nine
_____

(c) 14. ten million, seven thousand, four _____

Write the following numbers in order from least to greatest.

15. 175; 168; 186 _____

(d) 16. 213; 214; 211 _____

Tell what the highlighted digit stands for in the number below.

17. 31,528,067

     A. thousands   B. ten thousands   C. hundred thousands
     D. millions   E. ten millions   F. hundred millions

Choose the group of words that belongs in the blank.

18. 63,407,890 _____, four hundred seven thousand, eight hundred ninety

    A. sixty three million   B. sixty-three hundred thousand
    C. sixty-three   D. sixty-three million
    E. sixty three thousand

Rearrange the digits in each number to make them as large as possible.

19. 164,235 _____   20. 826,593 _____

Rearrange the digits in each number to make them as small as possible.

(e) 21. 973,475 _____   22. 839,741 _____

Lesson 10—Rounding and Estimating with Two-Digit Numbers

Sometimes we may not need to know the exact answer to a problem. In a case like that, the first thing to do is to **round** the numbers. Rounding a number makes it end in zero. Here's an example.

$$41 \longrightarrow 40 \qquad \text{Rounding to the nearest ten.}$$

See, we rounded 41 to the nearest ten, which just means we looked for the closest number that has a zero in the ones place.

Here's how to use rounding to find a number that's close to the sum of 23 and 34.

$$
\begin{array}{c}
23 + 34 \\
\downarrow \quad \downarrow \\
20 + 30 = 50 \\
2 + 3 = 5
\end{array}
\qquad
\begin{array}{l}
\text{Round the numbers} \\
\text{and then add in your} \\
\text{head.}
\end{array}
$$

As you can see, we rounded 23 to 20 and 34 to 30 before adding. Notice that when both numbers end in 0, they're easy to add in your head just by adding $2+3$ to get 5 and then tacking on a 0. Fifty isn't the answer to the original problem, but remember we don't always have to be exact. An answer that is close but not exact is actually called an **estimate**, and the method we just used is called **estimating**. Next, let's estimate the answer to a subtraction problem.

$$
\begin{array}{c}
78 - 62 \\
\downarrow \quad \downarrow \\
80 - 60 = 20 \\
8 - 6 = 2
\end{array}
\qquad
\begin{array}{l}
\text{Round the numbers} \\
\text{and then subtract} \\
\text{in your head.}
\end{array}
$$

Just as before, the first step was to round. We rounded 78 to 80 and 62 to 60. That left us with $80-60$, which you could easily subtract in your head by calculating $8-6$ to get 2 and then adding a 0 to the end. That means that an estimate of $78-62$ is 20.

Practice 10

a. Write thirty million, twelve thousand using digits. _____

b. Write the following numbers in order from least to greatest: 939; 938; 993

_____

c. Tell what number these tally marks represent. _____

Find estimates for each of the problems below by rounding each of the numbers to the nearest ten and then adding or subtracting (as required) in your head

d. 32 + 24 _____   **e.** 67 − 51 _____

Problem Set 10

Tell whether each sentence below is True or False.

1. When we round to the nearest ten, we're looking for the closest number that has a zero in the ones place. _____

2. An estimate is an answer that's close but not exact. _____

Tell what the highlighted digit stands for in the number below.

3. 142,378,905 _____

A. thousands	B. ten thousands	C. hundred thousands
D. millions	E. ten millions	F. hundred millions

Choose the group of words that belong in the blank.

4. 162,431,756 _____, four hundred thirty-one thousand, seven hundred fifty-six

      A. one hundred sixty two million   B. one hundred sixty-two thousand
      C. one hundred sixty-two million   D. one hundred and sixty-two million
      E. one hundred and sixty two million

Answer the question below.

(a) 5. Write fifty million, nineteen thousand using digits. _____

Write the following numbers in order from least to greatest.

6. 535; 524; 514 _____

(b) 7. 838; 883; 837 _____

Round each of the following numbers to the nearest ten.

8. 12_____   **9.** 41 _____   **10.** 59 _____

For each problem below, tell what number the tally marks represent.

11. ||
_____

12. 卌
_____

(c) 13. 卌 卌 |
_____

Tell whether a <, >, or = should go between each pair of numbers below.

14. 92,512 ____ 101,210   **15.** 80,228 ____ 80,182

Rearrange the digits in the numbers below to make them as large as possible.

16. 63,287 _____   **17.** 197,625 _____

Rearrange the digits in the numbers below to make them as small as possible.

18. 21,563 _____   **19.** 362,385 _____

Find estimates for each of the problems below by rounding each of the numbers to the nearest ten and then adding or subtracting (as required) in your head.

(d) 20.   43 + 33 _____   **21.**   61 + 52 _____

(e) 22.   89 − 53 _____

Lesson 11—Addition with Carrying

We've already talked about adding numbers by lining up the columns, but sometimes the sum of one column is too large to simply put it underneath the column being added. In this case, we need to split the number into two pieces. Here's an example.

$$
\begin{array}{r}
\overset{1}{3}5 \\
+\ 27 \\
\hline
62
\end{array}
$$
5+7=12, so we have to carry the 1.

Notice that because $5+7=12$, we had to break the 12 into two pieces so that it became $10+2$. Then we wrote the 2 below in the ones column, and the 10 became a little 1 written at the top of the tens column. It makes sense to put the 10 part of the 12 into the tens column as long as we show it as a 1, because in the tens column a 1 means 10. We then just added the entire tens column to get the overall sum of 62. The process that we used in this problem is called **carrying**, which just means putting part of the sum of a column into the next column. You always have to carry when a column adds up to more than 9. Here's another example.

$$
\begin{array}{r}
\overset{1}{9}6 \\
+\ 28 \\
\hline
124
\end{array}
$$
Carry the 1, then add up the tens column.

Since $6+8=14$, we put the 4 underneath the ones column and carried the 1 to the tens. After adding up the tens, we found that the answer is 124, and notice that we didn't need to carry a second time. Since the tens column was the last one, we didn't have to worry about the 12 bumping into digits from another column.

Practice 11

a. Write eight million, one hundred twenty-four using digits. _____

b. Add
$$
\begin{array}{r}
45 \\
+\ 39 \\
\hline
\end{array}
$$

c. Add
$$
\begin{array}{r}
56 \\
+\ 75 \\
\hline
\end{array}
$$

d. Tell what number these tally marks represent. _____

e. Find an estimate for $67 - 51$ by rounding each of the numbers to the nearest ten and then subtracting in your head. _____

Problem Set 11

Tell whether each sentence below is True or False.

1. A one in the tens column stands for ten. _____

2. You always have to carry when a column adds to more than 9. _____

Do the problems below.

3. Find the difference of 9 and 5.

_____

4. Find the difference of 8 and 6.

_____

For each problem below, choose the group of words that belongs in the blank.

5. 120,517,760 _____, five hundred seventeen thousand, seven hundred sixty

  A. twenty million   B. one hundred and twenty million
  C. one hundred twenty million   D. one hundred twenty thousand
  E. one hundred and twenty thousand

6. 476,608,142   four hundred seventy-six million, _____, one hundred forty-two

  A. six hundred thousand   B. six hundred and eight thousand
  C. sixty eight thousand   D. and six hundred and eight thousand
  E. six hundred eight thousand

Write each number below using digits.

7. four million, eight hundred seventy-six thousand, two hundred three _____

(a) 8. five million, four hundred ninety-two _____

Tell whether a <, >, or = should go between each pair of numbers below.

9. 10,513 ____ 9,891   10. 22,815 ____ 22,851

Answer each question below.

11. Rearrange the digits in 438,467 to make it as large as possible. _____

12. Rearrange the digits in 592,314 to make it as small as possible. _____

Add each pair of numbers below.

(b) 13.   58
          + 27
          ————

(c) 14.   78
          + 54
          ————

15.   67
      + 59
      ————

16.   66
      + 25
      ————

For each problem below, tell what number the tally marks represent.

17. 卌 ||

_____

(d) 18. 卌 卌 卌 |||

_____

19. 卌 卌 ||||

_____

Find estimates for each of the problems below by rounding each of the numbers to the nearest ten and then adding or subtracting (as required) in your head.

20. $51 + 42$ _____

21. $81 + 73$ _____

(e) 22. $89 - 64$ _____

Lesson 12—Adding More than Two

Sometimes we need to add more than two numbers. Here's an example.

$$\begin{matrix} 5 \\ 3 \end{matrix} \Big\} 8$$
$$\underline{+\ 9}$$
$$17$$

Add the numbers
two at a time.

To add these three numbers, we just did it in steps, starting with the 5 and the 3, which gave us 8. Then we took that and added it with the 9 to get 17. Here's another example.

27+36+18

Since this problem is written horizontally, the first step is to put the numbers on top of each other, making sure to put ones over ones and tens over tens. Then we can just add the numbers two at a time, starting with the ones.

$$\begin{matrix} 2 \\ 27 \\ 36 \end{matrix} \Big\} 13$$
$$\underline{+18}$$
$$81$$

Add the numbers
two at a time, and
carry when needed.

First we added the 7 and the 6 to get 13. Then, we took the 13 and added it to 8 to get 21. Since 21 was too large to fit, we wrote the 1 below and carried a 2, which was perfectly okay even though we've only carried 1s in previous lessons. Next, we added up all the digits in the tens column, including the 2 that we carried, and that gave us an overall sum of 81.

Just like when adding two numbers, it turns out we can add three or more numbers in any order. The formal name for this rule is the **associative property of addition**, and it allows us to shuffle all the numbers in our last example without changing the answer.

$$\begin{matrix} 2 \\ 18 \\ 27 \end{matrix} \Big\} 15$$
$$\underline{+36}$$
$$81$$

The numbers can be
added in any order.

Notice that the answer is still 81, which means that if you're not sure about an answer to an addition problem, one good way to check it is to just use the associative property to change the order of the numbers and add everything again. If you get the same answer the second time around, your first answer was probably right.

Practice 12

a. Write eleven million, five thousand, six using digits. _____

b. Tell what number these tally marks represent. _____

c. Find an estimate for $88 - 33$ by rounding each of the numbers to the nearest ten and then subtracting in your head. _____

Add each group of numbers below.

d.
$$
\begin{array}{r}
6 \\
7 \\
+\ 5 \\
\hline
\end{array}
$$

e.
$$
\begin{array}{r}
64 \\
47 \\
+\ 22 \\
\hline
\end{array}
$$

Problem Set 12

Tell whether each sentence below is True or False.

1. You cannot carry a 2 from the ones column into the tens column. _____

2. When adding three or more numbers, it doesn't matter which two are added first. _____

Add or subtract each pair of numbers below.

3.
$$
\begin{array}{r}
34 \\
+\ 11 \\
\hline
\end{array}
$$

4.
$$
\begin{array}{r}
85 \\
-\ 33 \\
\hline
\end{array}
$$

5.
$$
\begin{array}{r}
76 \\
-\ 61 \\
\hline
\end{array}
$$

Do each problem below.

6. Find the sum of 61 and 23.

7. Find the difference of 53 and 42.

+ _____

− _____

Write each number below using digits.

8. seventy thousand, four hundred one _____

(a) 9. fourteen million, three thousand, two _____

For each problem below, tell what number the tally marks represent.

10.

_____

(b)11. |||| |||| |||| ||||

_____

12. |||| |||| ||

_____

For each problem below, choose the group of words that belongs in the blank.

13. 6,105,823   six million, _____, eight hundred twenty-three

    A. one hundred five
    B. one hundred and five thousand
    C. one hundred five thousand
    D. and one hundred five thousand
    E. and one hundred and five thousand

14. 212,251,923   _____, two hundred fifty-one thousand, nine hundred twenty-three

    A. two hundred twelve million
    B. two hundred twelve thousand
    C. two hundred and twelve
    D. two hundred and twelve million
    E. two hundred and twelve thousand

Find estimates for each of the problems below by rounding each of the numbers to the nearest ten and then adding or subtracting (as required) in your head.

15. $32 + 54$ _____

16. $37 + 13$ _____

(c) 17. $48 - 21$ _____

Add each group of numbers below.

(d) 18.
$$\begin{array}{r} 8 \\ 6 \\ + \ 3 \\ \hline \end{array}$$

19.
$$\begin{array}{r} 7 \\ 4 \\ + \ 3 \\ \hline \end{array}$$

(e) 20.
$$\begin{array}{r} 23 \\ 35 \\ + \ 84 \\ \hline \end{array}$$

21.
$$\begin{array}{r} 32 \\ 84 \\ + \ 47 \\ \hline \end{array}$$

22.
$$\begin{array}{r} 96 \\ 37 \\ + \ 48 \\ \hline \end{array}$$

Lesson 13—Adding and Subtracting with Three-Digit Numbers

We've already talked about carrying, but sometimes you actually have to carry more than once. Here's an example.

$$\begin{array}{r} \overset{1\ 1}{957} \\ +\ 284 \\ \hline 1,241 \end{array}$$ Carrying more than once.

Notice that we added two 3-digit numbers, which is different that what we've done before. That's okay though, because the process for adding was still the same. We just added each of the columns starting with the ones. Since $7+4=11$, we put a 1 below and carried a 1 to the tens column. Then, in the tens column, $1+5+8$ is 14, so we had to carry again. However, in the tens column, a 14 really stands for 140. So to carry, we had to break 140 into two pieces: $100+40$. The 40 could be shown by putting a 4 below, and the 100 could be written as a 1 in the hundreds column. See, carrying twice is basically no different than carrying once, except the little 1 we carried stands for 100 this time instead of 10. To finish, we just added all of the digits in the hundreds column, giving us a sum of 1,241.

Next, let's try subtracting two 3-digit numbers. Remember, first we have to put the bigger number on top and line them up vertically.

$$\begin{array}{r} 679 \\ -534 \\ \hline 145 \end{array}$$ Subtract the columns starting with the ones.

Then we subtracted the columns, starting with the ones. In the ones column, $9-4$ is 5, so we wrote a 5 below. In the tens column, $7-3$ is 4. Finally, we subtracted the hundreds column to get 145. The main point of this example is to show that subtracting with bigger numbers is no different from subtracting with smaller numbers; you still just line everything up and subtract each column.

Practice 13

a. Write forty-two million, twelve using digits. _____

b. Tell what number these tally marks represent. _____

Add or subtract (as required) each group of numbers below.

c.
$$
\begin{array}{r}
37 \\
46 \\
+\ 18 \\
\hline
\end{array}
$$

d.
$$
\begin{array}{r}
563 \\
+\ 258 \\
\hline
\end{array}
$$

e.
$$
\begin{array}{r}
784 \\
-\ 432 \\
\hline
\end{array}
$$

Problem Set 13

Tell whether each sentence below is True or False.

1. You aren't allowed to carry twice in a problem. _____

2. Subtracting with bigger numbers is no different from subtracting with smaller numbers, you still just line everything up and subtract each column. _____

Add or subtract (as required) each pair of numbers below.

3.
$$
\begin{array}{r}
79 \\
+\ 15 \\
\hline
\end{array}
$$

4.
$$
\begin{array}{r}
52 \\
-\ 31 \\
\hline
\end{array}
$$

5.
$$
\begin{array}{r}
63 \\
+\ 19 \\
\hline
\end{array}
$$

Write each number below using digits.

6. one hundred forty-five thousand, thirty-seven _____

(a) 7. twenty million, nineteen _____

For each problem below, choose the group of words that belongs in the blank.

8. 352,111,292 _____, one hundred eleven thousand, two hundred ninety-two

    A. three hundred fifty-two   B. three hundred fifty two million
    C. three hundred fifty two thousand   D. three hundred fifty-two million
    E. three hundred and fifty-two million

9. 2,891,203   two million, _____, two hundred three

    A. eight hundred ninety-one million   B. eight hundred ninety-one thousand
    C. eight hundred ninety one thousand   D. eight hundred and ninety-one thousand
    E. eight hundred ninety one-thousand

For each problem below, tell what number the tally marks represent.

10. 卌 ||||

    _____

(b) 11. 卌 卌 卌 卌 ||

    _____

12. 卌 卌 卌 |||

    _____

Answer each question below.

13. Rearrange the digits in 230,928 to make it as large as possible. _____

14. Rearrange the digits in 821,593 to make it as small as possible. _____

Find estimates for each of the problems below by rounding each of the numbers to the nearest ten and then adding or subtracting (as required) in your head.

15. $51 + 12$ _____

16. $84 - 31$ _____

17. $66 + 12$ _____

Add or subtract (as required) each group of numbers below.

18.
$$
\begin{array}{r}
7 \\
8 \\
+\ 2 \\
\hline
\end{array}
$$

(c) 19.
$$
\begin{array}{r}
29 \\
66 \\
+\ 78 \\
\hline
\end{array}
$$

(d) 20.
$$
\begin{array}{r}
279 \\
+\ 146 \\
\hline
\end{array}
$$

(e) 21.
$$
\begin{array}{r}
932 \\
-\ 311 \\
\hline
\end{array}
$$

22.
$$
\begin{array}{r}
756 \\
-\ 642 \\
\hline
\end{array}
$$

Lesson 14—Rounding and Estimating with Three-Digit Numbers

Sometimes we need to round numbers to the nearest hundred. Here's an example.

$$611 \longrightarrow 600$$

Rounding 611 to
the nearest hundred.

Changing 611 to 610 isn't right if we're trying to round to the nearest hundred. To round to the nearest hundred, we have to change 611 into a number we would say when counting by hundreds. So rounding to the nearest hundred really means changing a number to the closest number that ends in two 0s. That's why the answer is 600. Here's a tougher example.

$$769 \longrightarrow 800$$

Rounding 769 to
the nearest hundred.

One way to do this would have been to turn the 6 and the 9 into 0s and keep the 7, but 700 is not the closest number to 769 that ends in two 0s, 800 is. By the way, we call changing the 7 to an 8 "rounding up" because we went up by 1 digit, but the main point is that keeping the digit that's in the hundreds place the same and changing all the numbers to zeros doesn't always work. Here's an even harder problem.

$$350 \longrightarrow 400$$

Round up if the digit
is 5 or more.

This was hard because 350 is just as close to 400 as it is 300, but in cases like this we always round up. Actually, the very best way to round is to just look at the digit to the right of the digit you're rounding to. In this instance, that would be the digit in the tens place. If the tens digit is less than 5, the hundreds digit should stay the same. If the tens digit is 5 or more, the hundreds digit should be rounded up. Next, let's use rounding to the nearest hundred to get an estimate of an addition problem.

$$921 + 415$$
$$\downarrow \qquad \downarrow$$
$$900 + 400 = 1,300$$
$$9 + 4 = 13$$

Round the numbers
and then add them
in your head.

First, we rounded each of the numbers to the nearest hundred. Then we just added 900 and 400, which is really the same as $9+4$ except that we're dealing with hundreds. So the answer is 1,300. The main point of this last example is to show that we can round numbers in the hundreds to get estimates as long as we're careful to follow the rules for rounding.

Practice 14

    a.   Write fifty million, sixty-eight using digits. _____

    b.   Tell what number these tally marks represent. _____

    c.   Round 650 to the nearest hundred. _____

    d.   Add
$$\begin{array}{r} 83 \\ 62 \\ +\ 49 \\ \hline \end{array}$$

    e.   Find an estimate for $758 + 312$ by rounding each of the numbers to the nearest hundred and then adding in your head. _____

Problem Set 14

Tell whether each sentence below is True or False.

    1.   When rounding a number to the nearest hundred, if the tens digit is less than 5, the hundreds digit should stay the same. _____

    2.   When rounding a number to the nearest hundred, if the tens digit is 5 or more, the hundreds digit should be rounded up. _____

Write each number below using digits.

    3.   two million, six hundred seventy-seven thousand, fourteen _____

  (a) 4.   ninety million, seventeen _____

For each problem below, choose the group of words that belongs in the blank.

5. 235,820,003 _____, eight hundred twenty thousand, three

    A. two hundred thirty-five million   B. two hundred and thirty-five million
    C. two hundred thirty five million   D. two hundred thirty-five thousand
    E. two hundred thirty five-million

6. 274,262,841   two hundred seventy-four million, _____, eight hundred forty-one

    A. two hundred sixty-two million   B. two hundred and sixty-two thousand
    C. two hundred sixty-two thousand   D. and two hundred sixty-two thousand
    E. two hundred sixty two thousand

For each problem below, tell what number the tally marks represent.

7. IIII IIII IIII IIII   **8.** IIII IIII IIII IIII IIII

_____   _____

(b) 9. IIII IIII IIII IIII IIII II

_____

Answer each question below.

10. Rearrange the digits in 239,064 to make it as large as possible. _____

11. Rearrange the digits in 331,652 to make it as small as possible. _____

Round each number below to the nearest hundred.

12. 322 _____   **13.** 734 _____

(c) 14. 153 _____

Add or subtract (as required) each group of numbers below.

(d) 15.
$$\begin{array}{r} 49 \\ 64 \\ + 53 \\ \hline \end{array}$$

16.
$$\begin{array}{r} 26 \\ 46 \\ + 34 \\ \hline \end{array}$$

17.
$$\begin{array}{r} 247 \\ + 184 \\ \hline \end{array}$$

18.
$$\begin{array}{r} 699 \\ - 288 \\ \hline \end{array}$$

19.
$$\begin{array}{r} 537 \\ - 325 \\ \hline \end{array}$$

Find estimates for each of the problems below by rounding each of the numbers to the nearest hundred and then adding in your head.

20. $423 + 509$ _____

21. $631 + 194$ _____

(e) 22. $152 + 310$ _____

Quiz 2

Tell whether each sentence below is True or False.

1. When doing a subtraction on paper, we always put the smaller number over the larger number. _____

2. When we round to the nearest ten, we're looking for the closest number that has a zero in the ones place. _____

Tell what the highlighted digit stands for in the number below.

3. 834,318,015 _____

    A. thousands   B. ten thousands   C. hundred thousands
    D. millions   E. ten millions   F. hundred millions

Write each number below using digits.

4. seventy million, five hundred thirty-seven thousand, six hundred _____

5. eighty million, twenty-nine _____

For each problem below, tell what number the tally marks represent

6. 卌 卌 卌 卌 |||

    _____

7. 卌 卌 卌 卌 卌 卌 |

    _____

Answer each question below.

8. Rearrange the digits in 723,401 to make it as large as possible. _____

9. Rearrange the digits in 637,619 to make it as small as possible. _____

Tell whether a <, >, or = should go between each pair of numbers below.

10. 11,120 _____ 9,978   **11.** 54,302 _____ 54,320

Do each problem below.

12. Find the sum of 62 and 19.   **13.** Find the difference of 85 and 34.

+ _____   − _____

14. Find the difference of 45 and 22.

− _____

Add or subtract (as required) each group of numbers below.

15.
```
  9
  4
+ 3
```

16.
```
  96
  24
+ 58
```

17.
```
  625
+ 159
```

18.
```
  629
+ 598
```

19.
```
  734
− 421
```

Round each number below to the nearest hundred.

20. 545 _____   **21.** 652 _____

65

Find estimates for each of the problems below by rounding each of the numbers to the nearest hundred and then adding in your head.

22. $340 + 105$ _____

23. $428 + 499$ _____

24. $251 + 512$ _____

Lesson 15—Adding and Subtracting Word Problems

There are lots of real-life situations where you have to add or subtract. Here's an example.

> Horatio and Fowler are collecting cans of food for charity. So far, Horatio has collected 48 cans and Fowler has collected 37. How many cans is this altogether?

This is obviously an addition problem because it asks how many cans have they collected *altogether*. So to add, we just put one number over the other and add the columns.

$$\begin{array}{r} {}^{1}48 \\ +\ 37 \\ \hline 85 \end{array}$$ Add because the problem says altogether.

In the ones column $8+7$ is 15, so we put the 5 below and carried the 1. Then, in the tens column, $1+4$ is 5 and $5+3$ is 8, which gave us an overall answer of 85 cans. Now let's try a real-life subtraction problem.

> Grandma Allen is famous for her gourmet chocolate chip cookies. On Saturday, she baked 97 of them, but then she gave 21 of those to the people in her Sunday school class. How many cookies does she have left?

The hardest thing about solving a real-world problem is figuring out whether we're supposed to add or subtract. Fortunately, this problem talks about *giving* something away, which is a clue that we need to subtract. The problem also asks how many cookies Grandma had *left,* which is another clue that something was subtracted.

$$\begin{array}{r} 97 \\ -\ 21 \\ \hline 76 \end{array}$$ "Gave" and "left" are clues to use subtraction.

Notice that we put the bigger number over the smaller number as always, and then we just subtracted the columns starting with the ones. Since $7-1$ is 6 and $9-2$ is 7, the answer was 76. So Grandma Allen has 76 gourmet chocolate chip cookies left.

Practice 15

   a. Round 195 to the nearest hundred. _____

   b. Add
$$\begin{array}{r} 91 \\ 64 \\ +\ 38 \\ \hline \end{array}$$

   c. Find an estimate for $899 - 203$ by rounding each of the numbers to the nearest hundred and then subtracting in your head. _____

Solve each of the word problems below

   d. Nathan and Craig enjoy collecting baseball cards. Nathan has 68 cards in his collection and Craig has 57. How many cards do they have altogether? _____

   e. Uncle Winters carves wooden toys on his days off. Last year he carved 45 toys but gave 21 of them away. How many toys did he keep? _____

Problem Set 15

Tell whether each sentence below is True or False.

   1. The hardest thing about solving a real-world problem is figuring out whether you're supposed to add or subtract. _____

   2. When a problem talks about giving something away, that's a clue you need to add. _____

Write each number below using digits.

   3. eleven million, eight hundred fifty thousand, two hundred sixty _____

   4. nine million, five _____

For each problem below, choose the group of words that belongs in the blank.

5. 624,936,005 _____, nine hundred thirty-six thousand, five

    A. six hundred twenty four million   B. six hundred and twenty-four million
    C. six hundred twenty-four thousand   D. six hundred and twenty four-million
    E. six hundred twenty-four million

6. 36,288,023 thirty-six million, _____, twenty-three

    A. two hundred eighty-eight thousand   B. two hundred eighty-eight million
    C. two hundred and eighty-eight   D. two hundred and eighty-eight thousand
    E. two hundred eighty eight thousand

For each problem below, tell what number the tally marks represent.

7. 卌 卌 卌 I

    _____

8. 卌 卌 卌 卌 卌 III

    _____

Answer each question below.

9. Write the following numbers in order from least to greatest: 975; 1,001; 970.

    _____

(a) 10. Round 896 to the nearest hundred. _____

11. Round 488 to the nearest hundred. _____

Add or subtract (as required) each group of numbers below.

(b) 12.
```
  36
  82
+ 29
```

13.
```
  76
  15
+ 48
```

14.
```
  329
+ 488
```

15.
```
  658
+ 275
```

16.
```
  623
− 411
```

17.
```
  959
− 625
```

Find estimates for each of the problems below by rounding each of the numbers to the nearest hundred and then subtracting in your head.

18. 723 − 612 _____

19. 589 − 211 _____

(c) 20. 690 − 170 _____

Solve each of the word problems below.

(d) 21. Lauren loves to pick daisies. Last week she picked 29 daisies, and this week she picked 17 daisies. How many daisies did she pick altogether? _____

(e) 22. Sam's Hamburger Joint is giving away free hamburgers. If they made 95 hamburgers and gave away 63 of them, how many do they have left? _____

Lesson 16—Roman Numerals—Part 1

You've probably seen **Roman numerals**, maybe in a book or on a clock or building. Roman numerals are just a different way to write numbers. For example, here are the numbers 1, 5, and 10 written as Roman numerals.

I   one
V   five
X   ten

Believe it or not, we can write any number from 1-39 using just these three Roman numerals. However, writing Roman numerals can be tricky. That's because Roman numerals don't use the place value system. Remember, place value just means the position of a number tells us what the number stands for, but with Roman numerals, an I always stands for 1, a V always stands for 5, and an X always stands for 10. Here's what the number 2 looks like as a Roman numeral.

II   two

This stands for 2 because with Roman numerals, we're supposed to add up all the values of the numerals starting from the left. Since I stands for 1, II means $1+1$. That also means that III stands for $1+1+1$, or 3, but the number 4 is not written as IIII. It's actually written like this.

IV   four

See, whenever a numeral of smaller value appears to the left of a numeral of larger value, we're supposed to subtract the smaller one. In this case, the I was before the V, which gives us $5-1$ or 4. Here are two more examples where we need to subtract.

IX   nine
XIV   fourteen

In the first one, since the I stands for 1 and the X stands for 10, I is smaller than X, which means we need to subtract I from X to get 9. In the second example, X stands for 10, but then the I is smaller than the V, so we had to calculate $5-1$, which is 4. That gave us 14 overall.

You can figure out what number a Roman numeral stands for by adding each of the individual numerals longways if you want. Just remember that if a smaller numeral is ever *above* a larger numeral, the smaller one has to be subtracted from the larger one.

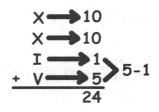

In the problem above, the I had to be subtracted from the V, since I is smaller than V. V minus I is the same as $5 - 1$, or 4, so that left us with $10 + 10 + 4$, or 24.

Practice 16

a. Tell what number XIX represents. _____

b. Write the Roman numeral for 6. _____

c. Find an estimate for $798 - 185$ by rounding each of the numbers to the nearest hundred and then subtracting in your head. _____

Solve each word problem below.

d. Christie loves reading books about horses. This year she read 24 books and last year she read 17 books. How many books did she read in all? _____

e. Todd has a die cast car collection. If he has 63 die cast cars and he traded 12 away, how many die cast cars does he have left? _____

Problem Set 16

Tell whether each sentence below is True or False.

1. The Roman numeral X stands for 10. _____

2. When a smaller Roman numeral appears to the left of a larger Roman numeral, you're supposed to subtract the smaller from the larger. _____

For each problem below, choose the group of words that belongs in the blank.

3. 192,831,570 _____, eight hundred thirty-one thousand, five hundred seventy

    A. one hundred ninety two million   B. one hundred and ninety two million
    C. one hundred ninety-two thousand   D. one hundred ninety-two million
    E. one hundred and ninety-two million

For each problem below, tell what number the tally marks represent.

4. |||| |||| |||| |||| ||||

    _____

5. |||| |||| |||| |||| |||| |||| ||

    _____

Answer each question below.

6. Write eight hundred one million, sixteen using digits. _____

7. Round 352 to the nearest hundred. _____

Tell whether a <, >, or = should go between each pair of numbers below.

8. 100,240 _____ 97,956   9. 81,281 _____ 81,280

Add each group of numbers below.

10.
$$\begin{array}{r} 51 \\ 82 \\ + 49 \\ \hline \end{array}$$

11.
$$\begin{array}{r} 68 \\ 48 \\ + 37 \\ \hline \end{array}$$

12.
$$\begin{array}{r} 479 \\ + 251 \\ \hline \end{array}$$

Tell what number each Roman numeral below represents.

13. IV _____   **14.** XII _____

(a) 15. XXIX _____

Write the Roman numeral for each number below.

16. 3 _____   **(b) 17.** 7 _____

18. 9 _____

Find estimates for each of the problems below by rounding each of the numbers to the nearest hundred and then subtracting in your head.

19. $728 - 118$ _____   **(c) 20.** $487 - 284$ _____

Solve each word problem below.

(d) 21. The Spartans played two basketball games last week. Their top player, Clayton, scored 21 points in the first game and 19 points in the second. How many points did he score in all? _____

(e) 22. Jenna has 34 paper doll cutouts at her house. One day, she decided to give 12 paper doll cutouts to her friend. How many paper doll cutouts does she have left? _____

Lesson 17—Roman Numerals—Part 2

In addition to the Roman numerals I, V, and X that we learned last lesson, there are also Roman numerals for larger numbers. Here are the next four.

L   fifty
C   hundred
D   five hundred
M   thousand

The good news is that working with bigger Roman numerals is no different than working with smaller ones. The same rules apply. Here's an example.

LX   sixty

The L stands for 50 and the X stands for 10, so we added $50+10$ to get 60. Here's another one.

CXL   one hundred forty

Since the rules for working with bigger and smaller Roman numerals are the same, we still subtract whenever a smaller numeral is to the left of a larger one. That means we had to subtract 10 from 50 because the X is before the L, which gave us an overall answer of 140. We can also change bigger Roman numerals to regular numbers longways, which really helps when there are a lot of letters to add.

```
  C ⟶ 100
  C ⟶ 100
  C ⟶ 100
  L ⟶  50
  X ⟶  10
+ I ⟶   1
        361
```

C means 100, so we put 100 next to each of the Cs. Then we filled in the rest of the numbers and added everything up to get 361. Here's one more problem.

```
  C ⟶ 100 ⎫
  D ⟶ 500 ⎬ 500-100
  I ⟶   1 ⎫
+ X ⟶  10 ⎬ 10-1
        409
```

Since this is such a hard problem, we broke it into two steps. The 100 was before the 500, so we calculated $500 - 100$ to get 400. Then, because the 1 was before the 10, we calculated $10 - 1$ to get 9. The last step was just to add 400 and 9, which gave us 409.

Practice 17

a. Tell what number CLXIV represents. _____

b. Write the Roman numeral for 34. _____

c. Find an estimate for $387 + 215$ by rounding each of the numbers to the nearest hundred and then adding in your head. _____

Solve each word problem below.

d. Sally counted 88 candies in the first bowl and 83 in the second. How many candies is this altogether? _____

e. The ice cream man had 97 chocolate-covered ice cream bars in his freezer. Then he sold 42 of them. How many chocolate-covered ice cream bars does he have left? _____

Problem Set 17

Tell whether each sentence below is True or False.

1. The Roman numeral L stands for 100. _____

2. The Roman numeral M stands for 1,000. _____

For the problem below, choose the group of words that belong in the blank.

3. 723,694,136 _____, six hundred ninety-four thousand, one hundred thirty-six

    A. seven hundred twenty-three million   B. seven hundred and twenty-three million
    C. seven hundred twenty three million   D. seven hundred twenty-three thousand
    E. seven hundred twenty three-million

For each problem below, tell what number the tally marks represent.

4. ⵌ ⵌ ⵌ ⵌ ⵌ ⵌ ⵌ

_____

5. ⵌ ⵌ ⵌ ⵌ ⵌ ⵌ ⵌ I

_____

Answer each question below.

6. Write ten million, three hundred thousand, eight using digits. _____

7. Round 293 to the nearest hundred. _____

8. Rearrange the digits in 623,078 to make it as large as possible. _____

9. Rearrange the digits in 314,923 to make it as small as possible. _____

Subtract each group of numbers below.

10. 535
    − 211
    _____

11. 785
    − 342
    _____

12. 698
    − 437
    _____

Tell what number each Roman numeral below represents.

13. CLI _____   (a) 14. CLIV _____

15. XVII _____

Write the Roman numeral for each number below.

16. 31 _____

(b) 17. 24 _____

18. 39 _____

Find estimates for each of the problems below by rounding each of the numbers to the nearest hundred and then adding in your head.

19. 623 + 180 _____

(c) 20. 785 + 214 _____

Solve each word problem below.

(d) 21. The first bookshelf has 75 books on it and the second has 58. How many books is this altogether? _____

(e) 22. The Alpha force started with a total of 68 missiles, but they used 45 of them in battle. How many missiles does the force have left? _____

Lesson 18—Simple Two-Step Word Problems

Some problems in real-life require us to do two steps to get the answer. Here's an example.

Samantha is 6 years older than Jackie, and Jackie is 4 years older than Nicole. If Nicole is 15 years old, how old is Samantha?

We're told how old Nicole is, but the problem never gives specifics about how Nicole's age compares with Samantha's. In a case like this, the best way to get the answer is to do the problem in steps, but we'll need to work backwards. We know Nicole is 15 years old, and we also know that Jackie is 4 years older than Nicole. That means Jackie is 19.

$$\begin{array}{r} 15 \\ +\ 4 \\ \hline 19 \end{array}$$ First, find
Jackie's age.

Since we know Jackie's age, we can now figure out Samantha's age because the problem says Samantha is 6 years older than Jackie. So we just have to add 19 and 6.

$$\begin{array}{r} ^1 19 \\ +\ 6 \\ \hline 25 \end{array}$$ Use Jackie's age
to find Samantha's.

So Samantha is 25. Next, let's try another two step problem.

The hardware store manager ordered 38 can crushers, and by the end of the first week, he had sold 13 of them. By the end of the second week, he had sold another 11. How many can crushers did he have at the start of the third week?

Probably the best way to do this problem is to just add the amounts the store sold in both weeks and then subtract that from the amount they started with, which is 38.

$$\begin{array}{r} 13 \\ +11 \\ \hline 24 \end{array} \qquad \begin{array}{r} 38 \\ -24 \\ \hline 14 \end{array}$$ First add,
then subtract.

Since 13+11 is 24, we subtracted 24 from 38 to get 14. We could have also done this problem by subtracting twice, which would have given us the same answer. However, subtraction is usually harder than addition so it's better to add first, then subtract.

Practice 18

a. Tell what number XXVII represents. _____

b. Write the Roman numeral for 59. _____

c. Find an estimate for $219 + 684$ by rounding each of the numbers to the nearest hundred and then adding in your head. _____

Solve each word problem below.

d. Jeremy is 7 years older than Devin, and Devin is 5 years older than Micah. If Micah is 18 years old, how old is Jeremy? _____

e. The store greeter started with 47 balloons and she plans to give them all away. During the first hour of the day, she gave away 14, and during the second hour, she gave away 12. How many balloons does she still need to give away? _____

Problem Set 18

Tell whether each sentence below is True or False.

1. Some word problems should be done in two steps. _____

2. On some addition word problems, it's best to work backwards. _____

For the problem below, choose the group of words that belong in the blank.

3. 456,816,139 _____, eight hundred sixteen thousand, one hundred thirty-nine

    A. four hundred fifty six million   B. four hundred and fifty-six million
    C. four hundred fifty-six million   D. four hundred fifty-six thousand
    E. four hundred fifty six-million

For each problem below, tell what number the tally marks represent.

4.

_____

5.

_____

Tell what number each Roman numeral below represents.

6. LVIII _____   **(a)** 7. LXVII _____

8. CLXX _____

Write the Roman numeral for each number below.

9. 35 _____   10. 53 _____

(b) 11. 69 _____

Add or subtract (as required) each group of numbers below.

12.   82
        63
      + 48
      _____

13.   74
        36
      + 27
      _____

14.   632
     + 188
     _____

15.   429
     + 283
     _____

16.   748
     - 321
     _____

17.   629
     - 227
     _____

Find estimates for each of the problems below by rounding each of the numbers to the nearest hundred and then adding in your head.

18. $387 + 193$ _____   **(c) 19.** $580 + 305$ _____

Solve each word problem below.

20. Denise needs to move 56 chairs to the gymnasium. So far, she's only moved 32. How many does she have left to move? _____

(d) 21. Nathaniel is 6 years older than Franklin, and Franklin is 7 years older than Owen. If Owen is 23 years old, how old is Nathaniel? _____

(e) 22. The salesman plans to make 58 calls today. During the first hour of the day, he made 16 calls, and during the second hour, he made another 21. How many calls does he still have to make? _____

Lesson 19—Multiplication Basics

Multiplication is just a fast way to show a number being added to itself a bunch of times. So, for example, if we wanted to add 5 to itself 8 times, we could write $5+5+5+5+5+5+5+5$. In cases like this, most people would use multiplication instead because it's faster. All we have to do is realize that eight 5s added together is the same as 8 times 5, which is equal to 40.

$$5+5+5+5+5+5+5+5 = 5 \times 8 = 40$$

Here's another example.

$$7+7+7 = 3 \times 7 = 21$$

Because there are three 7s being added together, that's the same as 3 times 7, which is 21. We could also have written this as 7×3 because we can multiply any two numbers in any order. This is called the **commutative property of multiplication**, and like the commutative property of addition, it's one of the most important rules in math.

Numbers that are multiplied are actually called **factors**. So in 3×7, 3 and 7 are both factors. The answer to a multiplication is called a **product**. That means that 21 is the product of 3×7.

$$\underset{3 \times 7}{\text{factors}} \quad \underset{= 21}{\text{product}}$$

The big benefit of multiplication is that it's faster than adding over and over, but multiplication is only faster if you know your multiplication facts. So memorizing the facts is really important. If you do forget one of the facts, though, you can look it up in the multiplication table on the next page.

The Multiplication Table

1	2	3	4	5	6	7	8	9	10	11	12
2	4	6	8	10	12	14	16	18	20	22	24
3	6	9	12	15	18	21	24	27	30	33	36
4	8	12	16	20	24	28	32	36	40	44	48
5	10	15	20	25	30	35	40	45	50	55	60
6	12	18	24	30	36	42	48	54	60	66	72
7	14	21	28	35	42	49	56	63	70	77	84
8	16	24	32	40	48	56	64	72	80	88	96
9	18	27	36	45	54	63	72	81	90	99	108
10	20	30	40	50	60	70	80	90	100	110	120
11	22	33	44	55	66	77	88	99	110	121	132
12	24	36	48	60	72	84	96	108	120	132	144

See how the table works? To find the product of two numbers, like 6 and 8, we found the row that starts with the first factor, 6. Then we looked for the column that begins with the second factor, 8. The spot where the row and column meet shows the product of the two numbers, which in this case is 48. The table is obviously useful, but it's still important to memorize your multiplication facts.

Practice 19

a. Write the Roman numeral for 11. _____

b. Rewrite 5×3 as the same number added to itself over and over. _____

c. Write 9+9+9+9+9 as a multiplication. _____

Solve each word problem below.

d. Ms. Redding is knitting a hat. She has 89 feet of yarn and she has used 15 feet so far. How much yarn does she have left? _____

e. Stephanie has 14 more gumdrops than Julie, and Julie has 11 more gumdrops than Amber. If Amber has 18 gumdrops, how many gumdrops does Stephanie have? _____

Problem Set 19

Tell whether each sentence below is True or False.

1. The commutative property of multiplication says we can multiply any two numbers in any order. _____

2. Numbers that are multiplied are called factors. _____

3. The answer to a multiplication is called a sum. _____

Tell what number each Roman numeral below represents.

4. LXXII _____   5. CLXVI _____

Write the Roman numeral for each number below.

6. 84 _____   (a) 7. 13 _____

Do each problem below.

8. Find the sum of 243 and 778.   9. Find the difference of 638 and 217.

+____   −____

10. Find the difference of 896 and 531.

$$-\underline{\quad\quad}$$

Add each group of numbers below.

11.
$$
\begin{array}{r}
72 \\
23 \\
+\ 19 \\
\hline
\end{array}
$$

12.
$$
\begin{array}{r}
51 \\
82 \\
+\ 48 \\
\hline
\end{array}
$$

Rewrite each multiplication below as the same number added to itself over and over.

(b) 13. 3×8 _____

14. 6×9 _____

15. 5×4 _____

Rewrite each expression below as a multiplication.

(c) 16. $2 + 2 + 2 + 2 + 2 + 2$ _____

17. $8 + 8 + 8 + 8 + 8 + 8 + 8 + 8 + 8$ _____

18. $11 + 11 + 11 + 11$ _____

Find estimates for each of the problems below by rounding each of the numbers to the nearest hundred and then subtracting in your head.

19. $199 - 118$ _____

20. $782 - 410$ _____

Solve each word problem below.

(d) 21. Lucy, the seamstress, started with 79 feet of fabric but then she cut off a 14 foot piece. How much fabric does she have left? _____

(e) 22. Kim has 16 more pages in her scrapbook than Jeanette, and Jeanette has 14 more pages in her scrapbook than Anne. If Anne has 75 pages in her scrapbook, how many pages does Kim have? _____

Lesson 20—Multiplying with 0, 1, and 2

In addition to the commutative property of multiplication, there are other important multiplication rules. For example, any number times 0 is always equal to zero.

$$11 \times 0 = 0$$

Any number times
0 is equal to 0.

This rule works for any number, big or small. Another neat rule is that any number multiplied by 1 is always equal to itself.

$$2 \times 1 = 2$$
$$4 \times 1 = 4$$

Any number times
1 is equal to itself.

Again, it doesn't matter how big or small the number is, any number times 1 is just itself.

The nice thing about the rules for multiplying numbers by 1 and 0 is that they make it so you don't need to memorize the facts for 1 and 0. However, you should memorize all of the facts for the other numbers, such as 2, but if you do forget a multiplication fact for 2, just remember that 2 multiplied by any number doubles the number.

$$2 \times 3 = 6$$
$$2 \times 4 = 8$$

6 is double 3.
8 is double 4.

The main point of the lesson is that there are several important rules for multiplying that can help us with the multiplication facts, but memorizing the facts is still important.

Practice 20

a. Write the Roman numeral for 71. _____

b. Rewrite 8×7 as the same number added to itself over and over. _____

c. Find the product of 2 and 9 using the rule for multiplying numbers by 2. _____

Solve each word problem below.

    d. Stan's Grocery started the day with 57 cans of tomato soup. Then somebody bought 24 cans. How many cans of soup does the grocery have now? _____

    e. Starbright Jewelers needs to sell 56 diamond rings in its going-out-of-business sale. The first day of the sale, the store sold 12 diamond rings. The second day they sold 13. How many diamond rings do they have left? _____

Problem Set 20

Tell whether each sentence below is True or False.

    1. Any number times 0 always equals 0. _____

    2. Any number times 1 always equals 1. _____

    3. Two multiplied by any number triples the number. _____

Tell what number each Roman numeral below represents.

    4. CXVIII_____   **5.** XXXIV _____

Write the Roman numeral for each number below.

    6. 67 _____   **(a) 7.** 81 _____

Add or subtract (as required) each group of numbers below.

    8.
$$\begin{array}{r} 73 \\ 68 \\ + 55 \\ \hline \end{array}$$

    9.
$$\begin{array}{r} 496 \\ + 519 \\ \hline \end{array}$$

    10.
$$\begin{array}{r} 695 \\ - 181 \\ \hline \end{array}$$

    11.
$$\begin{array}{r} 747 \\ - 623 \\ \hline \end{array}$$

Rewrite each multiplication below as the same number added to itself over and over.

12. 4×3 _____

(b) 13. 9×5 _____

Rewrite each expression below as a multiplication.

14. $6 + 6 + 6 + 6 + 6 + 6 + 6$ _____

15. $9 + 9 + 9 + 9 + 9 + 9 + 9 + 9 + 9$ _____

Find each product below using the rules for multiplying a number by 0, 1, and 2 in your head.

16. 3×0 _____

17. 49×1 _____

(c) 18. 7×2 _____

Find estimates for each of the problems below by rounding each of the numbers to the nearest hundred and then adding in your head.

19. $205 + 295$ _____   **20.** $391 + 620$ _____

Solve each word problem below.

(d) 21. Larry's Produce started the day with 45 green apples. Then somebody bought 21 of them. How many green apples does Larry have left? _____

(e) 22. The florist made 96 specialty bouquets for Valentine's Day. The first day the bouquets were on sale, the store sold 32 of them. The second day they sold 52. How many specialty bouquets do they have left? _____

Lesson 21—Multiplying with 5s and 9s

There are more rules that can be used to help remember some of the multiplication facts. One of them is that 5 times any number equals a number that ends in 5 or 0. Also, if you do forget one of your facts for 5, you can always just start counting by 5s. So for example, if you forget what 5×9 is, all you have to do is count by 5s until you reach the ninth number in the sequence.

$$5 \times 9$$

0, 5, 10, 15, 20, 25, 30, 35, 40, 45
0 1 2 3 4 5 6 7 8 9

There's also a rule to help us with the facts for 9 all the way up to 9×10. The first digit for each product is 1 less than the number being multiplied by 9. Here's an example.

$$9 \times 3 = 27 \qquad \text{The 2 is 1 less than 3.}$$

Also, the two digits in every multiplication fact for 9 through 9×10 add up to 9.

$$\begin{aligned} &\overset{2+7=9}{9 \times 3 = 27} \\ &\overset{3+6=9}{9 \times 4 = 36} \end{aligned} \qquad \text{The digits in the answer always add up to 9.}$$

This is important because as long as we know the first digit of the product (and we already know how to find that), we can always find the second digit because it has to be the difference between the first digit and 9.

Practice 21

a. Tell what number XL represents. _____

b. Rewrite 8×3 as the same number added to itself over and over. _____

c. Find the product of 9 and 4 using the rule for multiplying numbers by 9. _____

Solve each word problem below.

    d. The wrecking machine demolished 18 buildings last year and 16 buildings this year. How many buildings has it demolished altogether? _____

    c. Jackie sold 18 more fish than Emily, and Emily sold 17 more fish than Hannah. If Hannah sold 25 fish, how many did Jackie sell? _____

Problem Set 21

Tell whether each sentence below is True or False.

    1. Five times any number equals a number that ends in 5 or 0. _____

    2. The first digit in the product of 9×8 is 6. _____

Do each problem below.

    3. Find the sum of 723 and 199.   **4.** Find the difference of 893 and 271.

$$+ \underline{\qquad} \qquad\qquad - \underline{\qquad}$$

Tell what number each Roman numeral below represents.

    5. CXXI _____   **(a) 6.** XLII _____

Write the Roman numeral for each number below.

    7. 26 _____   **8.** 152 _____

Rewrite each multiplication below as the same number added to itself over and over.

    (b) 9. 8×4 _____

    10. 7×2 _____

Rewrite each expression below as a multiplication.

11. $3+3+3+3+3+3$ _____

12. $6+6+6+6+6+6+6+6+6$ _____

Find the answer to each multiplication problem below using what you know about multiplying by 5s.

13. 4×5 _____

14. 7×5 _____

15. 8×5 _____

Find the answer to each problem below using the rules for multiplying a number by 9 in your head.

(c) 16. 3×9 _____

17. 6×9 _____

18. 9×9 _____

Find estimates for each of the problems below by rounding each of the numbers to the nearest hundred and then subtracting in your head.

19. $491-320$ _____   **20.** $591-110$ _____

Solve each word problem below.

(d) 21. Speedsters Inc. sold 24 drag racers last year and 19 this year. How many drag racers is this altogether? _____

(e) 22. Cindy sold 11 more pretzels than Amanda, and Amanda sold 15 more pretzels than Holly. If Holly sold 26 pretzels, how many did Cindy sell? _____

Quiz 3

Tell whether each sentence below is True or False.

    1. On some addition word problems, it's best to work backwards. _____

    2. The answer to a multiplication is called a sum. _____

Tell what number each Roman numeral below represents.

    3. CCXXI _____   **4.** CCCVI _____

Write the Roman numeral for each number below.

    5. 32 _____   **6.** 121 _____

Add or subtract (as required) each group of numbers below.

$$
\begin{array}{r} 88 \\ \textbf{7.} \quad 76 \\ + 39 \\ \hline \end{array}
\qquad
\begin{array}{r} 199 \\ \textbf{8.} \quad + 188 \\ \hline \end{array}
\qquad
\begin{array}{r} 837 \\ \textbf{9.} \quad + 475 \\ \hline \end{array}
$$

$$
\begin{array}{r} 349 \\ \textbf{10.} \quad - 134 \\ \hline \end{array}
\qquad
\begin{array}{r} 796 \\ \textbf{11.} \quad - 236 \\ \hline \end{array}
$$

Rewrite each multiplication below as the same number added to itself over and over.

    12. 6×3 _____

    13. 9×4 _____

Rewrite each expression below as a multiplication.

14. $8+8+8+8+8+8+8+8$ _____

15. $7+7+7+7+7+7+7+7+7$ _____

Find each product below using what you know about multiplying numbers by 0, 1, 2, 5, and 9 in your head.

16. 8×0 _____

17. 32×1 _____

18. 4×2 _____

19. 6×5 _____

20. 7×9 _____

Find estimates for each of the problems below by rounding each of the numbers to the nearest hundred and then subtracting in your head.

21. $886 - 105$ _____   **22.** $494 - 381$ _____

Solve each word problem below.

23. Cindy collected 88 seashells on the beach, and then she used 15 of them for necklaces. How many seashells does she have left? _____

24. Heather is 15 years older than Suzanne, and Suzanne is 13 years older than Tiffany. If Tiffany is 19 years old, how old is Heather? _____

Lesson 22—Harder Multiplication Facts

There are strategies for multiplying with the numbers 3, 4, 6, 7, and 8. For instance, if you happen to forget one of your 3s facts, you could count by 3s. This is a pretty good approach because 3 is a small number so counting by 3s isn't too hard.

Counting by 3s:
0, 3, 6, 9, 12, 15, 18, 21, 24, 27

This also works for the 4s. Same goes for 6, 7, and 8, but as the numbers get bigger, it gets harder and harder to count your way to the answer.

Counting by 4s:
0, 4, 8, 12, 16, 20, 24, 28, 32, 36

Counting by 6s:
0, 6, 12, 18, 24, 30, 36, 42, 48, 54

Counting by 7s:
0, 7, 14, 21, 28, 35, 42, 49, 56, 63

Counting by 8s:
0, 8, 16, 24, 32, 40, 48, 56, 64, 72

As you can see, it gets harder and harder to count as the numbers get bigger. That's one reason why you should have all of your facts memorized. Also, in real-life, you won't always have time to remember a special rule or find the answer by counting.

Practice 22

a. Tell what number LXXV represents. _____

b. Rewrite 7×5 as the same number added to itself over and over. _____

    c. Finish the multiplication sequence for the number 8 by filling in the blanks: 0, 8, 16, _____, 32, _____, _____, 56, _____, 72, _____, 88, and 96.

Solve each word problem below.

    d. On the first day of the trip, Matt drove 65 miles. On the second day of the trip he drove 59 miles. How many miles did he drive altogether? _____

    e. Paul has 17 more army men than Adam, and Adam has 21 more army men than Ben. If Ben has 30 army men, how many does Paul have? _____

Problem Set 22

Tell whether each sentence below is True or False.

    1. If you forget one of your 3s facts, you could just start counting by 3s to get the answer. _____

    2. You need to memorize all the multiplication facts because in real life, you won't always have time to remember a special rule or find the answer by counting. _____

Tell what number each Roman numeral below represents.

    3. XXXVI _____   (a) **4.** LXXXV _____

Write the Roman numeral for each number below.

    5. 117 _____   **6.** 160 _____

Add or subtract (as required) each group of numbers below.

    7.
$$\begin{array}{r} 98 \\ 53 \\ + 19 \\ \hline \end{array}$$

    8.
$$\begin{array}{r} 235 \\ + 169 \\ \hline \end{array}$$

    9.
$$\begin{array}{r} 738 \\ - 104 \\ \hline \end{array}$$

Rewrite each multiplication below as the same number added to itself over and over.

(b) 10. 7×4 _____

11. 9×6 _____

Rewrite each expression below as a multiplication.

12. $7 + 7 + 7 + 7 + 7 + 7$ _____

13. $3 + 3 + 3 + 3 + 3 + 3 + 3 + 3$ _____

Find the answer to each problem below using the rules for multiplying a number by 0, 1, 2, and 9 in your head.

14. 4×0 _____

15. 6×1 _____

16. 8×9 _____

(c) 17.   Finish the multiplication sequence for the number 3 by filling in the blanks: 0, 3, 6, _____, 12, _____, _____, 21, _____, 27, _____, 33, and 36.

18.   Finish the multiplication sequence for the number 4 by filling in the blanks: 0, 4, _____, 12, 16, _____, _____, 28, 32, _____, 40, _____, and 48.

19.   Finish the multiplication sequence for the number 6 by filling in the blanks: 0, 6, 12, _____, 24, 30, _____, _____, 48, _____, _____, 66, and 72.

20.   Finish the multiplication sequence for the number 7 by filling in the blanks: 0, 7, _____, 21, _____, 35, _____, 49, _____, 63, _____, 77, and 84.

Solve each word problem below.

(d) 21. On the first day of vacation, the Henderson family drove 78 miles. On the second day of the trip they drove another 63 miles. How many miles did they drive altogether?
_____

(e) 22. Kate has 12 more ribbons than Emma, and Emma has 19 more ribbons than Christa. If Christa has 28 ribbons, how many ribbons does Kate have? _____

Lesson 23—Multiplying with Two-Digit Numbers

In addition to knowing the facts for 0 through 9, you should also know the multiplication facts for 10, 11, and 12. If you forget a multiplication fact for 10, just add 0 to the number you're multiplying 10 by. Here are a few examples.

$7 \times 10 = 70$ Add 0 to the number being multiplied by 10.

If we multiply 11 by any number from 1 through 9, the answer is just two of the digit we're multiplying by.

$2 \times 11 = 22$
$3 \times 11 = 33$
$4 \times 11 = 44$
     The answer is two of the digit that's being multiplied by 11.

Unfortunately, the pattern breaks down when we multiply 11 by 10 or more.

$10 \times 11 = 110$
$11 \times 11 = 121$
$12 \times 11 = 132$
     The pattern doesn't work for numbers bigger than 9.

There's no special rule for multiplying by 12, so you just have to memorize your 12s facts. As for bigger numbers, such as 13 or 14, you can multiply them on paper, and it's easy if you've memorized all of the multiplication facts. Here's an example.

Multiply 2 by each digit on top.

First, we lined up the numbers vertically, putting the bigger number on top. Then we just multiplied the 2 in the bottom by each of the digits in the top. Since 4×2 is 8, we wrote an 8 below, and then since 2×3 is 6, we wrote a 6 below the 3. You can figure out the answer to ANY multiplication problem, no matter how big the numbers, with only the knowledge of the multiplication facts. That's why the facts are so important.

Practice 23

   a. Write the Roman numeral for 325. _____

   b. Rewrite 7×7 as the same number added to itself over and over. _____

   c. Multiply $\begin{array}{r} 13 \\ \times\, 3 \\ \hline \end{array}$

Solve each word problem below.

   d. William can take 24 photographs on one roll of film, but he has only taken 12. How many photographs does he have left? _____

   e. Jamie had a total of 76 hair ties, but then she gave 23 hair ties to her friend Michelle and 12 to her friend Julie. How many hair ties does Jamie have left? _____

Problem Set 23

Tell whether each sentence below is True or False.

   1. To multiply a number by 10, just add 0 to the number you're multiplying 10 by. _____

   2. If we multiply 11 by any number from 1 through 9, the answer is just two of whatever digit we're multiplying by. _____

   3. We can figure out the answer to any multiplication problem, no matter how big the numbers, with only knowledge of the multiplication facts. _____

Answer each question below.

   4. Tell what number XXIX represents. _____

(a) 5. Write the Roman numeral for 215. _____

Rewrite each multiplication below as the same number added to itself over and over.

(b) 6. 6×4 _____

    7. 5×5 _____

Rewrite each expression below as a multiplication.

    8. $4+4+4+4+4+4+4+4+4$ _____

    9. $5+5+5+5+5+5+5+5$ _____

Multiply each pair of numbers in your head.

    10. 4×10 _____

    11. 8×10 _____

    12. 5×11 _____

    13.   Finish the multiplication sequence for the number 12 by filling in the blanks: 0, 12, 24, ____, 48, 60, ____, 84, 96, 108, ____, 132, and 144.

Find the answer to each multiplication problem below.

    14. 7×5 _____   **15.** 8×3 _____   **16.** 6×6 _____

(c) 17. $\begin{array}{r} 14 \\ \times\, 2 \\ \hline \end{array}$ **18.** $\begin{array}{r} 23 \\ \times\, 3 \\ \hline \end{array}$ **19.** $\begin{array}{r} 22 \\ \times\, 4 \\ \hline \end{array}$

    20. $\begin{array}{r} 32 \\ \times\, 3 \\ \hline \end{array}$

Solve each word problem below.

(d) 21. The cafeteria lady started with 59 bowls of custard. If she has passed out 23 bowls, how many does she have left? _____

(e) 22. Mary had a huge collection of 88 jean patches, but in a friendly gesture, she gave her friend Rachel 32 patches and her friend Allison another 21. How many patches does Mary have now? _____

Lesson 24—Multiplying by a Multiple of 10

You already know that you can multiply a number by 10 just by adding a 0 to the number. Well, it's just as easy to multiply a one-digit number by a number like 20, 30, 40 or any other number you say when you count by 10s in your head. These numbers—20, 30, 40, and so on—are actually called **multiples** of 10. A multiple of a number is just the number times another whole number, like 1, 2, and 3. Here's an example of multiplying a one-digit number by a multiple of 10.

$$2 \times 80 = 160 \quad \text{Add a zero.}$$
$$2 \times 8 = 16$$

First, we just multiplied the non-zero digits, 2 and 8, which gave us 16. Then, since there's one 0 in 80, we put a 0 after 16 to get 160. Here's one more example.

$$4 \times 70 = 280 \quad \text{Add a zero.}$$
$$4 \times 7 = 28$$

Once again, we just multiplied the non-zero digits, 4 and 7, to get 28. Then, because there's one 0 after the 7 in 70, we added a 0 to 28 which left us with 280.

Practice 24

a. Write the Roman numeral for 55. _____

b. Multiply $\begin{array}{r} 21 \\ \times\, 2 \\ \hline \end{array}$

c. Multiply 8×60 in your head. _____

Solve each word problem below.

d. The shoe store had a total of 11 pairs of floral flip-flops in stock, but they just received another 40 pairs. How many do they have now? _____

e. Carter scored 14 more points than Mike, and Mike scored 15 more points than Reggie. If Reggie scored 12 points, how many did Carter score? _____

Problem Set 24

Tell whether each sentence below is True or False.

1. A multiple of a number is just the number times another whole number, like 1, 2, 3, and so on. _____

2. The numbers 20, 30, and 40 are all multiples of 10. _____

Answer each question below.

3. Tell what number CCCL represents. _____

(a) 4. Write the Roman numeral for 65. _____

Rewrite each multiplication below as the same number added to itself over and over.

5. 5×9 _____

6. 8×8 _____

Rewrite each expression below as a multiplication.

7. $5 + 5 + 5 + 5 + 5 + 5$ _____

8. $7 + 7 + 7 + 7 + 7 + 7 + 7$ _____

Find the answer to each multiplication problem below.

9. 3×8 _____   10. 6×7 _____

11. 3×11 _____

(b) 12. 22
×3

13. 42
×2

14. 21
×4

15. Finish the multiplication sequence for the number 12 by filling in the blanks: 0, 12, 24, 36, 48, ____, 72, 84, ____, ____, 120, 132, and 144.

Multiply each pair of numbers in your head.

16. 9×10 _____

(c) 17. 3×20 _____

18. 5×30 _____

19. 7×50 _____

20. 6×80 _____

Solve each word problem below.

(d) 21. The paint store had a total of 12 cans of neon green paint in stock, but they just received another 45 cans. How many cans do they have now? _____

(e) 22. Yesterday at batting practice, Benny hit 11 more foul balls than Jerry, and Jerry hit 12 more foul balls than Matthew. If Matthew hit 15 foul balls, how many did Benny hit? _____

Lesson 25—Rounding and Estimating When Multiplying

We can estimate the answer to lots of different multiplication problems. Here's an example.

Estimate the answer to 32×3

If we wanted an exact answer, we would multiply the 3 in the bottom by each of the digits in the top, but since the question asks us to estimate, we first have to round 32 to the nearest ten.

$$32 \longrightarrow 30 \qquad \textbf{First round to the nearest ten.}$$

That leaves us with 30×3, so now we're multiplying a multiple of ten by a single-digit number. We can do that in our heads just by multiplying the non-zero digits and then adding a 0 to the answer.

$$3 \times 30 = 90$$
$$3 \times 3 = 9 \qquad \text{Add a zero.}$$

So the answer to the question is 90. That's not the actual answer to 32×3, but we weren't looking for the exact answer, just an estimate.

Practice 25

a. Write the Roman numeral for 75. _____

b. Multiply
$$\begin{array}{r} 24 \\ \times\, 2 \\ \hline \end{array}$$

c. Solve the word problem below.

The city bus started out with 75 passengers. After the first stop, 21 people got off. After the second stop, another 13 people got off. How many people are left on the bus?

_____

Find an estimate for each of the problems below by rounding the first number to the nearest ten and then multiplying the numbers that are left in your head.

    d. 32×2 _____

    e. 71×5 _____

Problem Set 25

Tell whether each sentence below is True or False.

    1.   An estimate is the same as an exact answer. _____

    2.   You can find an estimate for some multiplication problems by rounding first and then multiplying what's left in your head. _____

Answer each question below.

    3.   Tell what number CCVII represents. _____

(a) 4.   Write the Roman numeral for 85. _____

Rewrite each multiplication below as the same number added to itself over and over.

    5. 6×7 _____

    6. 8×2 _____

Rewrite each expression below as a multiplication.

    7. $2 + 2 + 2 + 2 + 2$ _____

    8. $6 + 6 + 6 + 6 + 6 + 6 + 6 + 6$ _____

Find the answer to each multiplication problem below.

    9. 7×3 _____   **10.** 4×11 _____

(b) 11.
$$\begin{array}{r} 22 \\ \times\ 2 \\ \hline \end{array}$$

12.
$$\begin{array}{r} 31 \\ \times\ 3 \\ \hline \end{array}$$

13.
$$\begin{array}{r} 32 \\ \times\ 4 \\ \hline \end{array}$$

14. Finish the multiplication sequence for the number 12 by filling in the blanks: 0, 12, 24, 36, 48, 60, 72, 84, 96, 108, _____, _____, and _____.

Solve each word problem below.

15. Dynamite Inc. destroyed 24 buildings last year and 19 buildings this year. How many buildings have they destroyed in the two years combined? _____

(c) 16. The subway had a total of 86 passengers on board. After the first stop, 23 passengers got off. After the second stop, another 12 passengers got off. How many passengers are left on the subway? _____

Find estimates for each of the problems below by rounding the first number to the nearest ten and then multiplying the numbers that are left in your head.

(d) 17. 33×3 _____

18. 24×2 _____

19. 52×4 _____

(e) 20. 81×5 _____

21. 72×3 _____

22. 91×8 _____

Lesson 26—Multiplying with Three-Digit Numbers

Sometimes we have to multiply with numbers that have more than two digits. We can solve these the same way as all the others. Here's an example.

$$431 \times 2$$

First, we put the bigger number over the smaller one. Then, we just multiply the bottom digit by each of the top digits.

Multiply 2 by each digit on top.

Notice that when we multiplied the 2 and the 3, we were really multiplying 2 by 30 because the 3 was in the tens column. But since 2 times 30 is 60, everything still worked out perfectly because when we put the 6 below, it went into the tens place, which made it equal to 60. Also, when we multiplied the 2 by the 4, we were actually multiplying 2 by 400, but that was also okay because we wrote the 8 in the hundreds column to make it stand for 800. Here's one more example.

Multiply 3 by each digit on top.

The main point of this lesson is that multiplying with bigger numbers is really no different than multiplying with smaller ones. You still just multiply the bottom digit by each of the top digits.

Practice 26

a. Write the Roman numeral for 1,100. _____

b. Solve the word problem below.

Tommy's surfboard is 10 inches longer than Michael's, and Michael's is 12 inches longer than Luke's. If Luke's surfboard is 64 inches long, how long is Tommy's surfboard? _____

   c. Find an estimate for 61×8 by rounding the first number to the nearest ten and then multiplying the numbers that are left in your head. _____

Multiply each pair of numbers below.

   d.
$$143 \\ \underline{\times\ 2}$$

   e.
$$622 \\ \underline{\times\ 3}$$

Problem Set 26

Tell whether each sentence below is True or False.

   1. You can multiply with bigger numbers as long as you know your multiplication facts. _____

   2. Multiplying with bigger numbers is really no different than multiplying with smaller ones. _____

Answer each question below.

   3. Tell what number CCLI represents. _____

 (a) 4. Write the Roman numeral for 2,200. _____

Rewrite each multiplication below as the same number added to itself over and over.

   5. 8×5 _____

   6. 9×2 _____

Rewrite each expression below as a multiplication.

   7. $7 + 7 + 7 + 7 + 7 + 7 + 7 + 7$ _____

   8. $3 + 3 + 3 + 3 + 3 + 3 + 3 + 3 + 3$ _____

Solve each word problem below.

9. El Capitan needs to walk 25 paces to get to the buried treasure. So far he has only walked 12. How many paces does he have left to walk? _____

(b) 10. Sandy's desk is 12 inches longer than Katie's, and Katie's desk is 18 inches longer than Christine's. If Christine's desk is 48 inches long, how long is Sandy's desk? _____

11. Finish the multiplication sequence for the number 12 by filling in the blanks: 0, 12, 24, 36, 48, 60, 72, 84, 96, _____, 120, _____, and _____.

Find estimates for each of the problems below by rounding the first number to the nearest ten and then multiplying the numbers that are left in your head.

(c) 12. 71×7 _____   13. 42×4 _____

14. 81×8 _____

Multiply each pair of numbers below.

15. 9×9 _____   16. 7×11 _____

17. $\begin{array}{r} 23 \\ \times\ 2 \\ \hline \end{array}$ 18. $\begin{array}{r} 41 \\ \times\ 8 \\ \hline \end{array}$

19.
$$\begin{array}{r} 72 \\ \times\ 4 \\ \hline \end{array}$$

(d) 20.
$$\begin{array}{r} 123 \\ \times\ 2 \\ \hline \end{array}$$

21.
$$\begin{array}{r} 621 \\ \times\ 4 \\ \hline \end{array}$$

(e) 22.
$$\begin{array}{r} 833 \\ \times\ 3 \\ \hline \end{array}$$

Lesson 27—Multiplication Word Problems

Some word problems require us to multiply. Here's an example.

> Major Zap, the crime-fighting hero, drinks 6 protein shakes a day. How many protein shakes will he drink during a whole week (which is 7 days)?

The best way to do a problem like this is to first picture it in your mind.

Since Major Zap drinks 6 shakes and there are 7 days in a week, the problem is really asking what 6 added to itself 7 times is. That's the same as 6×7, or 42. Here's another example.

> Granny Hen sold 8 cartons of eggs at the market today. If each carton held 12 eggs, how many eggs did she sell in all?

The first step is to imagine (or draw) the 8 cartons of eggs with 12 eggs in each carton.

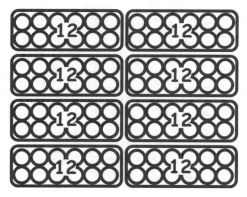

You can imagine it just as easily as drawing it, but this makes it easier to see that the problem is asking us to add 12 to itself 8 times, which is the same as 12×8. Since 12×8 is 96, Granny must have sold 96 eggs in total.

Practice 27

    a. Write the Roman numeral for 1,150. _____

    b. Find an estimate for 62×4 by rounding the first number to the nearest ten and then multiplying the numbers that are left in your head. _____

    c. Multiply $\begin{array}{r} 734 \\ \times\ 2 \\ \hline \end{array}$

Solve each word problem below.

    d. Tim started with 49 water balloons. After the first hour, he used 12 water balloons. After the second hour, he used another 18. How many water balloons does he have left to use? _____

    e. Michelle bought 6 packs of cola at the store. If each pack contains 12 cans of cola, how many cans of cola does she have in all? _____

Problem Set 27

Answer each question below.

    1. Tell what number LXXXV represents. _____

  (a) 2. Write the Roman numeral for 2,250. _____

Rewrite each multiplication below as the same number added to itself over and over.

    3. 9×4 _____

    4. 3×5 _____

Rewrite each expression below as a multiplication.

5. $4+4+4+4+4+4+4+4+4+4$ _____

6. $10+10+10+10+10+10+10+10$ _____

Multiply each pair of numbers in your head.

7. 4×4 _____   **8.** 8×11 _____

9. 4×12 _____

Find estimates for each of the problems below by rounding the first number to the nearest ten and then multiplying the numbers that are left in your head.

(b) 10. 42×3 _____   **11.** 81×4 _____

12. 51×9 _____

Multiply each pair of numbers below.

13.
$$\begin{array}{r} 33 \\ \times\ 2 \\ \hline \end{array}$$

14.
$$\begin{array}{r} 61 \\ \times\ 6 \\ \hline \end{array}$$

15.
$$\begin{array}{r} 92 \\ \times\ 4 \\ \hline \end{array}$$

16.
$$\begin{array}{r} 141 \\ \times\ 2 \\ \hline \end{array}$$

(c) 17.
$$\begin{array}{r} 523 \\ \times\ 3 \\ \hline \end{array}$$

18.
$$\begin{array}{r} 912 \\ \times\ 4 \\ \hline \end{array}$$

19.
$$\begin{array}{r} 811 \\ \times\ 7 \\ \hline \end{array}$$

Solve each word problem below.

(d) 20. Jenny has 59 different colored crayons and she plans to use them all at some point during the day. In her first picture, she used 15 different colored crayons. In her second picture, she used another 18. How many colored crayons does she have left to use?
_____

21. In order to stay in shape, Stewart runs 5 miles every day. How many miles will he run in one week (which is 7 days)? _____

(e) 22. Mrs. Preston bought 7 bags of peanut butter candies for her always-hungry brood. If each bag contained 15 candies, how many candies did she buy in all? _____

Lesson 28—Multiplication with Carrying

Sometimes we have to carry when multiplying, and the process is the same as with addition. Here's an example.

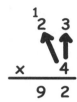

Multiply 2×4, then add the 1 that was carried.

See, when we multiplied the 3 and the 4, the answer was too big to fit below, so we carried the 1. Next, we multiplied the 2 and the 4 and then added the 1 that we carried, giving us an answer of 92. Here's another example.

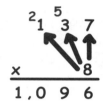

Carrying more than once.

Even though the numbers were larger in this one, we followed the same steps. We multiplied the 8 on the bottom by each number on top, but notice that we had to carry in both the tens and hundreds columns this time. Also, we had to carry a 5 in the tens column, which is fine because we can carry numbers bigger than 1. After multiplying everything, the final step was to put a comma between the 1 and the 0.

The main point of this lesson is that we sometimes have to carry when multiplying, but the process works the same as with addition.

Practice 28

a. Find an estimate for 68×3 by rounding the first number to the nearest ten and then multiplying the numbers that are left in your head. _____

Multiply each pair of numbers below.

b.
$$\begin{array}{r} 74 \\ \times\ 6 \\ \hline \end{array}$$

c.
$$\begin{array}{r} 692 \\ \times\ 7 \\ \hline \end{array}$$

Solve each word problem below.

    d. Tony is 12 years older than Ray, and Ray is 14 years older than Ben. If Ben is 23 years old, then how old is Tony? _____

    e. The computer company shipped 15 laptops to 6 different stores. How many laptops did they ship in all? _____

Problem Set 28

Tell whether each sentence below is True or False.

    1. We sometimes have to carry when multiplying, but the process works the same as with addition. _____

    2. On some multiplication problems, it's necessary to carry a number bigger than 1 into the tens column. _____

Answer each question below.

    3. Tell what number CVI represents. _____

    4. Write the Roman numeral for 2,110. _____

Rewrite each multiplication below as the same number added to itself over and over.

    5. 7×9 _____

    6. 9×3 _____

Rewrite each expression below as a multiplication.

    7. $4 + 4 + 4 + 4 + 4$ _____

    8. $5 + 5 + 5 + 5 + 5 + 5 + 5 + 5 + 5$ _____

Multiply each pair of numbers in your head.

    9. 6×11 _____   **10.** 7×12 _____   **11.** 8×12 _____

Find estimates for each of the problems below by rounding the first number to the nearest ten and then multiplying the numbers that are left in your head.

12. 82×3 _____   **(a) 13.** 48×4 _____

14. 79×6 _____

Multiply each pair of numbers below.

(b) 15.
$$\begin{array}{r} 27 \\ \times\, 3 \\ \hline \end{array}$$

16.
$$\begin{array}{r} 72 \\ \times\, 8 \\ \hline \end{array}$$

17.
$$\begin{array}{r} 95 \\ \times\, 6 \\ \hline \end{array}$$

18.
$$\begin{array}{r} 233 \\ \times\, 3 \\ \hline \end{array}$$

19.
$$\begin{array}{r} 416 \\ \times\, 4 \\ \hline \end{array}$$

(c) 20.
$$\begin{array}{r} 842 \\ \times\, 6 \\ \hline \end{array}$$

Solve each word problem below.

(d) 21. Annie is 11 years older than Tara, and Tara is 14 years older than Lacy. If Lacy is 26 years old, then how old is Annie? _____

(e) 22. The baton company shipped 18 batons to 4 different sporting goods stores. How many batons did they ship in all? _____

Quiz 4

Tell whether each sentence below is True or False.

1. You need to memorize all the multiplication facts because in real-life, you won't always have time to remember a special rule or find the answer by counting. _____

2. An estimate is the same as an exact answer. _____

Answer each question below.

3. Tell what number CCLXV represents. _____

4. Write the Roman numeral for 1,005. _____

Rewrite each multiplication below as the same number added to itself over and over.

5. 6×2 _____

6. 8×9 _____

Rewrite each expression below as a multiplication.

7. $3 + 3 + 3 + 3 + 3 + 3 + 3$ _____

8. $12 + 12 + 12 + 12 + 12 + 12$ _____

9. Finish the multiplication sequence for the number 8 by filling in the blanks: 0, 8, 16, ____, 32, ____, 48, ____, 64, ____, ____, 88, and 96.

10. Finish the multiplication sequence for the number 12 by filling in the blanks: 0, 12, ____, 36, ____, 60, ____, 84, 96, ____, 120, 132 and ____.

Multiply each pair of numbers in your head.

11. 0×17 _____   12. 4×10 _____

13. 9×11 _____

121

Find estimates for each of the problems below by rounding the first number to the nearest ten and then multiplying the numbers that are left in your head.

14. 31×8 _____

15. 48×5 _____

16. 67×7 _____

Multiply each pair of numbers below.

17.
$$\begin{array}{r} 41 \\ \times\ 2 \\ \hline \end{array}$$

18.
$$\begin{array}{r} 58 \\ \times\ 6 \\ \hline \end{array}$$

19.
$$\begin{array}{r} 86 \\ \times\ 7 \\ \hline \end{array}$$

20.
$$\begin{array}{r} 131 \\ \times\ 3 \\ \hline \end{array}$$

21.
$$\begin{array}{r} 362 \\ \times\ 4 \\ \hline \end{array}$$

22.
$$\begin{array}{r} 674 \\ \times\ 8 \\ \hline \end{array}$$

Solve each word problem below.

23. The Gamma Force started with a total of 86 missiles. If they used 23 missiles in the first battle and 32 missiles in the second battle, how many missiles do they have left? _____

24. The store had only 4 packages of batteries left. If each package contained 16 batteries, how many batteries is this in all? _____

Lesson 29—Multiplying Three Numbers

Sometimes it's necessary to multiply more than two numbers. Here's an example.

$$5 \times 6 \times 4$$

The way to do this is to multiply two of the numbers first, then take that first answer and multiply it by the third number.

$$\underbrace{5 \times 6}_{} \times 4$$
$$30 \quad \times 4 = 120$$

Go two at
a time.

See, first we multiplied the 5 and the 6 to get 30. Then, we took 30 and multiplied it by 4, which can be done in your head by multiplying 3 and 4 to get 12, and then adding a 0 at the end since there is one 0 in 30.

Remember, when you multiply two numbers, the order doesn't matter so 9×7 is the same as 7×9. It turns out that this rule also works with three numbers. In other words, when multiplying three numbers, it doesn't matter which two you multiply first, the answer will stay the same. Here's an example.

$$\underbrace{3 \times 5}_{} \times 4 \qquad \underbrace{5 \times 4}_{} \times 3$$
$$15 \quad \times 4 = 60 \qquad 20 \quad \times 3 = 60$$

Any order
will work.

On the left, we multiplied 3 by 5 first to get 15. Then, we multiplied that by 4 to get 60. On the right, we first multiplied 4 and 5 to get 20. Since 20×3 is 60, you can see that the answer is still the same. So again, the rule for multiplying in any order works not only for two numbers but also for three.

Practice 29

a. Find an estimate for 58×4 by rounding the first number to the nearest ten and then multiplying the numbers that are left in your head. _____

Multiply each group of numbers below.

b.
$$\begin{array}{r} 236 \\ \times\ 8 \\ \hline \end{array}$$

c. $3 \times 5 \times 7$ _____

123

Solve each word problem below.

   d. Sandy buried 12 more bones than Jake, and Jake buried 14 more bones than Duncan. If Duncan buried 15 bones, how many did Sandy bury? _____

   e. Juliana bought 6 boxes of animal crackers. If each box had 24 crackers in it, how many crackers did she buy altogether? _____

Problem Set 29

Tell whether each sentence below is True or False.

   1. When multiplying three numbers, you just multiply them two at a time. _____

   2. When multiplying three numbers, it doesn't matter which two we multiply first, the answer will stay the same. _____

Answer each question below.

   3. Tell what number CIII represents. _____

   4. Write the Roman numeral for 1,070. _____

Rewrite each multiplication below as the same number added to itself over and over.

   5. 5×2 _____

   6. 9×9 _____

Rewrite each expression below as a multiplication.

   7. $5+5+5+5+5+5+5$ _____

   8. $11+11+11+11+11+11+11$ _____

Find estimates for each of the problems below by rounding the first number to the nearest ten and then multiplying the numbers that are left in your head.

   9. 43×3 _____   **10.** 71×8 _____   **(a) 11.** 39×7 _____

Multiply each group of numbers below.

12.　$\begin{array}{r} 34 \\ \times\ 8 \\ \hline \end{array}$

13.　$\begin{array}{r} 57 \\ \times\ 7 \\ \hline \end{array}$

14.　$\begin{array}{r} 79 \\ \times\ 6 \\ \hline \end{array}$

15.　$\begin{array}{r} 512 \\ \times\ 4 \\ \hline \end{array}$

(b) 16.　$\begin{array}{r} 638 \\ \times\ 3 \\ \hline \end{array}$

17.　$\begin{array}{r} 726 \\ \times\ 5 \\ \hline \end{array}$

(c) 18.　$2 \times 6 \times 8$ _____

19.　$7 \times 5 \times 4$ _____

20.　$3 \times 9 \times 8$ _____

Solve each word problem below.

(d) 21.　Last year in the Mighty Tots football league, Runaway Ryan ran for 12 more touchdowns than Cody, and Cody ran for 16 more touchdowns than Leon. If Leon ran for 23 touchdowns, how many touchdowns did Runaway Ryan run for? _____

(e) 22.　Shirley, the caterer, baked 5 plates of brownies. If each plate had 22 brownies on it, how many brownies did she bake altogether? _____

Lesson 30—Points, Lines, and Line Segments

Geometry is the study of shapes, and the simplest idea in geometry is the idea of a **point**, which just looks like a little dot on paper. Points are always named with capital letters. Here's point P.

P
●

Points are named
with capital letters.

There are also lines in geometry. A **line** goes on forever in both directions, and to show that, we draw arrows on both ends.

The arrows show that
the line goes on forever
in both directions.

Notice that the line has two points. We can use these points to name the line, so the line above is line CD.

A **line segment** is just part of a line, which means it doesn't go on forever. Every line segment has two ends called **endpoints**. These are used to name the segment, so this is line segment GH.

A line segment stops
on both ends.

The important thing to keep in mind is that a line goes on forever in both directions, but a line segment stops on both ends. Sometimes you'll see two line segments joined together. This is a line with three points on it, S, T, and U.

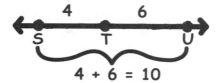

Add the two lengths
together to find
the length of SU.

It's a line because of the arrows, but the line also has segments on it because of the points. Line segment ST has a length of 4 and segment TU has a length of 6. To find the length of line segment SU, just add the lengths of segment ST and TU. Since $4+6$ is 10, segment SU has a length of 10.

Here's a tougher line segment problem where we're given the length of the bigger segment and one of the little segments and have to find the length of the other little segment.

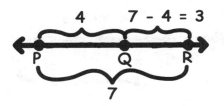

Subtract to find the length of QR.

The length of segment PQ is 4, and the length of the big segment PR is 7. Using that information, we can find the length of segment QR by subtracting the length of the segment PQ from the length of segment PR. Since $7 - 4$ is 3, line segment QR has a length of 3. Just remember that on problems like this, we always subtract the little segment whose length is known from the big segment to get the length of the other little segment.

Practice 30

Multiply each group of numbers below.

a.
$$
\begin{array}{r}
753 \\
\times\ 4 \\
\hline
\end{array}
$$

b.　$6 \times 5 \times 8$ _____

c.　Tell whether the picture below is a line, line segment or point. _____

d.　In the diagram below, the length of line segment MN is 3, and the length of line segment NO is 5. What is the length of line segment MO? _____

127

e. In the diagram below, the length of line segment PR is 6 inches, and the length of line segment QR is 4 inches. What is the length of line segment PQ? _____

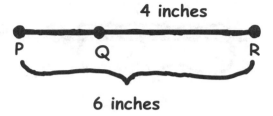

4 inches

P   Q   R

6 inches

Problem Set 30

Tell whether each sentence below is True or False.

1. Points are always named with lower case letters. _____

2. A line has two ends called endpoints. _____

Select the best possible choice to fill in the blanks below.

3. A _____ goes on forever in both directions.

    A. point   B. line segment   C. subtraction
    D. line   E. geometry

4. The dots at the ends of a line segment are called_____.

    A. endpoints   B. line dots   C. polka dots
    D. rays   E. none of the above

Answer each question below.

5. Write the Roman numeral for 3,100. _____

6. Rewrite 7×12 as the same number added to itself over and over. _____

Find estimates for each of the problems below by rounding the first number to the nearest ten and then multiplying the numbers that are left in your head.

7. 43×4 _____   8. 68×5 _____

Multiply each group of numbers below.

9. 23
    × 4
    ___

10. 55
     × 6
     ___

11. 96
     × 8
     ___

12. 146
     × 2
     ___

(a) 13. 365
         × 3
         ___

14. 632
     × 9
     ___

(b) 15. $7 \times 2 \times 5$ _____

16. $3 \times 6 \times 4$ _____

17. $9 \times 8 \times 2$ _____

Solve each word problem below.

18. Kyle is 10 years older than Darren, and Darren is 14 years older than Luke. If Luke is 27 years old, how old is Kyle? _____

19. Laura put 15 French fries in each holder. If there are 4 holders, how many French fries are there in total? _____

Answer each question below.

(c) 20. Tell whether the picture below is a line, line segment or point. _____

(d) 21. In the diagram below, the length of line segment GH is 6, and the length of line segment HI is 10. What is the length of line segment GI? _____

(e) 22. In the diagram below, the length of line segment JL is 18 inches, and the length of line segment KL is 12 inches. What is the length of line segment JK? _____

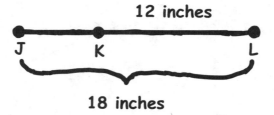

Lesson 31—Angles

When lines or segments cross, they form an **angle**. The technical word for cross is **intersect**, so line segments JK and KL below intersect at point K. The angle is just the space in the middle. JK and KL are called the sides of the angle, and point K is called the **vertex**. The vertex is the point where the sides of an angle intersect.

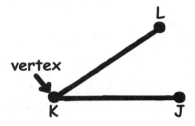

Segments KL and KJ
form the sides of the
angle. The vertex is K.

The angle above can be named angle K because K is the vertex. As long as you use the vertex, you can name an angle with just one letter. Here's another angle.

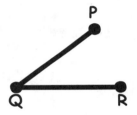

You can use the
vertex to name
the angle.

This angle could be called angle Q, but it could also be called angle PQR or angle RQP. The last two names are correct because the vertex, point Q, is in the middle. The other two letters, P and R, can be in any order as long as the vertex is the middle letter. Also, there's a special symbol for an angle. It looks like this: $\angle$. So the angle could be called $\angle Q$, $\angle PQR$, or $\angle RQP$.

Actually, sometimes you have to name an angle with three points because using just the vertex would cause confusion. Here's an example.

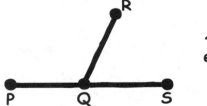

$\angle Q$ isn't specific
enough.

In this situation, if you were to tell somebody to look at angle Q, it wouldn't be clear which angle you meant, so you'd have to call the angle $\angle PQR$ or $\angle SQR$, depending on the angle you were talking about. Just remember, when there's more than one angle with the same vertex, use three letters.

Practice 31

Multiply each group of numbers below.

a.
$$\begin{array}{r} 477 \\ \times\,6 \\ \hline \end{array}$$

b. $6 \times 2 \times 8$ _____

c. In the diagram below, the length of line segment DF is 18 feet, and the length of line segment EF is 7 feet. What is the length of line segment DE? _____

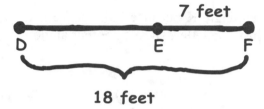

d. Name the vertex of the angle below. _____

    A. point A
    B. point B
    C. point C
    D. none of the above

e. Name the angle below in the simplest way possible. _____

    A. $\angle POQ$
    B. $\angle PQR$
    C. $\angle O$
    D. $\angle POR$
    E. $\angle QOR$

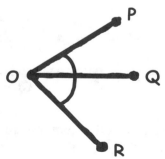

Problem Set 31

Tell whether each sentence below is True or False.

1. The sides of an angle intersect at the vertex. _____

2. We can always name an angle using just one point. _____

Answer each question below.

3. Tell what number CCCXX represents. _____

4. Write $11+11+11+11+11+11+11+11$ as a multiplication. _____

Multiply each group of numbers below.

5. $\begin{array}{r} 62 \\ \times\ 8 \\ \hline \end{array}$

6. $\begin{array}{r} 58 \\ \times\ 6 \\ \hline \end{array}$

7. $\begin{array}{r} 125 \\ \times\ 5 \\ \hline \end{array}$

(a) 8. $\begin{array}{r} 299 \\ \times\ 4 \\ \hline \end{array}$

9. $\begin{array}{r} 557 \\ \times\ 8 \\ \hline \end{array}$

10. $\begin{array}{r} 824 \\ \times\ 9 \\ \hline \end{array}$

(b) 11. $2 \times 6 \times 9$ _____

12. $7 \times 5 \times 8$ _____

13. $4 \times 3 \times 7$ _____

Find estimates for each of the problems below by rounding the first number to the nearest ten and then multiplying the numbers that are left in your head.

14. 33×7 _____

15. 87×6 _____

Answer each question below.

16. In the diagram below, the length of line segment GH is 12, and the length of line segment HI is 18. What is the length of line segment GI? _____

(c) 17. In the diagram below, the length of line segment UW is 15 feet, and the length of line segment UV is 10 feet. What is the length of line segment VW? _____

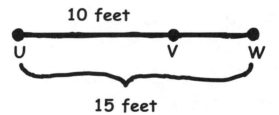

(d) 18. Name the vertex of the angle below. _____

A. point T
B. point R
C. point Q
D. none of the above

19. Name the angle below in the simplest way possible. _____

A. ∠BCD
B. ∠D
C. ∠B
D. ∠DCB
E. ∠C

(e) **20.** Name the angle below in the simplest way possible. _____

A. ∠TPR
B. ∠TPS
C. ∠P
D. ∠TSR
E. ∠S

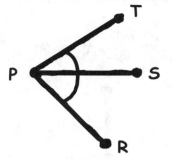

Solve each word problem below.

21. There were 56 cans of soda in the machine at the beginning of the week. On Monday, 15 cans of soda were bought, and on Tuesday, 16 more were bought. How many cans of soda are left? _____

22. Kristen bought 3 boxes of oranges. If each box contained 25 oranges, how many oranges did Kristen buy? _____

Lesson 32—Types of Angles

Angles can be big or small depending on how far apart the sides are, and some angles are shaped like an L. These are called **right angles**.

An angle that makes an L-shape is called a right angle.

It's sometimes hard to tell if an angle is truly a right angle, but if there is a little square in the angle, it's definitely a right angle, no matter which way it's turned.

The little square means it's a right angle.

Angles that are smaller than an L-shape are called **acute angles**. Here's an acute angle.

An angle smaller than an L-shape is called an acute angle.

Notice that the sides are squeezed together so there's less space inside than in a right triangle.

The last type of angle is called an **obtuse angle**, and it's bigger than an L-shape.

An angle bigger than an L-shape is called an obtuse angle.

An obtuse angle has more space inside of it than a right angle does.

The main point of this lesson is that there are three types of angles: a right angle, which has an L-shape, an acute angle, which is smaller than an L-shape, and an obtuse angle, which is bigger than an L-shape.

Practice 32

Multiply each group of numbers below.

a.
$$\begin{array}{r} 427 \\ \times\ 4 \\ \hline \end{array}$$

b. $3 \times 6 \times 8$ _____

c. In the diagram below, the length of line segment EG is 27 inches, and the length of line segment EF is 12 inches. What is the length of line segment FG? _____

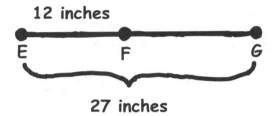

d. Which of the choices below shows an acute angle? _____

A.
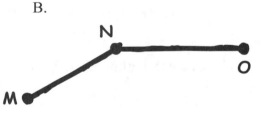

B.
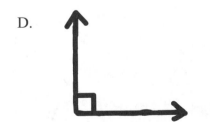

C.

D.

e. Name the type of angle below. _____

   A. acute
   B. right
   C. obtuse

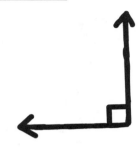

Problem Set 32

Tell whether each sentence below is True or False.

1. An acute angle has an L-shape. _____

2. A right angle is smaller than an L-shaped angle. _____

3. An obtuse angle is larger than an L-shaped angle. _____

Answer each question below.

4. Write the Roman numeral for 2,012. _____

5. Rewrite 7×10 as the same number added to itself over and over. _____

Multiply each group of numbers below.

(a) 6.
$$\begin{array}{r} 845 \\ \times\ 4 \\ \hline \end{array}$$

7.
$$\begin{array}{r} 998 \\ \times\ 6 \\ \hline \end{array}$$

8.
$$\begin{array}{r} 873 \\ \times\ 9 \\ \hline \end{array}$$

(b) 9. $3 \times 7 \times 4$ _____

10. $9 \times 2 \times 6$ _____

11. $5 \times 9 \times 4$ _____

Find estimates for each of the problems below by rounding the first number to the nearest ten and then multiplying the numbers that are left in your head.

12. 59×8 _____

13. 93×9 _____

Answer each question below.

14. In the diagram below, the length of line segment JK is 9, and the length of line segment KL is 15. What is the length of line segment JL? _____

(c) 15. In the diagram below, the length of line segment PR is 27 inches, and the length of line segment PQ is 21 inches. What is the length of line segment QR? _____

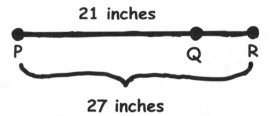

16. Name the vertex of the angle below. _____

   A. point R
   B. point S
   C. point T
   D. none of the above

17. Name the angle below in the simplest way possible. _____

   A. ∠OMN
   B. ∠MON
   C. ∠M
   D. ∠O
   E. ∠NOM

18. Name the angle below in the simplest way possible. _____

    A. $\angle A$
    B. $\angle C$
    C. $\angle BAC$
    D. $\angle BAD$
    E. $\angle CAD$

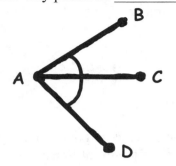

(d) 19. Which of the choices below shows an acute angle? _____

    A.

    B.

    C.

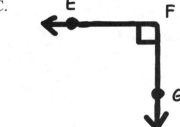

    D.

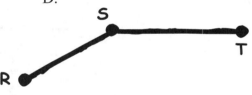

(e) 20. Name the type of angle below. _____

    A. obtuse
    B. acute
    C. right

Solve each word problem below.

21. Rachel is 13 years older than Elizabeth, and Elizabeth is 18 years older than Jen. If Jen is 22 years old, how old is Rachel? _____

22. Brice wants to play 4 rounds of golf this week. If he plays 18 holes each round, how many holes will he play altogether? _____

Lesson 33—Perpendicular and Parallel Lines

Sometimes two lines don't look like they cross (intersect) just because they haven't been drawn long enough, but since lines go on forever in both directions, they usually will intersect. Some lines don't intersect though, and we call those **parallel lines**.

Parallel lines never intersect.

Parallel lines never cross because they slant in exactly the same direction, which means they will always stay exactly the same distance apart.

A horizontal line is just a line that runs straight across from left to right and a vertical line is a line that runs straight up and down. When a horizontal and vertical line intersect, they create four right angles.

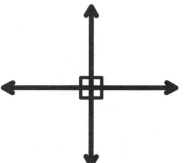

Vertical and horizontal lines intersect to form right angles.

Notice that there are four L-shaped angles in total. Here, the right angle symbol is on each angle, but you'll usually see the symbol on only one of the angles. One symbol is all that is needed to show that all four angles are right angles. Intersecting lines that form right angles are actually called perpendicular lines, and perpendicular lines don't have to be straight across and straight up and down to create right angles. If we rotate both of the lines above to the left a bit, all four angles will still be right angles.

Lines that intersect to form right angles are called perpendicular lines.

Practice 33

Multiply each group of numbers below.

a.
$$\begin{array}{r} 382 \\ \times\ 6 \\ \hline \end{array}$$

b. $6 \times 8 \times 0$ _____

c. Name the angle below in the simplest way possible. _____

    A. $\angle Q$
    B. $\angle O$
    C. $\angle NQO$
    D. $\angle NOP$
    E. $\angle NQP$

d. Which pair of lines below are parallel? _____

A.
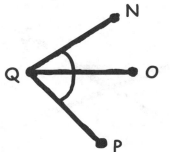

B.

C.

D.
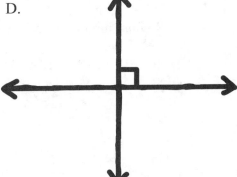

e. Which pair of lines below are perpendicular? _____

A.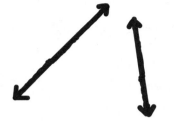

B.

C.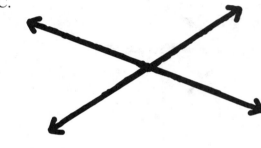

D.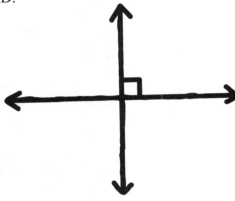

Problem Set 33

Tell whether each sentence below is True or False.

1. Parallel lines never cross because they slant in exactly the same direction. _____

2. Perpendicular lines are intersecting lines that form right angles. _____

Answer each question below.

3. Tell what number CCXII represents. _____

4. Write $12+12+12+12+12+12+12+12+12$ as a multiplication. _____

Multiply each group of numbers below.

(a) 5.
$$\begin{array}{r} 493 \\ \times\ 7 \\ \hline \end{array}$$

6.
$$\begin{array}{r} 554 \\ \times\ 8 \\ \hline \end{array}$$

7.
$$\begin{array}{r} 913 \\ \times\ 9 \\ \hline \end{array}$$

(b) 8. $9 \times 4 \times 0$ _____

9. $8 \times 7 \times 2$ _____

10. $6 \times 5 \times 6$ _____

Find estimates for each of the problems below by rounding the first number to the nearest ten and then multiplying the numbers that are left in your head.

11. 89×4 _____

12. 72×9 _____

Answer each question below.

13. In the diagram below, the length of line segment XY is 24 inches, and the length of line segment YZ is 30 inches. What is the length of line segment XZ? _____

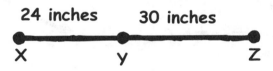

14. In the diagram below, the length of line segment TV is 36 yards, and the length of line segment TU is 16 yards. What is the length of line segment UV? _____

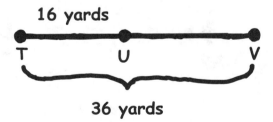

15. Name the angle below in the simplest way possible. _____

A. ∠G
B. ∠F
C. ∠FGH
D. ∠HGF
E. ∠H

(c) 16. Name the angle below in the simplest way possible. _____

A. ∠Q
B. ∠S
C. ∠RQT
D. ∠RST
E. ∠RQS

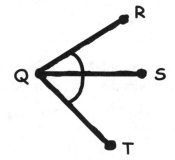

17. Which of the choices below shows an obtuse angle? _____

A.

B.

C.

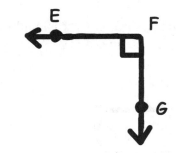

D.

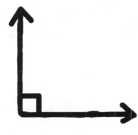

18. Name the type of angle below. _____

A. right
B. acute
C. obtuse

(d) 19. Which of the choices below shows a pair of parallel lines? _____

A.

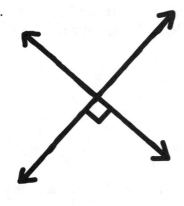

B.

C.

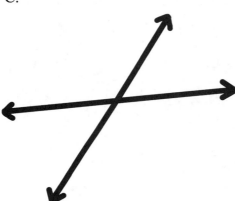

D.

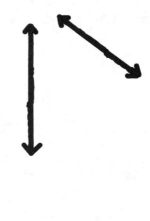

(e) 20. Which of the choices below shows a pair of perpendicular lines? _____

A.

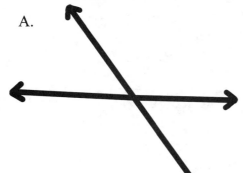

B.

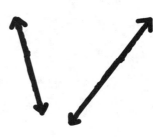

C.

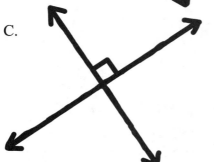

D.

Solve each word problem below.

21. Linus started with 25 gallons of gasoline in his car. He used 11 gallons to get to his first stop and 12 gallons to get to his second stop. How many gallons of gasoline does Linus have left? _____

22. Mrs. Shelton teaches 5 classes each day, and she has 23 students in each class. How many students does she have in all? _____

Lesson 34—Types of Triangles – Scalene, Isosceles, and Equilateral

Geometry shapes are called figures. One example of a figure is a triangle. All triangles have three sides and three angles, and the points where each of the sides connect are called the triangle's vertices, which is just the plural form for vertex.

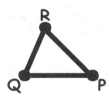

All triangles have
three sides and
three angles.

Vertices are used to name triangles, so the triangle above can be called ΔPQR. The little symbol in front of the letters just means triangle.

Some triangles are known for the lengths of their sides. For example, ΔPQR is called a **scalene triangle** because all of its sides have different lengths.

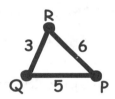

A scalene triangle
has lengths that are
all different sizes.

Another kind of triangle is one where two of the sides are equal. Triangles with two equal sides are called **isosceles triangles**. So ΔABC below is an isosceles triangle.

Triangles with two
equal sides are called
isosceles triangles.

Lastly, triangles where all three sides are the same length are called **equilateral triangles**. The triangle below, ΔDEF, is equilateral because all of its sides have a length of 7.

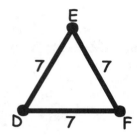

All three sides of an equilateral triangle are equal.

Practice 34

a. In the diagram below, the length of line segment AC is 48 feet, and the length of line segment AB is 22 feet. What is the length of line segment BC? _____

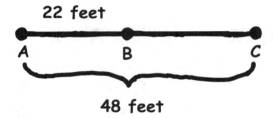

22 feet

48 feet

Tell whether each triangle below is scalene, isosceles, or equilateral.

b. _____

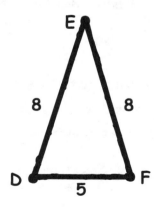

c. _____

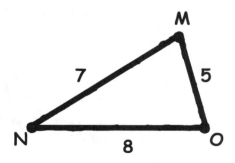

Solve each word problem below.

d. Sam is 17 years older than Jake, and Jake is 16 years older than Corey. If Corey is 33 years old, how old is Sam? _____

e. The doll-making shop needs to put 4 shoes in each of the 22 packages. How many shoes will this be altogether? _____

Problem Set 34

Tell whether each sentence below is True or False.

1. A scalene triangle is a triangle where all three sides are the same length. _____

2. An isosceles triangle is a triangle with two equal sides. _____

3. An equilateral triangle is a triangle where all three sides have different lengths. _____

Answer each question below.

4. Write the Roman numeral for 3,009. _____

5. Rewrite 8×11 as the same number added to itself over and over. _____

Multiply each group of numbers below.

6.
$$
\begin{array}{r}
513 \\
\times 8 \\
\hline
\end{array}
$$

7.
$$
\begin{array}{r}
566 \\
\times 5 \\
\hline
\end{array}
$$

8.
$$
\begin{array}{r}
983 \\
\times 7 \\
\hline
\end{array}
$$

9. $5 \times 4 \times 2$ _____

10. $7 \times 1 \times 8$ _____

11. $9 \times 4 \times 9$ _____

Find estimates for each of the problems below by rounding the first number to the nearest ten and then multiplying the numbers that are left in your head.

12. 49×3 _____

13. 81×7 _____

Answer each question below.

(a) 14. In the diagram below, the length of line segment LN is 56 feet, and the length of line segment LM is 14 feet. What is the length of line segment MN? _____

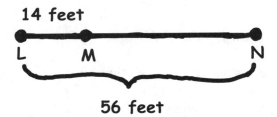

15. Name the angle below in the simplest way possible. _____

    A. ∠*U*
    B. ∠*VUW*
    C. ∠*TUV*
    D. ∠*TVW*
    E. ∠*TUW*

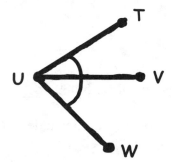

16. Which of the choices below shows a pair of parallel lines? _____

A.

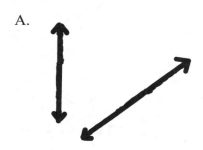

B.

C.

D.

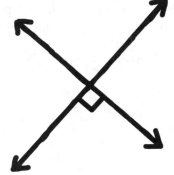

17. Which of the choices below shows a pair of perpendicular lines? _____

A.

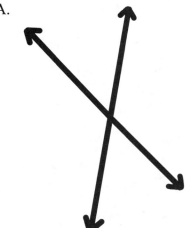

B.

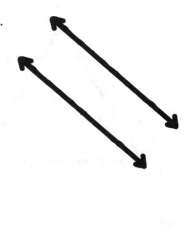

C.

D.

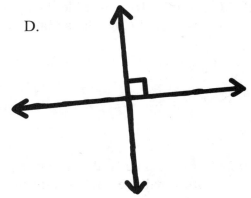

Tell whether each triangle below is scalene, isosceles, or equilateral.

(b) 18. _____

(c) 19. _____

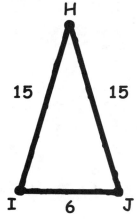

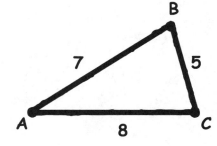

153

20. _____

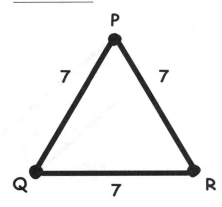

Solve each word problem below.

(d) 21. Matt is 18 years older than Nick, and Nick is 12 years older than James. If James is 24 years old, how old is Matt? _____

(e) 22. Moe's Tire Outlet was asked to put 4 new tires on each of the 25 used cars. How many tires will they put on altogether? _____

Lesson 35—Types of Triangles – Acute, Right, Obtuse

In addition to side lengths, you can tell the differences between triangles by looking at their angles. An **acute triangle** is a triangle that has all acute angles. Here's an example.

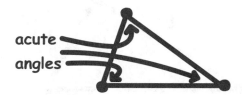

Acute triangles have all acute angles.

Remember, an acute angle is just an angle that is smaller than a right angle, and all three angles of this triangle are smaller than an L-shape.

Another kind of triangle is a right triangle. **Right triangles** are just triangles with one right angle.

Right triangles have one right angle.

Notice that this triangle has the right angle symbol on one of the angles. Whenever you see a box like that in a triangle, you know it's a right triangle.

The last group of triangles are called obtuse triangles. An **obtuse triangle** has one angle that's bigger than a right angle.

An obtuse triangle has one angle that is bigger than a right angle.

We can actually mention sides *and* angles when describing triangles. For example, a triangle could be equilateral because all of its sides are the same length and acute because all of its angles are smaller than a right angle. A triangle could also be both isosceles and right.

equilateral
acute

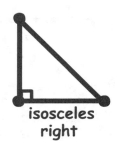

isosceles
right

You can use both sides and angles to describe a triangle.

155

Practice 35

a. Tell whether the triangle below is scalene, isosceles, or equilateral. _____

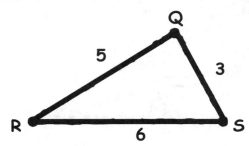

b. Tell whether the triangle below is acute, right, or obtuse. _____

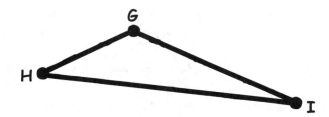

c. Describe the triangle below with the best of the following choices: isosceles acute, isosceles right, or isosceles obtuse. _____

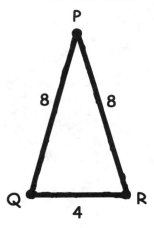

Solve each word problem below.

d. The postman needs to deliver 65 letters. The first hour he delivered 26 letters and the second hour he delivered 35 letters. How many letters does he have left to deliver?

_____

e.   Farmer Brown has 8 rows of pepper plants in his patch. If each row contains 28 pepper plants, how many pepper plants does he have in all? _____

Problem Set 35

Tell whether each sentence below is True or False.

1.   An acute triangle is one where all of the angles are L-shaped. _____

2.   A triangle with a right angle is called a right triangle. _____

3.   An obtuse triangle is made up of all acute angles. _____

Answer each question below.

4.   Tell what number CCCLI represents. _____

5.   Rewrite $12+12+12+12+12+12+12$ as a multiplication. _____

Multiply each group of numbers below.

6. $\begin{array}{r} 544 \\ \times\ 4 \\ \hline \end{array}$
7. $\begin{array}{r} 638 \\ \times\ 6 \\ \hline \end{array}$
8. $\begin{array}{r} 927 \\ \times\ 7 \\ \hline \end{array}$

9. $4\times6\times3$ _____
10. $5\times7\times5$ _____
11. $8\times7\times9$ _____

Find estimates for each of the problems below by rounding the first number to the nearest ten and then multiplying the numbers that are left in your head.

12. 53×5 _____
13. 68×9 _____

Answer each question below.

(a) 14. In the diagram below, the length of line segment UW is 63 yards, and the length of line segment UV is 42 yards. What is the length of line segment VW? _____

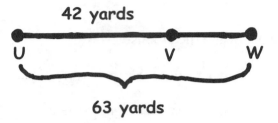

42 yards

U   V   W

63 yards

15. Which of the choices below shows a pair of perpendicular lines? _____

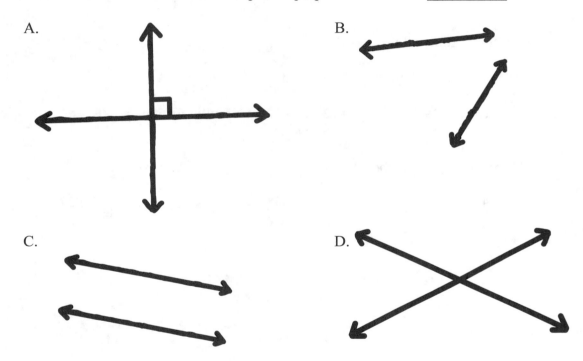

A.

B.

C.

D.

(b) 16. Tell whether the triangle below is scalene, isosceles, or equilateral. _____

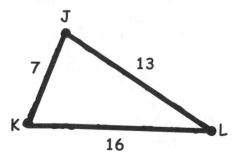

J

7   13

K   L

16

Tell whether each triangle below is acute, right, or obtuse.

17. _____

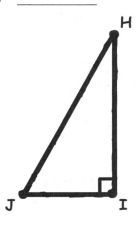

(c) 18. _____

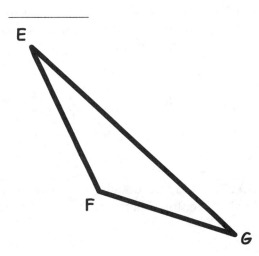

Describe each triangle below with the best of the following choices: equilateral acute, isosceles acute, or isosceles obtuse.

19. _____

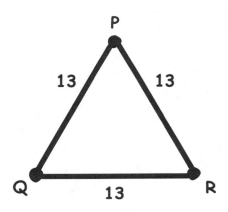

(e) 20. _____

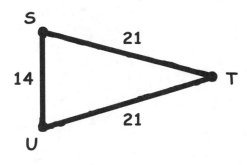

Solve each word problem below.

(d) 21. The ice skating rink has a total of 65 pairs of ice skates to rent. The first hour they rented 22 pairs and the second hour they rented 18 pairs. How many pairs of ice skates do they have left? _____

(e) 22. Maggie bought 4 packages of colored pens at the store. If each package contains 18 colored pens, how many colored pens did Maggie buy? _____

Quiz 5

Tell whether each sentence below is True or False.

1. The sides of an angle intersect at the vertex. _____

2. An acute triangle is one where all of the angles are larger than an L-shape. _____

Answer each question below.

3. Write the Roman numeral for 1,004. _____

4. Rewrite 4×11 as the same number added to itself over and over. _____

5. Rewrite $13 + 13 + 13 + 13 + 13$ as a multiplication. _____

Multiply each group of numbers below.

6.
$$\begin{array}{r} 57 \\ \times\ 7 \\ \hline \end{array}$$

7.
$$\begin{array}{r} 512 \\ \times\ 4 \\ \hline \end{array}$$

8.
$$\begin{array}{r} 638 \\ \times\ 3 \\ \hline \end{array}$$

9.
$$\begin{array}{r} 726 \\ \times\ 5 \\ \hline \end{array}$$

10. $3 \times 9 \times 0$ _____

11. $7 \times 5 \times 9$ _____

12. $2 \times 6 \times 8$ _____

Answer each question below.

13. Tell whether the picture below is a line, line segment or point. _____

14. In the diagram below, the length of line segment EF is 8, and the length of line segment FG is 19. What is the length of line segment EG? _____

15. In the diagram below, the length of line segment RT is 64 feet, and the length of line segment ST is 32 feet. What is the length of line segment RS? _____

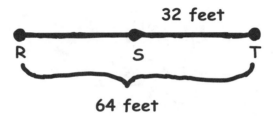

16. Name the vertex of the angle below. _____

    A. point G
    B. point H
    C. point I
    D. none of the above

17. Name the angle below in the simplest way possible. _____

    A. $\angle O$
    B. $\angle ROQ$
    C. $\angle PRQ$
    D. $\angle POQ$
    E. $\angle POR$

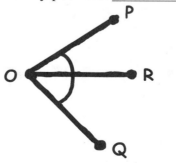

18. Which of the choices below shows an acute angle? _____

A.
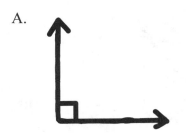

B.

C.
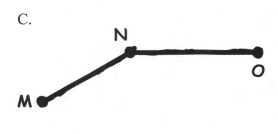

D.
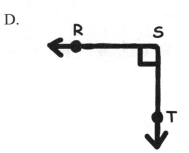

19. Which of the choices below shows a pair of perpendicular lines? _____

A.
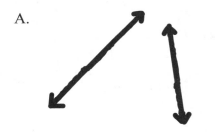

B.
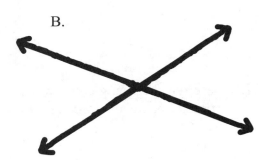

C.
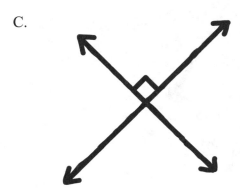

D.
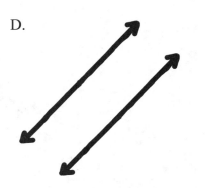

20. Tell whether the triangle below is scalene, isosceles, or equilateral. _____

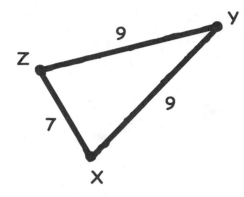

21. Tell whether the triangle below is acute, right, or obtuse. _____

22. Describe the triangle below with the best of the following choices: equilateral acute, isosceles acute, or isosceles obtuse. _____

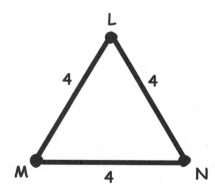

Solve each question below.

23. Last season, Jerome made 14 more free throws than Anthony, and Anthony made 16 more free throws than Brent. If Brent made 29 free throws, how many did Jerome make? _____

24. Jessica bought 6 packages of stickers at the store. If each package contains 24 stickers, how many stickers did Jessica buy? _____

Lesson 36—Polygons

A **polygon** is just a shape with straight sides that's closed all the way around. So, a triangle is a polygon because it has three straight sides and it's closed, which just means you can tell where the inside and outside are.

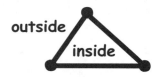

Triangles are polygons with three sides.

Triangles actually have the fewest number of sides of any polygon.

The next polygon after the triangle is called a **quadrilateral**, which is a four-sided figure. Here are a few examples.

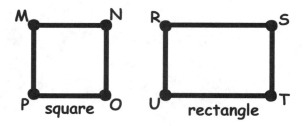

Quadrilaterals are polygons with four sides.

The figure on the left is a **square**, which is the simplest kind of quadrilateral. Notice that it has four sides, MN, NO, OP, and PM, and it also has four angles: M, N, O, and P. The figure on the right is a **rectangle**, which is also a quadrilateral.

Some polygons have more than four sides. A **pentagon** has five sides, a **hexagon** has six sides, and an **octagon** has eight sides. Here are examples of each.

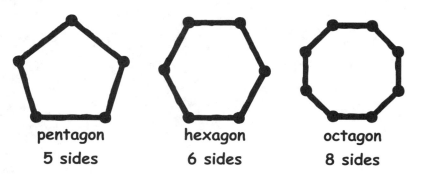

pentagon
5 sides

hexagon
6 sides

octagon
8 sides

Practice 36

a. Describe the triangle below with the best of the following choices: isosceles acute, isosceles right, or isosceles obtuse. _____

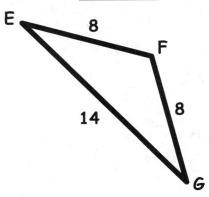

Tell whether each polygon below is a triangle, quadrilateral, pentagon, hexagon, or octagon.

b. _____

c. _____

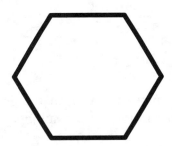

Solve each word problem below.

d. Gary had 85 stamps in his collection. Then he gave 21 stamps to Benjamin and 14 stamps to Tommy. How many stamps does he have now? _____

e. If the coaches bought 5 cases of bottled water and each case had 18 bottles, how many bottles of water did the coaches buy altogether? _____

Problem Set 36

Tell whether each sentence below is True or False.

1. A polygon is a closed shape with crooked sides. _____

2. A triangle is not a polygon. _____

3. A quadrilateral has four sides. _____

Multiply each group of numbers below.

4.
$$\begin{array}{r} 693 \\ \times\,6 \\ \hline \end{array}$$

5.
$$\begin{array}{r} 398 \\ \times\,5 \\ \hline \end{array}$$

6.
$$\begin{array}{r} 816 \\ \times\,9 \\ \hline \end{array}$$

7. $8 \times 9 \times 8$ _____

8. $5 \times 7 \times 6$ _____

9. $9 \times 4 \times 5$ _____

Find estimates for each of the problems below by rounding the first number to the nearest ten and then multiplying the numbers that are left in your head.

10. 19×9 _____

11. 83×7 _____

Answer each question below.

12. In the diagram below, the length of line segment AE is 72 feet, and the length of line segment AC is 32 feet. What is the length of line segment CE? _____

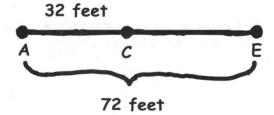

13. Tell whether the triangle below is scalene, isosceles, or equilateral. _____

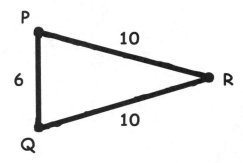

14. Tell whether the triangle below is acute, right, or obtuse. _____

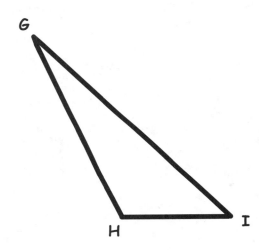

(a) 15. Describe the triangle below with the best of the following choices: isosceles acute, isosceles right, or isosceles obtuse. _____

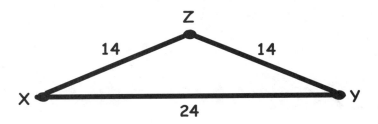

Tell whether the polygon below is a triangle, quadrilateral, pentagon, hexagon, or octagon.

16. _____

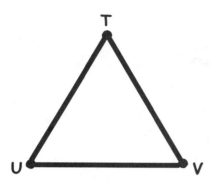

(b) 17. _____

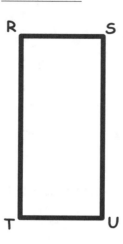

18. _____

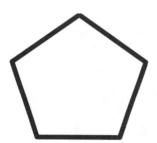

(c) 19. _____

20. _____

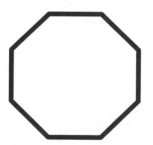

Solve each word problem below.

(d) 21. The carnival game operator started the day with 45 stuffed animals in his booth. He gave away 15 animals to winning contestants in the morning and 16 to winning contestants in the afternoon. How many stuffed animals does he have now?

_____

(e) 22. Katherine needed to buy balloons for her friend's birthday party. If she bought 5 packages and there were 25 balloons in each package, how many balloons did she buy altogether? _____

Lesson 37—Perimeter

Sometimes we have to calculate the distance around a polygon. For example, if we need to know the distance around a rectangular swimming pool, we would just add up the lengths of each side.

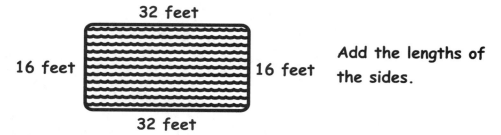

Add the lengths of the sides.

Starting with the left-hand side, $16+32$ is 48, and since the other two sides have the same lengths as the first two, we can just add 48 to 48 to get 96. So the distance around the pool is 96 feet. The distance around a polygon is actually called the **perimeter**.

When finding the perimeter of a square, we can either add the lengths of all the sides, or just multiply the length of one side by four, since all the sides have the same length.

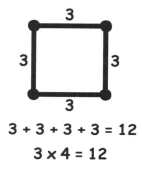

Add the lengths of the sides, or multiply one length by four.

$$3 + 3 + 3 + 3 = 12$$
$$3 \times 4 = 12$$

Notice that we get the same answer whether multiplying or adding. However, this only works with shapes that have sides that are all the same length. For example, to find the perimeter of this hexagon, you'd have to add the lengths of the sides since they aren't all the same.

Add the lengths of the sides to find the perimeter.

$$3 + 7 + 5 + 4 + 2 + 6 = 27$$

After adding up all of the sides, the sum turned out to be 27, so the perimeter is 27.

Practice 37

a. Tell whether the polygon below is a triangle, quadrilateral, pentagon, hexagon, or octagon. _____

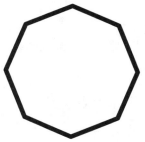

Find the perimeter of each polygon below.

b. _____

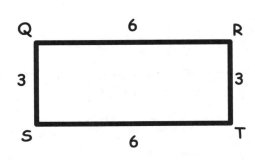

c. _____

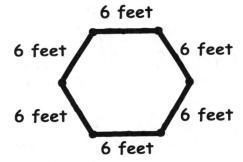

Solve each word problem below.

d. Carl is 23 years older than Mike, and Mike is 16 years older than Martin. If Martin is 19 years old, how old is Carl? _____

e. Each of the cheerleaders' bags can hold 4 pom-poms. If there are 15 bags, how many pom-poms are there in all? _____

Problem Set 37

Tell whether each sentence below is True or False.

1. The distance around a polygon is called the perimeter. _____

2. A square is a polygon and a quadrilateral. _____

173

Multiply each group of numbers below.

3. 368
     × 6

4. 199
     × 9

5. 684
     × 7

6. $6 \times 4 \times 4$ _____

7. $7 \times 9 \times 2$ _____

8. $5 \times 9 \times 0$ _____

Find estimates for each of the problems below by rounding the first number to the nearest ten and then multiplying the numbers that are left in your head.

9. 28×8 _____

10. 71×9 _____

Answer each question below.

11. In the diagram below, the length of line segment BE is 88 inches, and the length of line segment BD is 52 inches. What is the length of line segment DE? _____

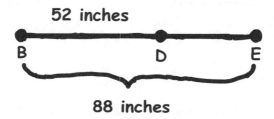

12. Tell whether the triangle below is scalene, isosceles, or equilateral. _____

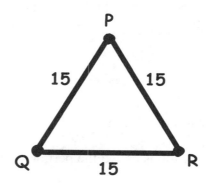

13. Tell whether the triangle below is acute, right, or obtuse. _____

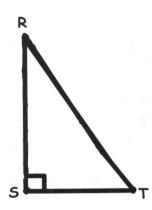

14. Describe the triangle below with the best of the following choices: isosceles acute, isosceles right, or isosceles obtuse. _____

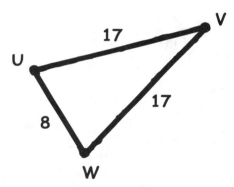

Tell whether the polygon below is a triangle, quadrilateral, pentagon, hexagon, or octagon.

15. _____   **(a) 16.** _____

Find the perimeter of each polygon below.

(b) 17. _____

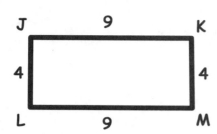

18. _____

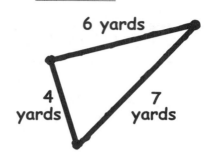

19. _____

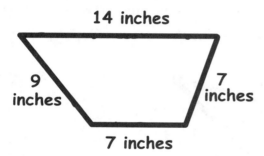

(c) 20. _____

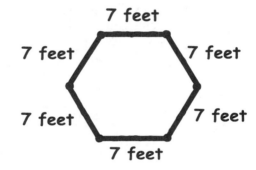

Solve each word problem below.

(d) 21. Amy is 22 years older than Kate, and Kate is 19 years older than Mary. If Mary is 18 years old, how old is Amy? _____

(e) 22. Each of the barrels can hold 28 gallons of radioactive sludge. If there are 6 barrels, how many gallons of radioactive sludge are there in all? _____

Lesson 38—Area

Sometimes we need to know how much space there is inside a polygon. For example, if we were planting flowers in a square flower bed, we'd need to know how much space was inside.

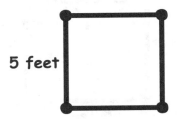

5 feet

How much space
is inside?

Notice that only one side length is given, but since the sides of a square have the same length, the other sides have to be 5 feet too. To measure the space inside, you can fill the square with smaller squares and then count them. Since the length and width of this square are measured in feet, we'll fill the square with little squares that are 1 foot long and 1 food wide and then start counting.

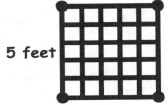

5 feet

Count the squares
to find the area.

After counting, it turns out that there are 25 smaller squares inside the large square, and since the space inside a polygon is called the **area**, we can say that the area of the flower bed is 25 square feet, or 25 sq. ft. for short (sq. means square and ft. means feet).

Drawing squares and counting takes a lot of time, but actually there is an easier way to find the area. All you have to do is multiply the length by the width. In the previous example, if we had multiplied 5×5, we would have gotten 25 again, which stands for 25 square feet. This method works for any square, no matter what size it is, and it also works on rectangles. Here's an example.

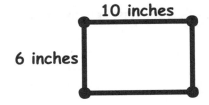

10 inches

6 inches

Multiply length
by width to find
the area.

To find the area of this rectangle, just multiply 10 and 6 in your head. Since the sides are in inches, the area has to be 60 square inches, or 60 sq. in. for short. The "in." stands for inches.

Practice 38

a. Find the perimeter of the polygon below. _____

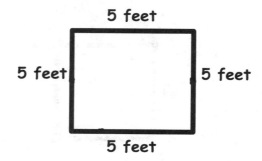

5 feet

5 feet   5 feet

5 feet

Find the area of each polygon below.

b. _____   c. _____

8 feet

8 feet

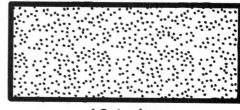

5 inches

12 inches

Solve each word problem below.

d. Bootsy has to pass out 75 snacks to his fellow scouts. If he passed out 16 snacks at the first table and 17 at the second table, how many are left to pass out? _____

e. Each squadron has a total of 22 rockets. If there are 6 squadrons, how many rockets are there in all? _____

Problem Set 38

Tell whether each sentence below is True or False.

1. All four sides of a square have the same length. _____

2. The space inside a polygon is called its area. _____

3. The area of a rectangle is equal to its length times its width. _____

Multiply each group of numbers below.

4. $\begin{array}{r} 828 \\ \times\,5 \\ \hline \end{array}$

5. $\begin{array}{r} 459 \\ \times\,7 \\ \hline \end{array}$

6. $2 \times 9 \times 9$ _____

7. $6 \times 8 \times 4$ _____

Find estimates for each of the problems below by rounding the first number to the nearest ten and then multiplying the numbers that are left in your head.

8. 47×7 _____

9. 51×8 _____

Answer each question below.

10. In the diagram below, the length of line segment RT is 75 inches, and the length of line segment ST is 33 inches. What is the length of line segment RS? _____

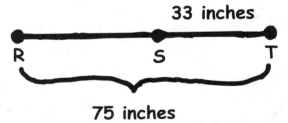

11. Tell whether the triangle below is acute, right, or obtuse. _____

12. Describe the triangle below with the best of the following choices: isosceles acute, equilateral acute, or equilateral obtuse. _____

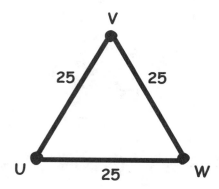

Tell whether the polygon below is a triangle, quadrilateral, pentagon, hexagon, or octagon.

13. _____

14. _____

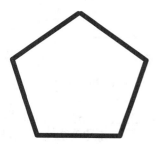

Find the perimeter of each polygon below.

(a) 15. _____

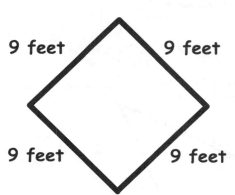

16. _____

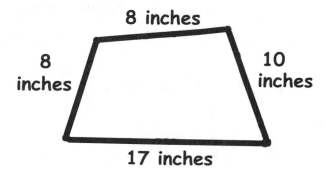

Find the area of each rectangle or square below.

17. _____

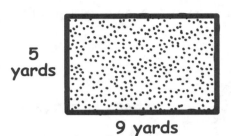

5 yards

9 yards

(b) 18. _____

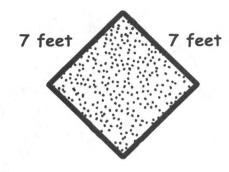

7 feet   7 feet

19. _____

3 feet

7 feet

(c) 20. _____

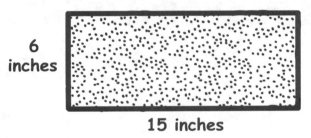

6 inches

15 inches

Solve each word problem below.

(d) 21.   Ashley needs to write 65 thank you notes in just a few days. If she wrote 11 notes the first day and 13 notes the second, how many notes does she still have to write?

_____

(e) 22.   Each jar has 22 jelly beans. If there are 4 jars, how many jelly beans are there in all?

_____

Lesson 39—Introduction to Fractions

Sometimes we need to talk about a part instead of a whole. For example, if two college roommates were going to share a pepperoni pizza, each roommate should get half of the pizza. The way to write that in math is with the fraction 1 over 2.

Each roommate should get $\frac{1}{2}$.

The bottom number in a fraction is called the **denominator**, and it tells how many pieces the pizza has been divided into. The top number is called the **numerator**, and it tells how many pieces you or the person you're talking about has.

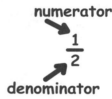

numerator

denominator

The top number is the numerator and the bottom is the denominator.

In this fraction, the numerator is 1, but in some fractions, the numerator is bigger than 1. For example, let's say a pan of brownies has been cut into 3 pieces, and the person who made it plans to give away 2 of the pieces. The fraction that describes the amount that will be given away is $\frac{2}{3}$.

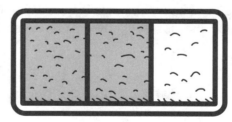

$\frac{2}{3}$ of a pan of brownies.

Another important thing to know is that when reading or saying the name of a fraction, we always go from the top to the bottom. The fraction $\frac{3}{4}$ should be pronounced "three fourths," and $\frac{1}{2}$, from the pizza problem, should be pronounced "one-half."

Also, we don't just use fractions to describe things we've cut into pieces, like pizzas or brownies. We can also use fractions to stand for a part of a group. For example, if Joey has 8 marbles and 7 of them are blue, then $\frac{7}{8}$ of his marbles are blue.

The main point of the lesson is that the bottom of a fraction (the denominator) tells how many pieces the whole is divided into, and the top (the numerator) tells how many pieces are being counted.

Practice 39

a. Find the perimeter of the polygon below. _____

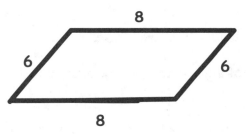

b. Find the area of the polygon below. _____

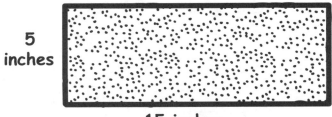

c. Write a fraction to show what part of the group the shaded piece represents.

_____

Solve each word problem below.

d. Leslie threw 12 more pitches than Amber, and Amber threw 19 more pitches than Megan. If Megan threw 43 pitches, how many pitches did Leslie throw? _____

e. Mrs. Cunningham ordered 3 sandwich platters for the block party. If each platter contained 21 sandwiches, how many sandwiches did Mrs. Cunningham order? _____

Problem Set 39

Tell whether each sentence below is True or False.

1. The denominator of a fraction tells how many equal pieces the whole has been divided into. _____

2. The numerator of a fraction tells how many pieces of the whole you have. _____

3. The numerator of a fraction can never be greater than 1. _____

Multiply each group of numbers below.

4.
$$\begin{array}{r} 732 \\ \times\ 4 \\ \hline \end{array}$$

5.
$$\begin{array}{r} 269 \\ \times\ 6 \\ \hline \end{array}$$

6. $9 \times 5 \times 2$ _____

7. $7 \times 8 \times 4$ _____

Find estimates for each of the problems below by rounding the first number to the nearest ten and then multiplying the numbers that are left in your head.

8. 74×6 _____   **9.** 59×7 _____

Answer each question below.

10. In the diagram below, the length of line segment LO is 68 feet, and the length of line segment LM is 18 feet. What is the length of line segment MO? _____

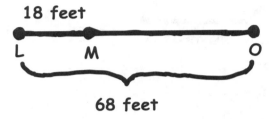

11. Describe the triangle below with the best of the following choices: isosceles acute, equilateral obtuse, or isosceles obtuse. _____

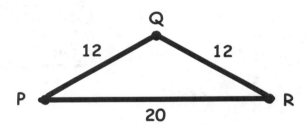

12. Tell whether the polygon below is a triangle, quadrilateral, pentagon, hexagon, or octagon. _____

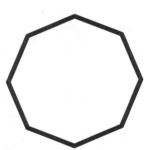

Find the perimeter of each polygon below.

(a) 13. _____

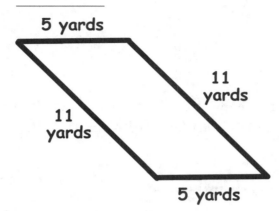

5 yards

11 yards

11 yards

5 yards

14. _____

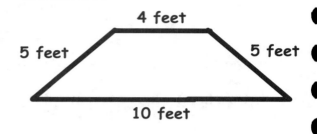

4 feet

5 feet

5 feet

10 feet

Find the area of each rectangle or square below.

(b) 15. _____

4 feet

12 feet

16. _____

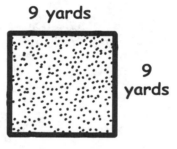

9 yards

9 yards

Write a fraction for the part of the whole that is shaded in each picture below.

17. _____

18. _____

Write a fraction to show what part of the group the shaded pieces represent.

(c) 19. _____

20. _____

Solve each word problem below.

(d) 21. Hoss weighs 18 pounds more than Dingo, and Dingo weighs 17 pounds more than Trixie. If Trixie weighs 19 pounds, how much does Hoss weigh? _____

(e) 22. Mr. Sterling ordered 6 small bundles of firewood for the winter. If each bundle contained 21 pieces of wood, how many pieces of wood did Mr. Sterling order? _____

Lesson 40—Adding with Four-Digit Numbers

We've already done problems that required us to carry twice, but sometimes it's necessary to carry three times. Here's an example.

$$
\begin{array}{r}
\overset{1\ \ 11}{5{,}689} \\
+\ 743 \\
\hline
6{,}432
\end{array}
$$

Carrying three times.

Even though the bottom number didn't have as many digits, we still put the bigger number over the smaller one and added the columns, just like we've always done. In the ones column, $9+3$ is 12, so we wrote a 2 below and carried the 1. As you can see, we actually had to carry three different times. However, it's the same process as before. After adding all of the columns, the sum turns out to be 6,432.

Here's another example, but this time we're adding *two* four-digit numbers.

$$
\begin{array}{r}
\overset{1\ \ 11}{9{,}756} \\
+8{,}497 \\
\hline
18{,}253
\end{array}
$$

Adding two four-digit numbers.

Once again, we just started with the ones and added each of the columns. Also, notice that we didn't have to carry the 1 in 18 because there were no more columns to the left. The main point of this lesson though is that carrying three times is no different than carrying twice. It just takes longer to finish the problem.

Practice 40

a. Add
$$
\begin{array}{r}
6{,}184 \\
+\ 5{,}238 \\
\hline
\end{array}
$$

b. Add
$$
\begin{array}{r}
8{,}775 \\
+\ 5{,}836 \\
\hline
\end{array}
$$

c. Write a fraction to show what part of the group the shaded piece represents.

_____

Solve each word problem below.

d. There are 48 spaces on the sign-up sheet. The first day, 12 people signed up, and the second day 15 more signed up. How many spaces are left on the sheet? _____

e. There are 5 full ice cube trays in the freezer. If each tray can hold 14 ice cubes, how many ice cubes are there altogether? _____

Problem Set 40

Tell whether each sentence below is True or False.

1. Carrying digits into the thousands column is not allowed. _____

2. Carrying three times is no different than carrying twice, it just takes longer to finish the problem. _____

Add each pair of numbers below.

3.
```
  4,196
+   395
```

(a) 4.
```
  3,236
+ 1,587
```

(b) 5.
```
  5,872
+ 4,458
```

Multiply each group of numbers below.

6. 765
    × 6

7. 967
    × 8

8. $2 \times 9 \times 8$ _____

9. $7 \times 7 \times 7$ _____

Answer each question below.

10. In the diagram below, the length of line segment NP is 99 feet, and the length of line segment OP is 33 feet. What is the length of line segment NO? _____

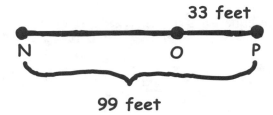

11. Describe the triangle below with the best of the following choices: isosceles acute, equilateral acute, or isosceles right. _____

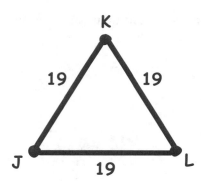

12. Tell whether the polygon below is a triangle, quadrilateral, pentagon, hexagon, or octagon. _____

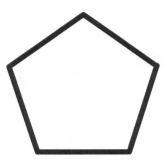

Find the perimeter of each polygon below.

13. _____

9 inches

9 inches

11 inches

19 inches

14. _____

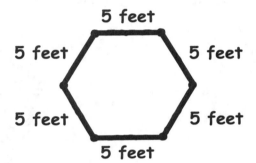

5 feet

5 feet

5 feet

5 feet

5 feet

5 feet

Find the area of each rectangle below.

15. _____

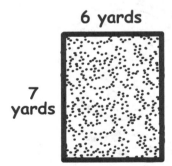

6 yards

7 yards

16. _____

7 inches

18 inches

17. _____

4 yards

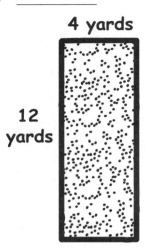

12 yards

18. _____

5 feet

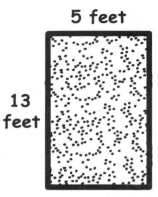

13 feet

19. Write a fraction telling what part of the whole is shaded. _____

(c) 20. Write a fraction to show what part of the group the shaded piece represents.
_____

Solve each word problem below.

(d) 21. The store had 94 copies of the book to start. The first day they sold 42 and the second day they sold 41. How many copies were left after the first two days? _____

(e) 22. There are 4 cartons of strawberries left in the store. If each carton contains 15 strawberries, how many strawberries are there altogether? _____

Lesson 41—Regrouping

In some subtraction problems, subtracting the columns won't work. Here's an example.

$$
\begin{array}{r}
84 \\
-\ 16 \\
\end{array}
$$

The 6 on bottom
is bigger than the
4 on top.

As you can see, the 4 is smaller than the 6. In a case like this, we have to take a 1 from the tens column. That turns the 8 into a 7. Next, we can give the 1 to the ones column, and since the 1 actually stands for a 10 that leaves us with 14 at the top of the ones column. From there, we just need to subtract the 14 and the 6.

$$
\begin{array}{r}
7\ 14 \\
\cancel{84} \\
-\ 16 \\
\hline
68 \\
\end{array}
$$

Moving a tens
from the tens
column to subtract.

Moving a 1 from one column to another is called **borrowing** or **regrouping**. Regrouping is necessary when a digit on top is smaller than a digit on bottom. The process always works, and the last example shows why. See, 84 just means $80+4$, which is the same as $70+10+4$ or $70+14$, so we didn't change the value of 84 when we borrowed. That means 68 has to be the right answer.

Here's another example.

$$
\begin{array}{r}
4\ 12 \\
\cancel{52} \\
-\ 43 \\
\hline
9 \\
\end{array}
$$

Regroup because
the number on bottom
is bigger than the
number on top.

Once again, regrouping was necessary because the 3 on bottom was larger than the 2 on top. So we just borrowed a 1 from the tens column, leaving us with 4 there. Since the 1 stands for 10, we crossed out the 2 and wrote 12 above the ones column. Next, we subtracted the columns, which gave us an answer of 9. The main point of this lesson, though, is that we have to regroup when the number on bottom is bigger than the number on top.

Practice 41

a. Add
$$\begin{array}{r} 7,165 \\ + 5,957 \\ \hline \end{array}$$

b. Subtract
$$\begin{array}{r} 84 \\ - 37 \\ \hline \end{array}$$

c. Write a fraction to show what part of the group the shaded pieces represent.

_____

Solve each word problem below.

d. Last month, Kenny caught 11 more fish than Chuck, and Chuck caught 19 more fish than Jed. If Jed caught 29 fish, how many fish did Kenny catch? _____

e. Jessica ordered 25 pizzas for the big party. If each pizza has 8 slices, how many slices of pizza are there in all? _____

Problem Set 41

Tell whether each sentence below is True or False.

1. Moving a 1 from one column to the other is called borrowing or regrouping.

_____

2. Regrouping is like changing $60+7$ to $50+17$. _____

Add or subtract (as required) each pair of numbers below.

(a) 3.
$$\begin{array}{r} 4,794 \\ + 3,816 \\ \hline \end{array}$$

4.
$$\begin{array}{r} 7,693 \\ + 5,329 \\ \hline \end{array}$$

(b) 5.
$$\begin{array}{r} 52 \\ - 18 \\ \hline \end{array}$$

6.
$$\begin{array}{r} 91 \\ -32 \\ \hline \end{array}$$

7.
$$\begin{array}{r} 75 \\ -36 \\ \hline \end{array}$$

8.
$$\begin{array}{r} 65 \\ -48 \\ \hline \end{array}$$

9.
$$\begin{array}{r} 81 \\ -59 \\ \hline \end{array}$$

Multiply each group of numbers below.

10.
$$\begin{array}{r} 992 \\ \times 8 \\ \hline \end{array}$$

11. $8 \times 5 \times 3$ _____

Answer each question below.

12. Describe the triangle below with the best of the following choices: isosceles acute, equilateral acute, or isosceles right. _____

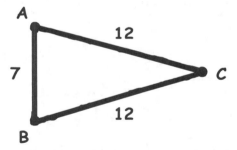

Find the perimeter of each polygon below.

13. _____

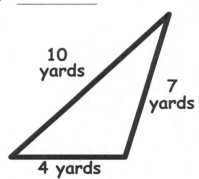

14. _____

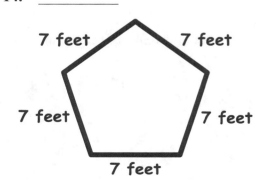

15. _____

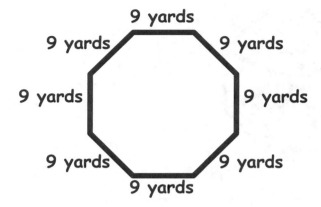

Find the area of each rectangle or square below.

16. _____

17. _____

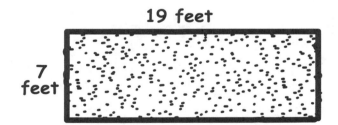

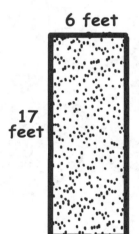

18. _____

19. Write a fraction telling what part of the whole is shaded. _____

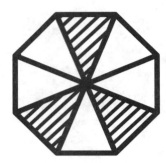

(c) 20. Write a fraction to show what part of the group the shaded pieces represent.
_____

Solve each word problem below.

(d) 21. Jules pedaled 14 more feet than Yvette, and Yvette pedaled 19 more feet than Bitsy. If Bitsy pedaled 31 feet, how many feet did Jules pedal? _____

(e) 22. Hannah ordered 32 flower arrangements for the wedding reception. If each arrangement had 6 flowers in it, how many flowers were there in all? _____

Lesson 42—Rounding and Estimating with Four-Digit Numbers

You've already learned how to round to the nearest ten and the nearest hundred. This approach actually works for rounding four-digit numbers to the nearest thousand, too. All we have to do is look at the hundreds digit. If it's 5 or greater, we round up. If it's 4 or less, we leave the thousands digit alone. Here's an example.

$$3,412 \longrightarrow 3,000$$

The hundreds digit is 4, so leave the thousands digit alone.

Since the hundreds digit is 4, we left the thousands digit alone. Here's another example.

$$9,500 \longrightarrow 10,000$$

The hundreds digit is 5, so round the thousands digit up.

Once again, we just looked at the hundreds digit, and since it was a 5, we rounded up. Remember though, a lot of times we round to help us find an estimate to an addition problem. Here's an example of that, and notice that both numbers have four digits.

$$7,368 + 4,152$$
$$\downarrow \qquad \downarrow$$
$$7,000 + 4,000 = 11,000$$
$$7 + 4 = 11$$

Round the numbers and then add them in your head.

First we rounded 7,368 to 7,000 and 4,152 to 4,000. From there we just added in our heads, and since 7 plus 4 is 11, the final answer was 11,000.

We can also round and estimate with four-digit subtractions. The process is the same as with addition. Here's an example.

$$3,972 - 2,800$$
$$\downarrow \qquad \downarrow$$
$$4,000 - 3,000 = 1,000$$
$$4 - 3 = 1$$

Round the numbers and then subtract them in your head.

Practice 42

Add or subtract (as required) each pair of numbers below.

a. Add $\begin{array}{r} 5,637 \\ + 4,694 \\ \hline \end{array}$

b. Subtract $\begin{array}{r} 31 \\ - 27 \\ \hline \end{array}$

c. Find an estimate for $1,219 + 2,984$ by rounding each of the numbers to the nearest thousand and then adding in your head. _____

Solve each word problem below.

d. Mr. Hubbell bought 75 steaks for the Fourth of July cookout. If he grilled 25 steaks during the first hour and 36 during the second, how many were left to grill after that? _____

e. Elaine bought 3 boxes of donuts for the office. If each box had 18 donuts, how many donuts did she buy altogether? _____

Problem Set 42

Tell whether each sentence below is True or False.

1. When rounding a four-digit number to the nearest thousand, we should always round up if the hundreds digit is 4 or less. _____

2. When rounding a four-digit number to the nearest thousand, we should always leave the thousands digit unchanged if the hundreds digit is 5 or more. _____

Add or subtract (as required) each pair of numbers below.

3. $\begin{array}{r} 4,765 \\ + 3,439 \\ \hline \end{array}$

(a) 4. $\begin{array}{r} 9,169 \\ + 1,942 \\ \hline \end{array}$

(b) 5. $\begin{array}{r} 62 \\ - 54 \\ \hline \end{array}$

6.
$$\begin{array}{r} 73 \\ -\ 46 \\ \hline \end{array}$$

7.
$$\begin{array}{r} 97 \\ -\ 28 \\ \hline \end{array}$$

8.
$$\begin{array}{r} 85 \\ -\ 49 \\ \hline \end{array}$$

Multiply each group of numbers below.

9.
$$\begin{array}{r} 295 \\ \times\ 6 \\ \hline \end{array}$$

10. $7 \times 9 \times 6$ _____

Round each number below to the nearest thousand.

11.   2,109 _____

12.   4,922 _____

13.   3,594 _____

Find estimates for each of the problems below by rounding each of the numbers to the nearest thousand and then adding or subtracting (as required) in your head.

(c) 14. $5,291 + 2,188$ _____

15. $7,904 - 1,803$ _____

16. $6,711 + 1,233$ _____

Answer each question below.

17.   Describe the triangle below with the best of the following choices: isosceles acute, isosceles obtuse, or isosceles right. _____

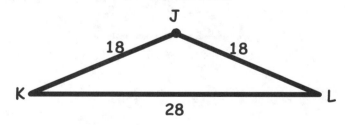

18. Find the perimeter of the polygon below. _____

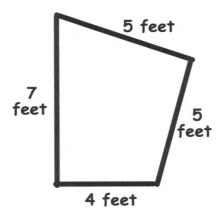

19. Find the area of the rectangle below. _____

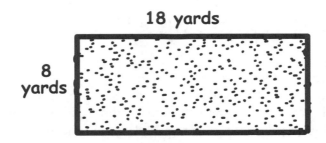

20. Write a fraction for the part of the whole that is shaded in the picture below.

_____

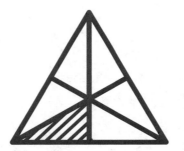

Solve each word problem below.

(d) 21. The church plans to give away 85 box lunches. If they gave away 33 box lunches the first hour and 29 the second hour, how many box lunches do they have left? _____

(e) 22. Jake's Sporting Goods bought 7 boxes of basketball jerseys. If each box contains 14 jerseys, how many did they buy altogether? _____

Quiz 6

Tell whether each sentence below is True or False.

1. The denominator of a fraction tells how many equal pieces the whole has been divided into. _____

2. Moving a 1 from one column to another is called borrowing or regrouping. _____

Add or subtract (as required) each pair of numbers below.

3.
$$\begin{array}{r} 2,394 \\ + 1,137 \\ \hline \end{array}$$

4.
$$\begin{array}{r} 8,256 \\ + 3,784 \\ \hline \end{array}$$

5.
$$\begin{array}{r} 42 \\ - 15 \\ \hline \end{array}$$

6.
$$\begin{array}{r} 71 \\ - 34 \\ \hline \end{array}$$

7.
$$\begin{array}{r} 43 \\ - 28 \\ \hline \end{array}$$

8.
$$\begin{array}{r} 86 \\ - 29 \\ \hline \end{array}$$

Multiply each group of numbers below.

9.
$$\begin{array}{r} 732 \\ \times 6 \\ \hline \end{array}$$

10.
$$\begin{array}{r} 825 \\ \times 9 \\ \hline \end{array}$$

Round each number below to the nearest thousand.

11. 3,252 _____

12. 6,581 _____

13. 8,861 _____

Find estimates for each of the problems below by rounding each of the numbers to the nearest thousand and then adding or subtracting (as required) in your head.

14. $4,252 + 2,918$ _____

15. $8,754 - 1,321$ _____

16. $5,120 + 4,955$ _____   17. $7,952 - 5,821$ _____

Answer each question below.

18. Describe the triangle below with the best of the following choices: isosceles acute, equilateral acute, or isosceles right. _____

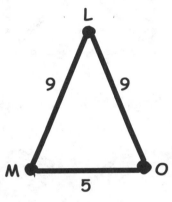

19. Find the perimeter of the polygon below. _____

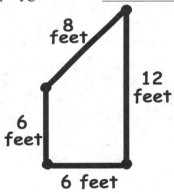

20. Find the area of the rectangle below. _____

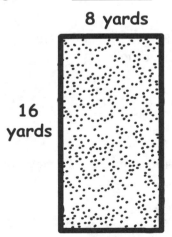

21. Write a fraction telling what part of the whole is shaded. _____

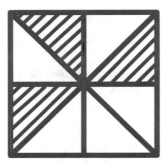

22. Write a fraction to show what part of the group the shaded pieces represent.

_____

Solve each word problem below.

23. Susan is 17 years older than Karen, and Karen is 24 years older than Kelsey. If Kelsey is 34 years old, how old is Susan? _____

24. There are 16 spiders in the cupboard. If each spider has 5 eyes, how many eyes are there in all? _____

Lesson 43—Decimal Basics – Tenths and Hundredths

We've already learned what all of the columns in a number stand for out to the hundred millions place, but there are also some columns to the right of the ones place that we never mentioned. Each of these has a value that's ten times greater than the digit to the right of it. For example, the column just to the right of the ones is called the **tenths**, and we use a dot, called a **decimal point**, to separate the tenths from the ones.

A digit in the tenths column stands for one tenth of one, which makes sense because the ones column is ten times the value of the tenths. Here's another number written out to the tenths place. It means 4 ones + 6 tenths.

4.6 The 6 is in the tenths place.

There's actually another column to the right of the tenths called the **hundredths**.

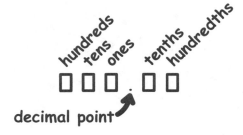

Since each column is ten times greater than the one to the right of it, a hundredth is equal to one tenth of one tenth and one hundredth of one. Here's a number that goes out to the hundredths.

847.56 The 6 is in the hundredths place.

The number means 8 hundreds + 4 tens + 7 ones + 5 tenths + 6 hundredths.

There are even numbers that have nothing to the left of the decimal point. Here's an example.

0.27   Some numbers have
nothing to the left
of the decimal point.

It may seem strange to put a 0 in front of the decimal point when there are no ones, but it's done like that to make the decimal point more visible.

Also, sometimes you may be told what a number stands for and then asked to write the number using digits. Here's an example of that.

5 tens + 8 ones + 9 tenths + 3 hundredths

58.93

On this problem, we wrote down the tens and ones digits and then drew in the decimal point. Next we wrote the 9 and the 3, the digits for the tenths and hundredths places.

The main point of the lesson is that there are places to the right of the ones column, and the first two of these are the tenths and hundredths.

Practice 43

a. Subtract $\begin{array}{r} 53 \\ -27 \\ \hline \end{array}$

b. Find an estimate for $6,818 - 4,207$ by rounding each of the numbers to the nearest thousand and then subtracting in your head. _____

c. Write the number 6 tens + 5 ones + 3 tenths + 5 hundredths using digits. _____

Solve each word problem below.

d. There were 55 pieces of paper in the tray to start. Then Sally printed a 13-page document and Ed printed a 29-page document. How many pieces of paper are in the tray now? _____

e. There are 6 loaves of bread and 28 slices in each loaf. How many slices are there altogether? _____

Problem Set 43

Tell whether each sentence below is True or False.

1. We always put a 0 to the left of the decimal point when there are no whole numbers. _____

2. The column that's just to the right of the ones is called the tenths. _____

For each problem below, choose the word that belongs in the blank.

3. A one in the _____ column stands for one tenth of one.

A. hundreds   B. tens   C. ones
D. tenths   E. hundredths

4. One tenth is ten times greater than one _____.

A. million   B. thousand   C. hundred
D. ten   E. hundredth

Add or subtract (as required) each pair of numbers below.

5.
$$4,166 + 2,934$$

6.
$$7,899 + 3,224$$

(a) 7.
$$86 - 37$$

8.
$$67 - 29$$

9.
$$82 - 46$$

Multiply each group of numbers below.

10.
$$\begin{array}{r} 593 \\ \times\ 6 \\ \hline \end{array}$$

11.
$$\begin{array}{r} 644 \\ \times\ 9 \\ \hline \end{array}$$

Find estimates for each of the problems below by rounding each of the numbers to the nearest thousand and then adding or subtracting (as required) in your head.

(b) 12. $4,181+3,276$ _____

13. $8,922-4,710$ _____

14. $5,954+2,183$ _____

15. $7,925-2,813$ _____

Answer each question below.

16. Tell which digit is in the tenths place in 43.28. _____

(c) 17. Write the number 9 tens + 2 ones + 5 tenths + 6 hundredths using digits. _____

18. Find the perimeter of the polygon below. _____

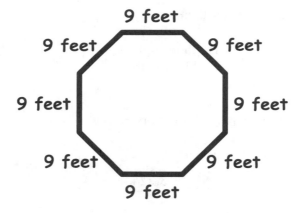

9 feet
9 feet   9 feet
9 feet   9 feet
9 feet   9 feet
9 feet

19. Find the area of the rectangle below. _____

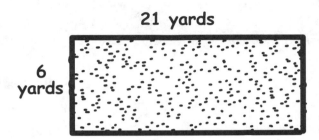

21 yards

6 yards

20. Write a fraction to show what part of the group the shaded pieces represent.

_____

Solve each word problem below.

(d) 21. There were 67 books on the librarian's cart to start. She shelved 21 of them, took a coffee break, and then shelved 24 more. How many books are on her cart now?

_____

(e) 22. There are 7 boxes and 22 doodads in each box. How many doodads are there in all?

_____

Lesson 44—Decimals and Fractions

In the last lesson, we learned about numbers with a decimal point, which are often called **decimals** for short. Well, it turns out that since both fractions and decimals stand for parts of a whole, it's possible to turn a decimal into a fraction. Here's an example.

$$0.1 = \frac{1}{10}$$

This decimal and this fraction mean the same thing.

Both the decimal and the fraction stand for one tenth, and both can be pronounced that way too. Here's another example.

$$0.3 = \frac{3}{10}$$

Two ways of showing three tenths.

It's also possible to start with a fraction and change it into a decimal. Here's an example of that.

$$\frac{9}{10} = 0.9$$

The fraction was changed into a decimal.

Decimals that go out to the hundredths place can also be written as fractions. Here's an example.

$$0.59 = \frac{59}{100}$$

Decimals with hundredths can also be written as fractions.

Also, we pronounce both 0.59 and $\frac{59}{100}$ as "fifty-nine hundredths." Finally, here's an example of changing a fraction with 100 in the bottom into a decimal.

$$\frac{9}{100} = 0.09$$

A 100 in the bottom means there has to be two places after the decimal point.

We couldn't write the $\frac{9}{100}$ as 0.9, because 0.9 is the same as $\frac{9}{10}$. So first we put a 0 to the left of the decimal point, just so people would see the point, and then we put a 0 in the tenths place and a 9 in the hundredths place. Nine over 100 written as a decimal, then, is 0.09 and both are pronounced "nine hundredths."

Practice 44

a. Find an estimate for $8,282 - 6,150$ by rounding each of the numbers to the nearest thousand and then subtracting in your head. _____

b. Write $\dfrac{3}{100}$ as a decimal. _____

c. Write 0.07 as a fraction. _____

Solve each word problem below.

d. Walter is 24 years older than Stan, and Stan is 18 years older than Kyle. If Kyle is 31 years old, how old is Walter? _____

e. The villagers have 24 buckets of water to use for mixing concrete. If each bucket contains 5 gallons, how many gallons of water are there in all? _____

Problem Set 44

Tell whether each sentence below is True or False.

1. Numbers that have a decimal point are called *decimals* for short. _____

2. Whenever you change a fraction that has 100 in the bottom into a decimal, you have to put two places to the left of the decimal point. _____

For each problem below, choose the group of words that belong in the blank.

3. The numbers $\dfrac{1}{10}$ and 0.1 are both pronounced "_____" and they mean the same thing.

   A. one hundred   B. one hundred tens   C. one tenth
   D. one hundredth   E. one hundred tenths

4. The number 0.76 is pronounced "_____."

    A. seventy-six thousands   B. seventy-six hundreds   C. seventy-six tens
    D. seventy-six tenths   E. seventy-six hundredths

Add or subtract (as required) each pair of numbers below.

5.
$$\begin{array}{r} 6,865 \\ + 4,937 \\ \hline \end{array}$$

6.
$$\begin{array}{r} 53 \\ - 28 \\ \hline \end{array}$$

7.
$$\begin{array}{r} 72 \\ - 18 \\ \hline \end{array}$$

Multiply each group of numbers below.

8.
$$\begin{array}{r} 366 \\ \times 5 \\ \hline \end{array}$$

9. $7 \times 5 \times 4$ _____

Find estimates for each of the problems below by rounding each of the numbers to the nearest thousand and then subtracting in your head.

(a) 10. $8,945 - 1,213$ _____   **11.** $7,785 - 3,674$ _____

12. Write the number 8 tens + 7 ones + 6 tenths + 4 hundredths using digits. _____

Write each fraction below as a decimal.

13. $\dfrac{1}{10}$ _____   **14.** $\dfrac{23}{100}$ _____

(b) 15. $\dfrac{5}{100}$ _____

Write each number below as a fraction.

   16. 0.7 _____   **17.** 0.51 _____

(c) 18. 0.03 _____

Answer each question below.

   19. Find the perimeter of the polygon below. _____

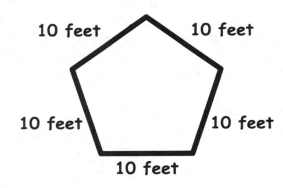

   20. Find the area of the rectangle below. _____

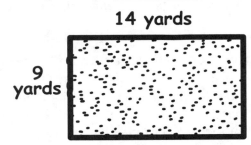

Solve each word problem below.

(d) 21. Kendra is 24 years older than Stacey, and Stacey is 17 years older than Annie. If Annie is 16 years old, how old is Kendra? _____

(e) 22. The restaurant supply company has to send out 23 packages of steak knives. If each package contains 8 knives, how many knives are there in all? _____

Lesson 45—Decimals in Words

A decimal point is used to separate the ones from the tenths place, which means it separates the whole-number part of a number from the part that's less than one. Separating the two parts is also important when saying or writing a decimal. Here's an example.

34.62
thirty-four and sixty-two hundredths

We did this by writing the whole number part of the number before the decimal part. Also, notice that we still used a hyphen for numbers from 21 through 99, and that we wrote the word *and* for the decimal point. Another important thing to remember when writing or saying a decimal is the *ths* ending in *tenths* and *hundredths*. Those endings tell us that we're dealing with parts of a number that are to the right of the decimal point. Here's another example.

347.51
three hundred forty-seven and fifty-one hundredths

With this number, the whole number part was again written first, followed by the *and* and then the decimal part.

It's also important to be able to take decimals written as words and write them using digits. Here's an example.

one thousand, five hundred seven and forty-eight hundredths

Here, we just need to write the whole number part, including the comma, after the thousands place. Then, since the *and* stands for the decimal point, we have to draw the point next. Finally, we just write the decimal part of the number to get the answer.

1,507.48

Practice 45

a. Find an estimate for $6,821 + 2,211$ by rounding each of the numbers to the nearest thousand and then adding in your head. _____

b. Choose the group of words that belongs in the blank.

312.89   three hundred twelve _____

   A. eighty-nine   B. eighty-nine hundredths
   C. eighty nine hundredths   D. and eighty nine hundredths
   E. and eighty-nine hundredths

c. Write the number eight hundred thirteen and twenty-four hundredths using digits.

_____

Solve each word problem below.

d. The lumberjacks have cut down 58 trees over the last three days. The first day, they cut down 23 trees, and in the second day they cut down 19. How many trees did they cut down on the third day? _____

e. The pet store has 15 goldfish in each tank. If there are 3 tanks of goldfish in the store, how many goldfish does the store have in all? _____

Problem Set 45

Tell whether each sentence below is True or False.

1. The decimal point separates the whole-number part of a number from the part that's less than one._____

2. The word "and" can be used to stand for the decimal point when saying or writing a decimal that has digits to the left of the point. _____

3. Hundredths means the same thing as hundreds. _____

Add or subtract (as required) each pair of numbers below.

4.
$$\begin{array}{r} 6,795 \\ +\ 6,415 \\ \hline \end{array}$$

5.
$$\begin{array}{r} 74 \\ -\ 16 \\ \hline \end{array}$$

6.
$$\begin{array}{r} 81 \\ -\ 56 \\ \hline \end{array}$$

Multiply each group of numbers below.

7.
$$746$$
$$\times\ 4$$

8. $5 \times 5 \times 8$ _____

Find estimates for each of the problems below by rounding each of the numbers to the nearest thousand and then adding in your head.

(a) 9. $4,750 + 6,129$ _____

10. $8,153 + 7,823$ _____

Write each fraction below as a decimal.

11. $\dfrac{31}{100}$ _____

12. $\dfrac{7}{100}$ _____

Write each number below as a fraction.

13. 0.9 _____

14. 0.01 _____

For each problem below, choose the group of words that belongs in the blank.

(b) 15. 491.35   four hundred ninety-one _____

    A. thirty-five
    C. thirty-five hundredths
    E. and thirty-five hundredths

    B. and thirty-five
    D. and thirty five hundredths

16. 519.75   five hundred nineteen _____

    A. seventy-five hundreds
    C. and seventy-five hundreds
    E. and seventy five hundredths

    B. seventy-five hundredths
    D. and seventy-five hundredths

Answer each question below.

(c) 17. Write the number six hundred thirty-seven and fifty-two hundredths using digits.

_____

18. Write the number nine hundred fifty-four and thirty-eight hundredths using digits.
_____

19. Find the perimeter of the polygon below. _____

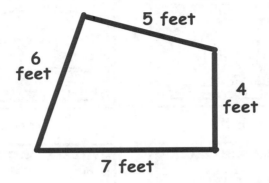

20. Find the area of the rectangle below. _____

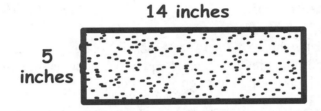

Solve each word problem below.

(d) 21. Stacey, the interior decorator, has decorated 45 houses over the last three years. The first year she decorated 13 houses, and the second year she decorated 18. How many houses did she decorate in the third year? _____

(e) 22. There are 18 candy canes in each box. If there are 9 boxes of candy canes in the store, how many candy canes are there in all? _____

Lesson 46—Dollars and Decimals

People use two kinds of money. First, there is paper money, also known as bills or dollars. Here are some examples.

one dollar bill

ten dollar bill

five dollar bill

twenty dollar bill

In addition to paper money, there are coins, or cents. For example, there is the penny, which is equal to one cent, the nickel, which is equal to five cents, the dime, which is equal to ten cents, and the quarter, which is equal to twenty-five cents.

When talking about dollars, we use a symbol called the **dollar sign**, which looks like this: $. The dollar sign always goes in front of the number. Here are some examples of dollar amounts written with numbers.

one dollar:	$1	The dollar sign ($) always goes before the number.
five dollars:	$5	
ten dollars:	$10	

Writing cents requires a symbol that looks like this: ¢. It's called the **cent sign** and it always goes after the number. Here are some examples of cent amounts written with numbers.

one cent:	1¢	The cent sign (¢) always goes after the number.
five cents:	5¢	
ten cents:	10¢	

Each of the coins we just mentioned is worth less than a dollar, which means that each coin is just a fraction of a dollar. For example, it takes one hundred pennies to make a dollar, so a penny is $\frac{1}{100}$ of a dollar. It takes twenty nickels to make a dollar, so a nickel is $\frac{1}{20}$ of a dollar. It takes ten dimes to make a dollar, so a dime is $\frac{1}{10}$ of a dollar, and it takes four quarters to make a dollar, so a quarter is $\frac{1}{4}$ of a dollar.

Finally, we can use everything we've learned above to do some tough problems. For example, since a penny is equal to $\frac{1}{100}$ of a dollar, we know that nine pennies has to be equal to $\frac{9}{100}$ of a dollar. Also, since it takes four quarters to make a dollar, it has to take three times as many quarters to make $3, and since 3×4 is 12, that's twelve quarters.

Practice 46

    a. Write the number three hundred sixty-one and twenty-five hundredths using digits. _____

    b. What fraction of a dollar is 13 pennies? _____

    c. If it takes 10 dimes to make $1, how many dimes does it take to make $2? _____

Solve each word problem below.

    d. Tyler drove 18 more miles than Dillon, and Dillon drove 24 more miles than Garret. If Garret drove 43 miles, how many miles did Tyler drive? _____

    e. Each of the identical desks has 3 drawers. If there are 19 desks, how many drawers are there in total? _____

Problem Set 46

Tell whether each sentence below is True or False.

    1. The dollar sign looks like this: ¢. _____

221

2. The cent symbol goes before the number of cents not after them. _____

Add or subtract (as required) each pair of numbers below.

3.
$$\begin{array}{r} 6,875 \\ +\ 4,166 \\ \hline \end{array}$$

4.
$$\begin{array}{r} 96 \\ -\ 37 \\ \hline \end{array}$$

Find estimates for each of the problems below by rounding each of the numbers to the nearest thousand and then subtracting in your head.

5. $3,756 - 1,321$ _____

6. $7,974 - 6,352$ _____

Write each fraction below as a decimal.

7. $\dfrac{57}{100}$ _____

8. $\dfrac{4}{100}$ _____

Write each number below as a fraction.

9. 0.43 _____

10. 0.03 _____

Write each number below using digits.

(a) 11. three hundred forty-two and fifty-one hundredths. _____

12. two hundred eighty-three and twenty-nine hundredths. _____

Write each of the amounts below using the cent symbol.

13. fifty-three cents _____

14. nine cents _____

Answer each question below.

15. What fraction of a dollar is a dime? _____

16. What fraction of a dollar is a quarter? _____

(b) 17. What fraction of a dollar is 11 pennies? _____

(c) 18. If it takes 4 quarters to make $1, how many quarters does it take to make $4?
_____

19. If it takes 20 nickels to make $1, how many nickels does it take to make $2?
_____

20. Find the perimeter of the polygon below. _____

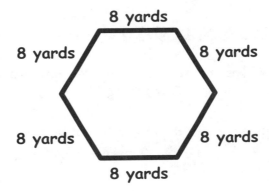

Solve each word problem below.

(d) 21. Dr. Rubin collected 17 more specimens than Dr. McKnight, and Dr. McKnight collected 15 more specimens than Dr. Albert. If Dr. Albert collected 22 specimens, how many specimens did Dr. Rubin collect? _____

(e) 22. Each stack of construction paper has 25 sheets. If there are 9 stacks of construction paper, how many sheets of construction paper are there in total? _____

Lesson 47—Dollars, Cents, and Decimals

You can change cents into dollars and dollars into cents very easily. Here's an example.

$$30¢ \longrightarrow 30. \longrightarrow \$0.30$$

Get rid of the cent sign, move the decimal point two places, and add a dollar sign.

To change 30¢ into dollars, we first got rid of the cent sign. Next, we moved the decimal point in 30 two places to the left; this may seem strange, but there is actually a decimal point to the right of the 0 in 30 since 30 is the same as 30.0. Finally, we put in a zero before the decimal point and added a dollar sign. Notice that we left the 0 in the hundredths place instead of just dropping it, because anytime we change cents into dollars, there have to be two digits to the right of the decimal point.

Dollars and cents can also be written together. Here's an example.

Twelve dollars and forty-eight cents
$12.48

Notice that the decimal point separates the dollars from the cents, and there's a dollar sign in front. So, when writing an amount of money that has both dollars and cents, use a decimal point to separate the two parts.

Practice 47

a. Write 21¢ using a dollar sign and a decimal point. _____

b. Write 4¢ using a dollar sign and a decimal point. _____

c. Choose the group of words that belong in the blank.

$62.38   Sixty-two dollars _____.

A. thirty-eight cents
B. and thirty-eight hundredths
C. and thirty eight cents
D. and thirty-eight cents
E. and thirty eight hundredths

Solve each word problem below.

d. The auto show had 75 different hot rods on display in three separate buildings. The first building had 27 hot rods and the second had 35. How many hot rods were in the third building? _____

e. Mrs. Kensington bought each of the girls in her art class 6 magic markers. If there are 27 girls in the class, how many magic markers did Mrs. Kensington buy in all? _____

Problem Set 47

Tell whether each sentence below is True or False.

1. To change cents into dollars, just drop the cent sign and move the decimal point two places to the right. _____

2. Any time we change cents into dollars, there have to be two digits to the right of the decimal point. _____

Add or subtract (as required) each pair of numbers below.

3.
$$\begin{array}{r} 5,927 \\ + 3,986 \\ \hline \end{array}$$

4.
$$\begin{array}{r} 74 \\ - 28 \\ \hline \end{array}$$

Find estimates for each of the problems below by rounding each of the numbers to the nearest thousand and then adding in your head.

5. $6,129 + 7,946$ _____

6. $5,833 + 3,705$ _____

7. $9,377 + 9,830$ _____

Write each number below using digits.

8. one hundred ninety-three and thirty-eight hundredths. _____

9. five hundred sixty-one and two hundredths. _____

Answer each question below.

10. Write $\dfrac{6}{100}$ as a decimal. _____

11. Write 0.91 as a fraction. _____

12. If one penny is $\dfrac{1}{100}$ of a dollar, 17 pennies is what fraction of a dollar? _____

13. What coin equals $\dfrac{1}{4}$ of a dollar? _____

    A. Penny   B. Nickel
    C. Dime   D. Quarter

Write each of the amounts below using a dollar sign and a decimal point.

(a) 14. 71¢ _____

15. 96¢ _____

(b) 16. 5¢ _____

17. thirty-two dollars and forty one cents _____

For each problem below, choose the group of words that belong in the blank.

(c) 18. $59.24   Fifty-nine dollars _____.

    A. twenty-four cents   B. and twenty-four hundredths
    C. and twenty four cents   D. and twenty-four cents
    E. and twenty four hundredths

19. $88.97   Eighty-eight dollars_____.

    A. ninety-seven cents   B. and ninety-seven hundredths
    C. and ninety-seven cents   D. and ninety seven cents
    E. and ninety seven hundredths

20. Find the area of the rectangle below. _____

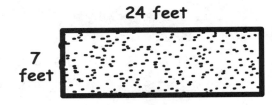

24 feet

7
feet

Solve each word problem below.

(d) 21. The store had 65 tin soldiers displayed on three different shelves. The first shelf had 25 soldiers and the second had 29. How many soldiers were on the third shelf?

_____

(e) 22. Pastor Thompson bought each member of the hand bell choir 4 bells. If there are 18 members in the choir, how many bells did Pastor Thompson buy in all? _____

Lesson 48—Adding and Subtracting with Decimals

Adding and subtracting decimals works basically the same way as adding and subtracting whole numbers. Here's an example.

$$
\begin{array}{r}
5.6 \\
+\ 2.3 \\
\hline
7.9
\end{array}
$$

Line up the decimal points, then add the columns.

First, we just put one number on top of the other. It doesn't matter which number is put on top, but it is extremely important to make sure that the decimal points are lined up. If the decimal points aren't lined up, it's possible that tenths won't be added to tenths or ones with ones. After the decimal points were lined up, we just added the columns, just as when adding whole numbers. Then, we put the decimal point in the answer directly beneath the decimal points in the numbers that were added, giving us an answer of 7.9.

Here's another example, except this time it's a subtraction rather than an addition.

$$
\begin{array}{r}
9.85 \\
-\ 7.24 \\
\hline
2.61
\end{array}
$$

Line up the decimal points, then subtract the columns.

We solved this problem the same way we solved the first one, except we had to subtract instead of add. Once again, we put the numbers on top of each other, but this time we made sure the larger number was on top since we're subtracting. Next, we lined up the decimal points, which is really important. Then, we just subtracted the columns, starting from the right. Last of all, we put the decimal point in the answer underneath the points in the numbers that were subtracted, and that left us with 2.61.

The main point of the lesson is that when adding and subtracting with decimals, we have to make sure the decimal points are lined up, and then put the decimal point in the answer directly below the decimal points in the numbers being added or subtracted.

Practice 48

a. If it takes 20 nickels to make $1, how many nickels does it take to make $5?

_____

b. Write 9 cents using a dollar sign and a decimal point. _____

c. Add $73.85 + 51.13$

$$+ \underline{\hspace{3cm}}$$

Solve each word problem below.

d. Dean is 23 years older than Levi, and Levi is 28 years older than Jeffrey. If Jeffrey is 19 years old, how old is Dean? _____

e. Each of the pouches has 9 gummy kangaroos. If there are 32 pouches, how many gummy kangaroos are there in all? _____

Problem Set 48

Tell whether each sentence below is True or False.

1. To add two decimals, the decimal points must be lined up. _____

2. When subtracting two decimals, the decimal points don't need to be lined up.
    _____

Add or subtract (as required) each pair of numbers below.

3. $\begin{array}{r} 8,469 \\ + 7,647 \\ \hline \end{array}$

4. $\begin{array}{r} 64 \\ - 38 \\ \hline \end{array}$

Find estimates for each of the problems below by rounding each of the numbers to the nearest thousand and then subtracting in your head.

5. $7,368 - 5,265$ _____

6. $8,706 - 4,201$ _____

7. $7,975 - 5,743$ _____

Write each number below using digits.

8. seven hundred nineteen and fifty-four hundredths. _____

9. six hundred forty-four and eighty-three hundredths. _____

Answer each question below.

10. Write $\dfrac{9}{100}$ as a decimal. _____

11. Write 0.63 as a fraction. _____

12. If one penny is $\dfrac{1}{100}$ of a dollar, 19 pennies is what fraction of a dollar?

(a) 13. If it takes 4 quarters to make $1, how many quarters does it take to make $3? _____

Write each of the amounts below using a dollar sign and a decimal point.

14. 67 cents _____

(b) 15. 8 cents _____

Add or subtract (as required) each group of decimals below.

16.
$$
\begin{array}{r}
13.2 \\
+\ 12.4 \\
\end{array}
$$

17.
$$
\begin{array}{r}
67.3 \\
-\ 15.2 \\
\end{array}
$$

(c) 18. $73.42 + 24.53$

19. $47.98 - 21.52$

$$
\begin{array}{r}
+ \underline{\hspace{3cm}}
\end{array}
$$

$$
\begin{array}{r}
- \underline{\hspace{3cm}}
\end{array}
$$

20.   Find the perimeter of the polygon below. _____

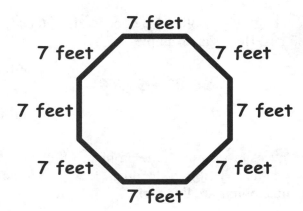

Solve each word problem below.

(d) 21.   Carrie is 18 years older than Melanie, and Melanie is 27 years older than Kylie. If Kylie is 21 years old, how old is Carrie? _____

(e) 22.   Each bottle of soda contains 24 ounces. If there are 8 bottles, how many ounces of soda are there in all? _____

Lesson 49—Adding and Subtracting with Dollars and Cents

Adding and subtracting with dollars and cents is almost exactly like adding and subtracting with plain decimals. Here's an example.

$6.23 + $1.74

Adding amounts that contain both dollars and cents.

The only difference between this problem and the problems in the last lesson is the dollar signs. To solve it, we just put one number on top of the other, leaving out the dollar signs temporarily, and then make sure the decimal points are lined up.

$$\begin{array}{r} 6.23 \\ +\ 1.74 \\ \hline 7.97 \end{array}$$

Line up the decimal points, then add the columns.

After adding the columns, we put a decimal point directly beneath the decimal points in the numbers being added. Finally, we put a dollar sign in front of our answer, which leaves us with $7.97.

Next, here's a subtracting cents problem.

54¢ - 21¢

Subtracting with cents.

Notice that this problem doesn't even have any decimals, since both numbers are just cents. That means all we have to do here is subtract the numbers and then put the cent sign after the answer, which leaves us with 33¢.

It's also possible to subtract two cent amounts and then change the answer to dollars.

97¢ - 83¢

The answer can be written in dollars.

After subtracting, we get an answer of 14¢. However, since we want to find the answer to be written in dollars, we have to get rid of the cents sign, move the decimal point, and then write a dollar sign at the beginning.

14¢ ⟶ 14 ⟶ $0.14

Changing 14¢ into dollars.

The final answer, then, is $0.14.

Practice 49

a. Write fifty-seven cents using a dollar sign and a decimal point. _____

b. Subtract $49.98 - 21.52$

c. Write the sum of 53¢ and 44¢ in dollar form.

$+$ _____

Solve each word problem below.

d. The Beta Force started the war with 88 missiles. In the first battle, they used 14 missiles. In the second battle, they used 23 missiles. How many missiles were left after that? _____

e. Each new employee receives 3 new company T-shirts when they are hired. If there are 28 employees, how many T-shirts have been given out in all? _____

Problem Set 49

Tell whether each sentence below is True or False.

1. To subtract two amounts that are written in cents, we just subtract the numbers and then put a cent sign after the result. _____

2. We can add two numbers that are not in dollar form and then change them to dollar form later. _____

Find estimates for each of the problems below by rounding each of the numbers to the nearest thousand and then adding in your head.

    3. $4,283 + 6,199$ _____

    4. $9,710 + 5,229$ _____

    5. $6,801 + 9,950$ _____

Answer each question below.

    6. Write four hundred eighty-seven and forty-nine hundredths using digits. _____

    7. Write $\dfrac{8}{100}$ as a decimal. _____

    8. Write 0.71 as a fraction. _____

    9. If one penny is $\dfrac{1}{100}$ of a dollar, 37 pennies is what fraction of a dollar? _____

Write each of the amounts below using a dollar sign and a decimal point.

(a) 10. ninety-seven cents _____

    11. three cents _____

Add or subtract (as required) each group of decimals below.

    12.
$$\begin{array}{r} 34.4 \\ +\,25.1 \\ \hline \end{array}$$

    13.
$$\begin{array}{r} 56.4 \\ -\,24.1 \\ \hline \end{array}$$

    14. $62.32 + 31.57$

(b) 15. $88.45 - 45.14$

$$+\ \underline{\hspace{3cm}}$$

$$-\ \underline{\hspace{3cm}}$$

Add or subtract (as required) each dollar amount below.

16. $4.24 + $3.35

17. $9.57 − $7.13

+ _____

− _____

18. Write the difference of 89¢ and 42¢ in cent form.

− _____

(c) 19. Write the sum of 62¢ and 23¢ in dollar form.

+ _____

20. Find the area of the rectangle below. _____

16 inches

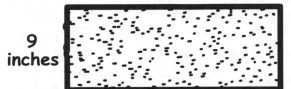

9 inches

235

Solve each word problem below.

(d) 21   The music store started out with 65 copies of the new top-selling CD. The first day the CD was on sale, they sold 24 copies. The second day, they sold 17 copies. How many copies were left after that? _____

(e) 22   Each box in the store contains 8 cereal bars. If there are 16 boxes, how many cereal bars are there in all? _____

Quiz 7

Tell whether each sentence below is True or False.

1. The word "and" can be used to stand for the decimal point when saying or writing a decimal that has digits to the left of the point. _____

2. When subtracting two decimals, the decimal points don't need to be lined up. _____

Add or subtract (as required) each pair of numbers below.

3. $\begin{array}{r} 5,638 \\ + \ 4,792 \\ \hline \end{array}$

4. $\begin{array}{r} 72 \\ - \ 34 \\ \hline \end{array}$

Find estimates for each of the problems below by rounding each of the numbers to the nearest thousand and then subtracting in your head.

5. $9,282 - 4,150$ _____

6. $8,794 - 2,153$ _____

7. $6,873 - 1,732$ _____

Answer each question below.

8. Write seven hundred thirty-four and sixty-eight hundredths using digits. _____

9. Write $\dfrac{69}{100}$ as a decimal. _____

10. Write 0.29 as a fraction. _____

11. If one penny is $\dfrac{1}{100}$ of a dollar, 23 pennies is what fraction of a dollar? _____

For each problem below, choose the group of words that best belongs in the blank.

12. $75.36   Seventy-five dollars _____.

      A. and thirty-six hundredths   B. and thirty-six
      C. and thirty six cents   D. and thirty-six cents
      E. and thirty six hundredths

13. $46.62   Forty-six dollars_____.

      A. sixty-two cents   B. and sixty two hundredths
      C. and sixty-two cents   D. and sixty two cents
      E. and sixty-two hundredths

Write each of the amounts below using a dollar sign and a decimal point.

14. ninety-nine cents _____

15. two cents _____

Add or subtract (as required) each group of decimals below.

16. $\begin{array}{r} 64.5 \\ + 12.3 \\ \hline \end{array}$ 17. $75.81 + 42.15$

$+$ _____

18. $89.64 - 36.21$

$-$ _____

Add or subtract (as required) each amount below.

19. $5.67 + $3.12

+ _____

20. Write the difference of 56¢ and 34¢ in cent form.

– _____

21. Write the sum of 41¢ and 17¢ in dollar form.

+ _____

22. Find the perimeter of the polygon below. _____

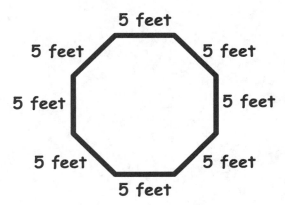

5 feet

5 feet   5 feet

5 feet   5 feet

5 feet   5 feet

5 feet

Solve each word problem below.

23. Last week, Ryan worked 13 more hours than Adam, and Adam worked 15 more hours than Alex. If Alex only worked 12 hours, how many hours did Ryan work? _____

24. There are 6 snack crackers in each package. If there are 31 packages, how many snack crackers are there altogether? _____

Lesson 50—Regrouping Twice

Sometimes it's necessary to regroup twice. Here's an example.

$$
\begin{array}{r}
5\overset{12}{\cancel{6}}\overset{18}{\cancel{38}} \\
-\ 479 \\
\hline
159
\end{array}
$$

Regrouping
more than
once.

Notice that we had to regroup in both the tens and the hundreds columns. First, since 8 was less than 9, we borrowed a 1 from the tens column, which gave us 18 in the ones column. However, in the tens column, we also had to regroup because 2 is less than 7, so we took 1 out of the hundreds, and gave it to the tens column. We then just subtracted 7 from 12 to get 5. Finally, we subtracted 5 and 4 in the hundreds column to get an answer of 159. Here's another example.

$$
\begin{array}{r}
6\overset{14}{\cancel{7}}\overset{12}{\cancel{52}} \\
-\ 183 \\
\hline
569
\end{array}
$$

Regrouping
more than
once.

Once again, we had to borrow in the ones column because 2 is smaller than 3, and we also had to borrow in the tens column because 4 is smaller than 8. After regrouping twice and subtracting the columns, we got an answer of 569.

The main point of this lesson is that regrouping twice isn't really any different than regrouping once.

Practice 50

    a. Subtract $94.76 - 52.41$

b. Write the difference of 79¢ and 54¢ in dollar form.

– _____

c. Subtract
$$\begin{array}{r} 512 \\ -\ 248 \\ \hline \end{array}$$

Solve each word problem below.

d. The subway started out with 67 people on board. After the first stop, 23 people got off. After the second stop, another 22 people got off. How many people were still on the subway after that? _____

e. There are 9 bunnies in each bus. If there are 17 buses, how many bunnies are there altogether? _____

Problem Set 50

Tell whether each sentence below is True or False.

1. It is illegal to regroup twice in a subtraction problem. _____

2. When you move a 1 from the hundreds to the tens column, that's like adding a 10 to the tens column. _____

Find estimates for each of the problems below by rounding each of the numbers to the nearest thousand and then subtracting in your head.

3. $9,347 - 5,214$ _____

4. $8,754 - 2,153$ _____

5. $7,847 - 5,736$ _____

Answer each question below.

6.   Write nine hundred twenty-three and sixty-five hundredths using digits. _____

7.   Write $\dfrac{51}{100}$ as a decimal. _____

8.   Write 0.53 as a fraction. _____

Write each of the amounts below using a dollar sign and a decimal point.

9.   eighty-two cents _____

10.   nine cents _____

Add or subtract (as required) each group of decimals below.

11. $\begin{array}{r} 74.6 \\ -\ 51.5 \\ \hline \end{array}$

12. $54.73 + 65.14$

$+\underline{\hspace{3cm}}$

(a) 13. $95.63 - 32.41$

$-\underline{\hspace{3cm}}$

Add or subtract (as required) each dollar amount below.

14. $\$9.47 + \$5.41$

15. $\$8.79 - \$4.52$

$+\underline{\hspace{2cm}}$

$-\underline{\hspace{2cm}}$

16. Write the difference of 78¢ and 64¢ in cent form.

$$-\ \underline{\hspace{3cm}}$$

(b) 17. Write the difference of 94¢ and 33¢ in dollar form.

$$-\ \underline{\hspace{3cm}}$$

Subtract each pair of numbers below.

(c) 18.
$$\begin{array}{r} 923 \\ -\ 574 \\ \hline \end{array}$$

19.
$$\begin{array}{r} 741 \\ -\ 258 \\ \hline \end{array}$$

20.
$$\begin{array}{r} 852 \\ -\ 473 \\ \hline \end{array}$$

Solve each word problem below.

(d) 21. When the play started, there were 98 people in the audience. After the first act, 24 people left. After the second act, another 27 people left. How many people were still in the audience after that? _____

(e) 22. There are 4 wild boars at each table. If there are 15 tables, how many wild boars are there altogether? _____

Lesson 51—Regrouping with Zeros

Regrouping can sometimes be difficult when there's a zero on top. Here's an example.

$$\begin{array}{r} \overset{5\ 10}{\cancel{60}} \\ -\ 43 \\ \hline 17 \end{array}$$
The zero
becomes a ten.

Since 0 is less than 3, we had to regroup by borrowing a 1 from the tens column. That 1 became a 10 in the tens column, and next we just added the 10 to the 0 that was there to get 10. Finally, we subtracted the columns to get 17.

Sometimes it's necessary to borrow from the tens column even if there is a zero in that column. Here's an example like that.

$$\begin{array}{r} \overset{9}{2\ \cancel{10}\ 15} \\ \cancel{305} \\ -\ 176 \\ \hline 129 \end{array}$$
Borrow from the next
column over when there
is a zero.

In the ones column, 5 is smaller than 6, so we had to regroup. However, in the tens column, there wasn't anything to borrow, at least at first. In cases like this, we have to go all the way over to the hundreds column, borrow a 1 from it, and then give that to the tens column. This left us with a 10 in the tens column, which we then borrowed a 1 from. That gave us a 9 in the tens column and a 15 in the ones. We then just subtracted the columns to get 129. Here's one last example.

$$\begin{array}{r} \overset{9}{3\ \cancel{10}\ 10} \\ \cancel{400} \\ -\ 253 \\ \hline 147 \end{array}$$
A problem with
two zeros on top.

This problem had two zeros in the top, but it's not really any harder than the previous example. Notice that once again, when we tried to borrow from the tens, there weren't any, so we had to borrow from the hundreds first, give that to the tens, and then borrow from the tens to give to the ones. After that, we were able to just subtract the columns to get 147.

The main point of this lesson is that if you need to regroup but there's nothing in the column on the left, just borrow something from the next column over.

Practice 51

a. Write the difference of 99¢ and 21¢ in dollar form.

－ _____

b. Subtract
$$\begin{array}{r} 647 \\ -\,359 \\ \hline \end{array}$$

c. Subtract
$$\begin{array}{r} 700 \\ -\,183 \\ \hline \end{array}$$

Solve each word problem below.

d. Margo is 25 years older than Jess, and Jess is 18 years older than Valerie. If Valerie is 22 years old, how old is Margo? _____

e. There are 6 big rigs at the truck stop. If each big rig has 18 wheels, how many wheels are there altogether? _____

Problem Set 51

Tell whether each sentence below is True or False.

1. You sometimes have to borrow a 1 from the hundreds column before you can subtract in the ones column. _____

2. Whenever we borrow a 1 from a column and give it to a column that has 0, the 0 becomes a 10. _____

Find estimates for each of the problems below by rounding each of the numbers to the nearest thousand and then adding in your head.

3. $6,150 + 4,299$ _____

4. $7,901 + 7,186$ _____

5. $8,713 + 3,932$ _____

Answer each question below.

6. Write eight hundred ninety-one and fifty-three hundredths using digits. _____

7. Write $\dfrac{89}{100}$ as a decimal. _____

8. Write 0.17 as a fraction. _____

Write each of the amounts below using a dollar sign and a decimal point.

9. forty-five cents _____

10. six cents _____

Add or subtract (as required) each group of decimals below.

11. $94.12 + 33.67$ **12.** $85.74 - 23.42$

$+$ _____ $-$ _____

Add or subtract (as required) each dollar amount below.

13. $\$6.32 + \$3.65$ **14.** $\$8.64 - \$1.61$

$+$ _____ $-$ _____

(a) 15. Write the difference of 67¢ and 15¢ in dollar form.

$-$ _____

Subtract each pair of numbers below.

(b) 16.
$$
\begin{array}{r}
532 \\
-\ 167 \\
\hline
\end{array}
$$

17.
$$
\begin{array}{r}
827 \\
-\ 439 \\
\hline
\end{array}
$$

18.
$$
\begin{array}{r}
90 \\
-\ 23 \\
\hline
\end{array}
$$

19.
$$
\begin{array}{r}
602 \\
-\ 175 \\
\hline
\end{array}
$$

(c) 20.
$$
\begin{array}{r}
800 \\
-\ 326 \\
\hline
\end{array}
$$

Solve each word problem below.

(d) 21. Angie is 32 years older than Jennifer, and Jennifer is 17 years older than Lorie. If Lorie is 14 years old, how old is Angie? _____

(e) 22. There are 7 identical houseboats at the dock. If each boat can hold 14 people, how many people can all the boats hold? _____

Lesson 52—Comparing Decimals

Sometimes it's necessary to compare two decimals to see which one is greater. Here's an example.

57.8 > 5.78

Notice that these numbers have the exact same digits, and they're even in the same order. However, the numbers are not equal because of the decimal point. In 57.8, the decimal point is between the 7 and the 8. In 5.78, it's between the 5 and the 7. That means that the whole number part of 57.8 is 57, and the whole number part of 5.78 is 5. Since 57 is definitely greater than 5, 57.8 has to be greater than 5.78. So one way to compare two decimals is to compare their whole number parts; whichever has the bigger whole number part has to be the greater number.

Sometimes when comparing two decimals, the whole number parts are the same. Here's an example.

3.21 > 3.25

Notice that the whole number part of both numbers is 3. In situations like this, we have to look at the digits to the right of the decimal point starting with the tenths. Both numbers have a 2 in the tenths place, so next we have to compare the hundredths. In 3.21, the hundredths digit is 1, but in 3.25, the hundredths digit is 5. Since 1 is less than 5, 3.21 is less than 3.25. Here's one last example.

98.7 > 98.72

The whole number parts are the same, and so are the digits in the tenths place. However, when comparing the hundredths, it appears that 98.7 doesn't have any digits in the hundredths place. In cases like this, just remember that 98.7 is the same as 98.70, which allows us to compare a 0 with a 2 to see that 98.7 is the lesser number. Here, again, are the rules for comparing decimals.

Comparing Decimals

1.	Find the decimal points and look at the whole number parts. The number with the bigger whole number is greater.
2.	If the whole number parts are the same, compare the digits to the right of the decimal point, until you find one that's bigger than another. The number with the bigger digit is greater.

Practice 52

a. Subtract
$$\begin{array}{r} 500 \\ -\ 283 \\ \hline \end{array}$$

Tell whether a <, >, or = should go between each pair of decimals below.

b. 71.83 _____ 71.89

c. 27.34 _____ 27.3

Solve each word problem below.

d. The department store started out with 68 puffy coats. If the store sold 23 puffy coats the first month and 22 the second month, how many were left after that? _____

e. The florist put 8 pinecones in each centerpiece. If she made 25 centerpieces, how many pinecones did she use in all? _____

Problem Set 52

Tell whether each sentence below is True or False.

1. When comparing two decimals, the one with the bigger whole number part is always greater. _____

2. If the whole number parts of two decimals are the same, we have to look at the digits to the right of the decimal point in order to compare them. _____

Find estimates for each of the problems below by rounding each of the numbers to the nearest thousand and then subtracting in your head.

3. $6,918 - 1,307$ _____   4. $9,925 - 2,813$ _____

Answer each question below.

5. Write six hundred eighty-four and fifty-seven hundredths using digits. _____

6. Write $\dfrac{39}{100}$ as a decimal. _____

7. Write 0.43 as a fraction. _____

8. Write twenty-nine cents using a dollar sign and decimal point. _____

Add or subtract (as required) each group of decimals below.

9. $86.27 + 52.71$ 10. $76.48 - 31.26$

    +_____   −_____

Subtract the two dollar amounts below.

11. $\$29.57 - \$13.25$

    −_____

12. Write the difference of 83¢ and 31¢ in dollar form.

    −_____

Subtract each pair of numbers below.

(a) 13.
$$\begin{array}{r} 972 \\ -\ 184 \\ \hline \end{array}$$

14.
$$\begin{array}{r} 80 \\ -\ 32 \\ \hline \end{array}$$

15.
$$\begin{array}{r} 703 \\ -\ 456 \\ \hline \end{array}$$

(b) 16.
$$\begin{array}{r} 900 \\ -\ 538 \\ \hline \end{array}$$

Tell whether a <, >, or = should go between each pair of decimals below.

17. 49.6 _____ 4.96

18. 86.37 _____ 86.57

(c) 19. 62.51 _____ 62.56

20. 45.23 _____ 45.2

Solve each word problem below.

(d) 21. The rescue team needs to find 78 kittens. They found 13 kittens on the first day and 24 on the second. How many kittens were left after that? _____

(e) 22. There are 7 blocks in each stack. If there are 19 stacks of blocks, how many blocks are there in all? _____

Lesson 53—Filling in the Holes – Part 1

When adding two decimals, the decimal points must be lined up, but sometimes that requires an extra step. Here's an example.

$$\begin{array}{r} 63.5 \\ + 24.19 \\ \hline \end{array}$$

There's a hole above the 9.

After lining up the decimal points, there's no number over the 9. In situations like this, most people fill the hole with a zero, which is allowed since 63.5 is the same as 63.50. Then they add the columns from right to left.

$$\begin{array}{r} 63.50 \\ + 24.19 \\ \hline 87.69 \end{array}$$

Fill the hole with a zero, then add the columns.

Notice that the decimal point in the answer went directly beneath the decimal point in the numbers being added. Here's another example.

$$\begin{array}{r} 15. \\ + \ 4.32 \\ \hline \end{array}$$

A problem with two holes on top.

This time there are holes above both the 3 and the 2. But again, it's possible to fill those holes with zeros and then add the columns.

$$\begin{array}{r} 15.00 \\ + \ 4.32 \\ \hline 19.32 \end{array}$$

Fill both of the holes with zeros.

After adding the columns, we got a final answer of 19.32. The main point of this lesson is that when adding decimals, the decimal points have to be lined up, and if there are any holes, you can fill them with zeros.

Practice 53

a. Tell whether a <, >, or = should go between 32.9 _____ 32.92

b. Add $65.6 + 24.16$

c. Add $52 + 13.78$

+ _____

+ _____

Solve each word problem below.

d. There are 15 more roly-polies than June bugs, and there are 13 more June bugs than fireflies. If there are 21 fireflies, how many roly-polies are there? _____

e. Tara drinks 8 glasses of water each day. How many glasses will she drink in 26 days? _____

Problem Set 53

Tell whether each sentence below is True or False.

1. Sometimes when you line up the decimal points, there are holes in the top number. _____

2. If there are holes in a number, they need to be filled with stars. _____

Find estimates for each of the problems below by rounding each of the numbers to the nearest thousand and then adding in your head.

3. $5,809 + 7,276$ _____

4. $8,763 + 4,951$ _____

Answer each question below.

5. Write 0.77 as a fraction. _____

6. Write forty-eight cents using a dollar sign and decimal point. _____

Add the two dollar amounts below.

7. $32.52 + $15.41

$$+ \underline{\hspace{3cm}}$$

8. Write the difference of 59¢ and 15¢ in dollar form.

$$- \underline{\hspace{3cm}}$$

Subtract each pair of numbers below.

9. 772
     − 284

10. 423
      − 198

11. 504
      − 125

12. 600
      − 348

Tell whether a <, >, or = should go between each pair of decimals below.

13. 9.43 _____ 94.3

14. 35.28 _____ 35.48

15. 17.33 _____ 17.32

(a) 16. 56.9 _____ 56.96

Add each pair of decimals below.

(b) 17. $42.7 + 23.18$ **18.** $32.7 + 15.25$

+ _____   + _____

19. $46.2 + 12.5$ **(c) 20.** $83 + 21.93$

+ _____   + _____

Solve each word problem below.

(d) 21.   There are 29 more bananas than apples, and there are 16 more apples than oranges. If there are 25 oranges, how many bananas are there? _____

(e) 22.   The sword smith can make 6 fighting swords each week. How many fighting swords can he make in 28 weeks? _____

Lesson 54—Decimals and Carrying

Sometimes it's necessary to carry when adding decimals. Here's an example.

$$
\begin{array}{r}
\overset{1}{6}5.8 \\
+\ 32.4 \\
\hline
98.2
\end{array}
$$

Carrying from the
tenths to the ones.

Notice that when we added the 8 and the 4 in the ones column, the answer was bigger than 9, so we had to carry. The carrying step worked because 10 tenths is the same as a one. Also, notice that after adding the rest of the columns, we put the decimal point in the answer directly below the points in the numbers being added. Here's another example.

$$
\begin{array}{r}
\overset{1}{5}\overset{1}{4}.76 \\
+\ 23.89 \\
\hline
78.65
\end{array}
$$

Carrying from hundredths
to tenths and from tenths
to ones.

After lining up the decimal points, we just added the columns. This time, we had to carry from both the hundredths to the tenths and from the tenths to the ones, and it was okay to carry from the hundredths to the tenths because 10 hundredths is the same as 1 tenth.

The main point of this lesson is that carrying with decimals is basically the same as carrying with whole numbers.

Practice 54

a. Tell whether a <, >, or = should go between 13.79 _____ 13.7

b. Add $25 + 14.78$

c. Add
$$
\begin{array}{r}
79.45 \\
+\ 23.68 \\
\hline
\end{array}
$$

$$
\begin{array}{r}
+\ \underline{\hspace{3cm}}
\end{array}
$$

Solve each word problem below.

d. Yesterday, the three space rangers shot 65 pieces of space junk with their laser guns. If the first ranger shot 17 pieces, and the second ranger shot 24, how many did the third ranger shoot? _____

e. There are 16 pawns in a chess set. If there are 7 chess sets, how many pawns are there in all? _____

Problem Set 54

Tell whether each sentence below is True or False.

1. You cannot carry a one from the tenths column to the ones column. _____

2. It's legal to carry a 1 from the hundredths column to the tenths column. _____

Find estimates for each of the problems below by rounding each of the numbers to the nearest thousand and then subtracting in your head.

3. $9,257 - 8,152$ _____   **4.** $7,919 - 2,718$ _____

Answer each question below.

5. Write $\dfrac{87}{100}$ as a decimal. _____

6. Write fifty cents using a dollar sign and decimal point. _____

Subtract the two dollar amounts below.

7. $\$95.78 - \$35.62$

$-$ _____

8. Write the sum of 45¢ and 34¢ in dollar form.

+ _____

Subtract each pair of numbers below.

9. 531
  − 197

10. 801
  − 416

11. 400
  − 254

Tell whether a <, >, or = should go between each pair of decimals below.

12. 15.6 _____ 1.56

13. 52.45 _____ 52.65

14. 93.83 _____ 93.82

(a) 15. 26.14 _____ 26.1

Add each pair of decimals below.

(b) 16. 64.7 + 25.21

17. 57 + 31.92

+ _____

+ _____

18. 73.8
  + 27.9

(c) 19. 67.84
  + 45.57

20. 98.62
  + 53.49

Solve each word problem below.

(d) 21. Last week, the three royal knights defeated 54 of their foes. If the first royal knight defeated 18 foes, and the second royal knight defeated 23, how many did the third royal knight defeat? _____

(e) 22. There are 18 sail boats in the harbor. If each boat has 2 sails, how many sails are there in all? _____

Lesson 55—Decimals and Regrouping

It's sometimes necessary to regroup when subtracting decimals. Here's an example.

$$
\begin{array}{r}
{\scriptstyle 7\ 14} \\
6\cancel{8}.\cancel{4} \\
-\ 23.5 \\
\hline
44.9
\end{array}
$$

Borrowing from the
ones column to give
to the tenths.

When subtracting the tenths, 4 was less than 5, so we had to regroup by borrowing a 1 from the ones column. That changed the 8 to a 7 and gave us 14 in the tenths column. It's okay to take 1 from the ones column and give it to the tenths because 1 is equal to 10 tenths. After subtracting the rest of the columns, we put the decimal point in the answer directly below the decimal points in the numbers being subtracted, which left us with 44.9.

It's also possible to regroup with numbers that go out to the hundredths. Here's an example.

$$
\begin{array}{r}
{\scriptstyle 5\ 12\ 15} \\
9\cancel{6}.\cancel{3}\cancel{5} \\
-\ 42.89 \\
\hline
53.46
\end{array}
$$

Regrouping with
the hundredths
and tenths.

This time we had to regroup in both the tenths and the hundredths columns. Since 5 was smaller than 9, we borrowed from the tenths column. Then, since the 2 was smaller than the 8 in the tenths, we borrowed from the ones column to get 12. After subtracting all of the columns, we put the decimal point in the answer to get 53.46.

The main point of this lesson is that regrouping with decimals is basically the same as regrouping with whole numbers.

Practice 55

a. Add
$$
\begin{array}{r}
82.45 \\
+\ 49.66 \\
\hline
\end{array}
$$

b. Subtract
$$
\begin{array}{r}
53.4 \\
-\ 21.7 \\
\hline
\end{array}
$$

c. Subtract
$$
\begin{array}{r}
63.51 \\
-\ 42.78 \\
\hline
\end{array}
$$

Solve each word problem below.

d. Andrew has 22 more action figures than Josiah, and Josiah has 19 more action figures than Michael. If Michael has 21 action figures, how many does Andrew have? _____

e. The building has 3 separate dining halls. If there are 26 tables in each dining hall, how many tables are there altogether? _____

Problem Set 55

Tell whether each sentence below is True or False.

1. It is illegal to borrow a 1 from the ones column and give it to the tenths. _____

2. You can borrow a 1 from the tenths column and give it to the hundredths, as long as the 1 becomes a 10 in the hundredths column. _____

Answer each question below.

3. Write $\dfrac{47}{100}$ as a decimal. _____

4. Write 0.29 as a fraction. _____

5. Write 0.31 as a fraction. _____

6. Write eighty-two cents using a dollar sign and decimal point. _____

7. Write the difference of 92¢ and 41¢ in dollar form.

_____

Subtract each pair of numbers below.

8.
$$703 \\ -\,526$$

9.
$$800 \\ -\,192$$

Tell whether a <, >, or = should go between each pair of decimals below.

10. 42.52 _____ 42.32

11. 27.91 _____ 27.93

12. 531.2 _____ 531.29

Add each pair of decimals below.

13. $26.5 + 11.34$

14. $72 + 45.73$

+ _____

+ _____

15.
$$\begin{array}{r} 82.7 \\ + 16.9 \\ \hline \end{array}$$

(a) 16.
$$\begin{array}{r} 57.68 \\ + 43.37 \\ \hline \end{array}$$

Subtract each pair of decimals below.

(b) 17.
$$\begin{array}{r} 94.2 \\ - 31.6 \\ \hline \end{array}$$

18.
$$\begin{array}{r} 75.5 \\ - 32.8 \\ \hline \end{array}$$

(c) 19.
$$\begin{array}{r} 85.24 \\ - 31.76 \\ \hline \end{array}$$

20.
$$\begin{array}{r} 93.51 \\ - 21.65 \\ \hline \end{array}$$

Solve each word problem below.

(d) 21. Taffy took 17 more photos than Paisley, and Paisley took 15 more photos than Ellie. If Ellie took 22 photos, how many did Taffy take? _____

(e) 22. The building has 5 stories. If there are 23 offices on each story, how many offices are there altogether? _____

Lesson 56—Filling in the Holes – Part 2

Sometimes it's necessary to fill in holes with zeros when subtracting decimals. Here's an example.

$$18.57$$
$$- \ 3.9 \ \ \ $$

A decimal problem with a hole on the bottom.

Notice that there is a hole under both the 1 and the 7. In cases like this, we always fill the hole on the right, but not the one on the left.

```
   7 15
 18.57  ← Fill in the hole
-  3.90    with a zero, then
 14.67     subtract the columns.
```

Since the 5 in the tenths column was less than the 9, we had to regroup. After subtracting all of the columns and placing the decimal point, we got a final answer of 14.67.

Sometimes we have to subtract a decimal from a whole number. Here's an example.

$$5 - 2.5 = 2.5$$

Subtracting a decimal from a whole number.

This problem could be done in your head because 2.5 is half of 5, so $5 - 2.5$ is just 2.5. However, many times subtracting decimals from whole numbers is too difficult to do in your head. Here's an example like that.

```
  79.
-14.68
```

Lining up the decimal points leaves us with holes on top.

First, we have to fill in the holes to the right of the point in 79 with two zeros. It's okay to do that because 79 is the same as 79.00. Next, we can just subtract the columns.

```
    9
  8 10 10
 79.00   ← Fill the holes with
-14.68      zeros then subtract.
 64.32
```

Practice 56

a. Subtract
$$\begin{array}{r} 74.23 \\ -\ 51.86 \end{array}$$

b. Subtract $19.28 - 5.3$

$$-\ \underline{\hspace{3cm}}$$

c. Subtract $83 - 22.71$

$$-\ \underline{\hspace{3cm}}$$

Solve each word problem below.

d. Caleb bought 75 dog biscuits for his dogs, Buddy and Norman. Last week, Buddy ate 13 dog biscuits and Norman ate 18. How many dog biscuits does Caleb have left? _____

e. Each taco combo comes with 3 tacos. If The Tasty Taco sold 25 taco combos, how many tacos were sold in all? _____

Problem Set 56

Tell whether each sentence below is True or False.

1. Sometimes you can subtract a decimal from a whole number in your head. _____

2. When we add a decimal point and two zeros at the end of a whole number, we don't make the number any bigger or smaller. _____

Write each fraction below as a decimal.

3. $\dfrac{19}{100}$ _____

4. $\dfrac{2}{100}$ _____

Write each decimal below as a fraction.

    5. 0.63 _____

    6. 0.07 _____

Answer each question below.

    7. Write twenty-four cents using a dollar sign and decimal point. _____

    8. Write the sum of 77¢ and 12¢ in dollar form.

        + _____

Tell whether a <, >, or = should go between each pair of decimals below.

    9. 32.863 ____ 328.63   **10.** 841.56 ____ 841.53

    11. 52.13 ____ 52.23   **12.** 721.6 ____ 721.62

Add each pair of decimals below.

    13. $63 + 26.28$ **14.** $\begin{array}{r}46.8\\+\ 23.6\\\hline\end{array}$

        + _____

    15. $\begin{array}{r}72.49\\+\ 31.85\\\hline\end{array}$

Subtract each pair of numbers below.

16.
700
− 426

(a) 17.
73.45
− 21.68

(b) 18. 25.71 − 4.8

(c) 19. 47 − 15.21

20. 56 − 21.36

Solve each word problem below.

(d) 21. Betty bought 63 cat snacks for her cats, Lucy and Frisky. Last week, Lucy ate 12 cat snacks and Frisky ate 21. How many cat snacks does Betty have left? _____

(e) 22. Each spaghetti platter comes with 5 meatballs. If the restaurant sold 23 spaghetti platters, how many meatballs were sold in all? _____

Quiz 8

Tell whether each sentence below is True or False.

1. Whenever we borrow a 1 from a column and give it to a column that has 0, the 0 becomes a 10. _____

2. When we add a decimal point and two zeros at the end of a whole number, we don't make the number any bigger or smaller. _____

Answer each question below.

3. Write $\dfrac{77}{100}$ as a decimal. _____

4. Write 0.53 as a fraction. _____

5. Write fifty-one cents using a dollar sign and decimal point. _____

6. Write the difference of 95¢ and 32¢ in dollar form.

$-$ _____

Subtract each pair of numbers below.

7.
$$\begin{array}{r} 821 \\ -357 \\ \hline \end{array}$$

8.
$$\begin{array}{r} 536 \\ -238 \\ \hline \end{array}$$

9.
$$\begin{array}{r} 608 \\ -159 \\ \hline \end{array}$$

10.
$$\begin{array}{r} 900 \\ -573 \\ \hline \end{array}$$

Tell whether a <, >, or = should go between each pair of decimals below.

11. 26.34 _____ 26.54

12. 370.21 _____ 370.23

13. 142.98 _____ 142.9

Add each pair of decimals below.

14. $64.74 + 24.1$

15. $91 + 37.82$

+ _____

+ _____

16.
54.9
+ 12.8

17.
51.58
+ 45.63

Subtract each pair of decimals below.

18.
64.5
− 23.7

19.
92.53
− 31.76

20. $54.68 - 2.4$

− _____

21. $64 - 31.43$

22. $93 - 62.19$

− _____

− _____

Solve each word problem below.

23. Lucky chased 12 more cats than Buster, and Buster chased 15 more cats than Spike. If Spike chased 17 cats, how many did Lucky chase? _____

24. The store has 8 packs of gum on the shelf. If each pack has 12 pieces, how many pieces of gum are there altogether? _____

Lesson 57—More Regrouping

Sometimes we have to subtract two four-digit numbers. Here's an example.

$$
\begin{array}{r}
3\,{}^{14}\!\!\!\!\!\!\!\!\!\!\!\!{}^{12}\!\!\!\!\!\!\!\!\!\!{}^{16} \\
\cancel{4{,}536} \\
-\,2{,}978 \\
\hline
1{,}558
\end{array}
$$

Subtracting with four-digit numbers.

First, we put the 4,536 over 2,978, and then we just subtracted the columns. Notice that we had to borrow in the ones, tens, and hundreds columns. Since 6 is less than 8 in the ones column, we had to borrow from the tens, and then since 2 is less than 7 in the tens column, we had to borrow from the hundreds. Finally, in the hundreds column, 4 is less than 9, so we had to borrow from the thousands column too. After subtracting all of the columns, we got a final answer of 1,558. Here's an even messier example.

$$
\begin{array}{r}
{}^{9}\ {}^{9} \\
5\,{}^{10}\!{}^{10}\!{}^{10}{}^{17} \\
\cancel{6{,}007} \\
-\,4{,}389 \\
\hline
1{,}618
\end{array}
$$

When the top number has lots of zeros, regrouping is even messier.

Notice that in the ones column, 7 is smaller than 9, but when we go to the tens column to borrow a 1, there's nothing there, and then when we move over to the hundreds, there's still nothing. In cases like this, we have to go all the way over to the thousands just to find something to borrow. Then, we take one from the thousands and give it to the hundreds, one from the hundreds and give it to the tens, and one from the tens and give it to the ones.

The main point of the lesson is that regrouping with four-digit numbers is really no different than regrouping with two or three-digit numbers. It's just that with four digits, the regrouping steps look complicated, and the problem can take awhile to work out.

Practice 57

a. Subtract 48 – 26.72

b. Subtract
$$
\begin{array}{r}
4{,}326 \\
-\,1{,}578 \\
\hline

\end{array}
$$

c. Subtract
$$\begin{array}{r} 6,004 \\ -\,2,179 \\ \hline \end{array}$$

Solve each word problem below.

d. Each of the 78 frogs was allowed to order only one of the three appetizers being offered. The waiter noted that 15 ordered appetizer #1 (fly soup) and 19 ordered appetizer #2 (swamp noodles). How many ordered appetizer #3 (leafy nuggets)?

_____

e. The store has 9 cartons of eggs on the top shelf. If each carton has 18 eggs, how many eggs are there altogether? _____

Problem Set 57

Tell whether each sentence below is True or False.

1. It is illegal to regroup three times in a subtraction problem. _____

2. You can borrow a 1 from the thousands column and give it to the hundreds, as long as the 1 becomes a 10 in the hundreds column. _____

Write each fraction below as a decimal.

3. $\dfrac{67}{100}$ _____

4. $\dfrac{8}{100}$ _____

Write each decimal below as a fraction.

5. 0.59 _____

6. 0.09 _____

Answer each question below.

7. Write ninety-four cents using a dollar sign and decimal point. _____

8. Write the sum of 63¢ and 15¢ in dollar form.

$$+ \underline{\hspace{3cm}}$$

Tell whether a <, >, or = should go between each pair of decimals below.

9. 64.54 ____ 64.14   **10.** 735.62 ____ 735.63

11. 897.5 ____ 897.51   **12.** 431.75 ____ 4,317.5

Add each pair of decimals below.

13. $57 + 32.46$ **14.** $\begin{array}{r} 73.5 \\ + 46.9 \\ \hline \end{array}$

$$+ \underline{\hspace{3cm}}$$

15. $\begin{array}{r} 65.78 \\ + 32.66 \\ \hline \end{array}$

Subtract each pair of decimals below.

16. $28.17 - 7.5$ **(a) 17.** $75 - 41.96$

$$- \underline{\hspace{3cm}} \qquad\qquad - \underline{\hspace{3cm}}$$

Subtract each pair of numbers below.

(b) 18.
$$\begin{array}{r} 5,647 \\ -\ 1,859 \\ \hline \end{array}$$

19.
$$\begin{array}{r} 6,305 \\ -\ 1,476 \\ \hline \end{array}$$

(c) 20.
$$\begin{array}{r} 7,006 \\ -\ 4,398 \\ \hline \end{array}$$

Solve each word problem below.

(d) 21. Each of the 56 turtles at this month's turtle Olympics could only compete in one of the three events being offered. The records showed that 24 signed up for the first event (the hurdle races) and 18 signed up for the second event (the high jump). How many turtles signed up for the third event (the marathon)? _____

(e) 22. The store has 9 packages of cheese on the shelf. If each package has 24 slices of cheese in it, how many slices of cheese are there altogether? _____

Lesson 58—Money Word Problems – Part 1

You can use addition and subtraction of decimals to do problems that involve adding or subtracting money. Here's an example.

Yesterday, Sue picked up some cans of soda pop for $5.79 and a container of ice cream for $3.34 at her local grocery store. How much did she spend in all?

To do this problem, we put the bigger number over the smaller one, add the columns, and then write in the dollar sign and decimal point to get $9.13.

$$\begin{array}{r} \overset{1\ 1}{5.79} \\ +\ 3.34 \\ \hline \$9.13 \end{array}$$ Line up the decimal points and add the columns.

Notice that we also had to carry twice in this problem. Here's a tougher one.

Gary bought a pair of boxing shoes for $55 and headgear for $29.75. How much did he spend altogether?

Here we're adding a whole number and a decimal, so we have to be careful when lining up the numbers. Remember, the decimal points have to be lined up, and then the holes can be filled with zeros.

$$\begin{array}{r} \overset{1}{55.00} \\ +\ 29.75 \\ \hline \$84.75 \end{array}$$ Fill in the holes with zeros, then add the columns.

After filling in the holes with zeros, we just added the columns. The last step was to put in the decimal point and write a dollar sign at the beginning, which gave us $84.75 as the final answer.

Practice 58

a. Subtract $38 - 21.54$

b. Subtract $\begin{array}{r} 7{,}326 \\ -\ 2{,}459 \\ \hline \end{array}$

$$\begin{array}{r} - \\ \hline \end{array}$$

c. Subtract
$$\begin{array}{r} 5,004 \\ -\ 1,879 \\ \hline \end{array}$$

Solve each word problem below.

d. Meg bought a pair of gloves for $13.50 and a scarf for $11.25. How much did she spend in all? _____

e. At Jim's Sporting Goods, Aaron bought a hockey mask for $33 and a junior hockey stick for $22.75. How much did he spend altogether? _____

Problem Set 58

Tell whether each sentence below is True or False.

1. When you're adding decimals in real life, you never have to line up the decimal points. _____

2. Sometimes, in the real world, you have to fill in holes to add one dollar amount to another. _____

Write each fraction below as a decimal.

3. $\dfrac{29}{100}$ _____

4. $\dfrac{4}{100}$ _____

Write each decimal below as a fraction.

5. 0.39 _____

6. 0.03 _____

Answer each question below.

7. Write seventy-six cents using a dollar sign and decimal point. _____

8. Write the difference of 82¢ and 21¢ in dollar form.

    – _____

Tell whether a <, >, or = should go between each pair of decimals below.

9. 70.15 _____ 70.05   **10.** 353.27 _____ 353.28

11. 619.8 _____ 619.83

Add each pair of decimals below.

12. 94 + 51.38

13. 81.5
        + 39.6
        _____

    + _____

14. 73.58
        + 26.94
        _____

Subtract each pair of decimals below.

15. 89.42
        – 31.76
        _____

16. 47.21 – 6.3

    – _____

(a) 17. $58 - 34.72$

$$\underline{}$$

Subtract each pair of numbers below.

(b) 18.
$$
\begin{array}{r}
6,731 \\
- 2,894 \\
\hline
\end{array}
$$

19.
$$
\begin{array}{r}
7,504 \\
- 2,819 \\
\hline
\end{array}
$$

(c) 20.
$$
\begin{array}{r}
8,002 \\
- 3,164 \\
\hline
\end{array}
$$

Solve each word problem below.

(d) 21. Lauren bought a pair of running shoes for $35.40 and some running shorts for $16.25. How much did she spend in all? _____

(d) 22. At the True Blue Vintage Toy Company, Mr. Leland bought a model railroad car for $24 and a jack-in-the-box for $15.25. How much did he spend altogether? _____

Lesson 59—Thousandths and Decimals

There's a place just to the right of the hundredths called the **thousandths**. The decimal 0.001 stands for "one thousandth," and as a fraction it looks like this.

$$0.001 = \frac{1}{1,000}$$

Thousandths are just to the right of hundredths.

Whenever 1,000 is in the bottom of a fraction, and we want to change the fraction to a decimal, we have to put three digits to the right of the decimal point. Here's an example.

$$\frac{136}{1,000} = 0.136$$

Thousandths have three digits after the decimal point.

Since there are three digits to the right of the decimal point, 136 over 1,000 is the same as 0.136, and both are pronounced "one hundred thirty-six thousandths."

It's also important to know how to write a decimal with thousandths when given what the number stands for. Here's an example.

2 tenths + 3 hundredths + 9 thousandths
0.239

To write this as a decimal, put a zero, then a decimal point, and then just write each number in the place it should go to get the answer, 0.239.

You can change decimals into fractions without much effort, too. Here's an example.

$$0.009 = \frac{9}{1,000}$$

Just put the 9 over 1,000.

Notice that we wrote $\frac{9}{1,000}$ not $\frac{009}{1,000}$. That's because we never start a whole number with zero.

To write a decimal that goes to the thousandths place in words, follow the same approach as with tenths and hundredths. So 3.467 in words is "three and four hundred sixty-seven thousandths." Notice that we still use the word *and* to stand for the decimal point. Also, addition and subtraction problems with decimals that go to thousandths are done in the same way as those that only go out to tenths or hundredths. We just line up the decimal points and then add or subtract the columns.

Practice 59

    a. Subtract $63 - 42.79$

        $-$ _____

    b. Write $\dfrac{2}{1,000}$ as a decimal. _____

    c. Write 0.007 as a fraction. _____

Solve each word problem below.

    d. Sweetpea painted 13 more eggs than Muffin, and Muffin painted 18 more eggs than Juliet. If Juliet painted 27 eggs, how many did Sweetpea paint? _____

    e. Mrs. Johnson bought a bag of dog food for $17 and a bag of cat food for $11.35. How much did she spend in all? _____

Problem Set 59

Tell whether each sentence below is True or False.

    1. The fraction $\dfrac{7}{1,000}$ is pronounced "seven thousandths." _____

    2. Whenever you want to change a fraction with 1,000 in its bottom into a decimal, you need to put three places to the right of the decimal point. _____

Tell what each of the highlighted digits stands for in the numbers below.

3. 4.6<mark>9</mark>2

    A. hundreds   B. tens   C. ones
    D. tenths   E. hundredths   F. thousandths

4. 0.53<mark>1</mark>

    A. hundreds   B. tens   C. ones
    D. tenths   E. hundredths   F. thousandths

Answer each question below.

5. Write sixty-one cents using a dollar sign and decimal point. _____

6. Write the sum of 35¢ and 19¢ in dollar form.

    + _____

7. If it takes 20 nickels to make $1, how many nickels does it take to make $6? _____

Tell whether a <, >, or = should go between each pair of decimals below.

8. 513.27 _____ 513.28   **9.** 25.681 _____ 25.68

Answer each question below.

10. Write 5 tenths + 2 hundredths + 8 thousandths using digits. _____

11. Write 0 tenths + 0 hundredths + 5 thousandths using digits. _____

Add or subtract (as required) each pair of decimals below.

12.
$$\begin{array}{r} 94.31 \\ -\ 52.78 \\ \hline \end{array}$$

13. $47 + 25.54$

$$+\ \underline{\hspace{3cm}}$$

(a) 14. $76 - 21.83$

$$-\ \underline{\hspace{3cm}}$$

Subtract each pair of numbers below.

15.
$$\begin{array}{r} 6,308 \\ -\ 3,179 \\ \hline \end{array}$$

16.
$$\begin{array}{r} 9,003 \\ -\ 4,276 \\ \hline \end{array}$$

Write each fraction below as a decimal.

17. $\dfrac{521}{1,000}$ _____

(b) 18. $\dfrac{9}{1,000}$ _____

Write each decimal below as a fraction.

19. 0.183 _____

(c) 20. 0.003 _____

283

Solve each word problem below.

(d) 21. Itty Bitty colored 11 more pictures than Rocky, and Rocky colored 23 more pictures than Peek-a-boo. If Peek-a-boo colored 28 pictures, how many did Itty Bitty color? _____

(e) 22. Mindy bought a new shirt for $23 and a pair of pants for $32.25. How much did she spend in all? _____

Lesson 60—Money Word Problems – Part 2

Whenever people buy things, they usually end up getting change back from the cashier. Here's an example.

> Roland bought a design-your-own stock car kit for $12.72. If he gave the cashier $15, how much should he have received in change?

We have to subtract to solve this problem because we're being asked how much Roland got back in change. So we'll first put the larger number over the smaller one and then get rid of the dollar signs (temporarily). Next, we'll line up the decimal points, fill in the holes with zeros, and then subtract the columns.

$$
\begin{array}{r}
\overset{9}{\cancel{}} \\
4\ \overset{10}{\cancel{10}}\ 10 \\
1\cancel{5}.\cancel{00} \\
-\ 12.72 \\
\hline
\$2.28
\end{array}
$$

Fill in the holes with zeros, then subtract.

Notice that when we went to borrow from the tenths column, there was nothing there, so we had to go over to the ones column. After we subtracted all the columns, we got 228, but then we had to put in the decimal point and dollar sign, which made the final answer $2.28. Here's another example.

> Wendy may love her little Yorkshire terrier too much. For example, yesterday, she bought the dog its own canopy bed with a goose down pillow. If the total bill was $72.39 and she gave the cashier $80, how much should she have received in change?

Once again we have to subtract, which means we need to put the bigger number on top, line up the decimals (remember, 80 has a decimal point just to the right of the 0), and fill in the holes.

$$
\begin{array}{r}
9\quad 9 \\
7\ \overset{10}{\cancel{10}}\ \overset{10}{\cancel{10}}\ 10 \\
\cancel{80}.\cancel{00} \\
-\ 72.39 \\
\hline
\$7.61
\end{array}
$$

Fill in the holes with zeros, then subtract.

Notice that when we tried to regroup, we had to go all the way over to the tens column to get something to borrow. After subtracting the numbers, we put in the decimal point in and wrote the dollar sign in front to get $7.61

Practice 60

a. Subtract $\begin{array}{r} 4,006 \\ -\ 1,327 \\ \hline \end{array}$

b. Write $\dfrac{5}{1,000}$ as a decimal. _____

c. Write 0.009 as a fraction. _____

Solve each word problem below.

d. Mark bought a radio-controlled car for $21.97. If he gave the cashier $25, how much should he have received in change? _____

e. Yesterday, Jessie bought a new hardback novel for $11.67. If she gave the cashier $20, how much should she have received in change? _____

Problem Set 60

Tell whether each sentence below is True or False.

1. To figure out how much change a cashier owes you, you need to subtract the cost of the item from the amount you gave the cashier. _____

2. To figure out how much change you should get back on a purchase, you may have to regroup. _____

Tell what each of the highlighted digits stands for in the numbers below.

3. 865.7⬛3

    A. hundreds   B. tens   C. ones
    D. tenths   E. hundredths   F. thousandths

4. 210.64**2**

    A. hundreds   B. tens   C. ones
    D. tenths   E. hundredths   F. thousandths

Answer each question below.

5. Write thirty-three cents using a dollar sign and decimal point. _____

6. Write the difference of 64¢ and 42¢ in dollar form.

    −
    _____

7. If it takes 4 quarters to make $1, how many quarters does it take to make $8?
_____

Tell whether a <, >, or = should go between each pair of decimals below.

8. 621.43 ____ 621.44   9. 43.726 ____ 43.72

Answer each question below.

10. Write 8 tenths + 3 hundredths + 5 thousandths using digits. _____

11. Write 0 tenths + 0 hundredths + 2 thousandths using digits. _____

Add or subtract (as required) each pair of decimals below.

12.   86.43
     − 41.95   13.   56 + 34.87

                             +
                          _____

14. $68 - 43.97$

$$-\underline{\qquad\qquad}$$

Subtract each pair of numbers below.

15.
$$\begin{array}{r} 7,051 \\ -\ 4,362 \\ \hline \end{array}$$

(a) 16.
$$\begin{array}{r} 5,002 \\ -\ 3,148 \\ \hline \end{array}$$

Write each fraction below as a decimal.

17. $\dfrac{397}{1,000}$ _____

(b) 18. $\dfrac{8}{1,000}$ _____

Write each decimal below as a fraction.

19. 0.231 _____

(c) 20. 0.001 _____

Solve each word problem below.

(d) 21. Julie bought a new dress for $31.46. If she gave the cashier $35, how much should she have received in change? _____

(e) 22. Yesterday, Benny bought a new baseball mitt at the store. If the total bill was $34.56 and he gave the cashier $50, how much should he have received in change? _____

Lesson 61—Money Word Problems – Part 3

Knowing how to change cents into dollars is useful knowledge for the real world. Here's an example.

> Trip wants to buy a model rocket car. The problem is he may not have enough money. The price on the box says $13.25, but that doesn't include the tax. If the tax is 93¢, what will Trip have to pay in dollars?

We could try to add 13.25 and 93, but that would be wrong because we'd be adding dollars to cents, and dollars always have to be added to dollars and cents to cents. So the first thing we need to do is change 93¢ into dollars by moving the decimal point two places to the left.

$$93¢ \longrightarrow 93. \longrightarrow \$0.93 \qquad \text{Changing 93¢ into dollars.}$$

Now that both numbers are written in dollars, we can put one number on top of the other, line up the decimal points, add the columns, and then put in the decimal point and dollar sign to get the final answer.

$$
\begin{array}{r}
\overset{1}{1}3.25 \\
+\ 0.93 \\
\hline
\$14.18
\end{array}
\qquad
\begin{array}{l}
\text{Since both numbers} \\
\text{are in dollars, just} \\
\text{add the columns.}
\end{array}
$$

Here's another example.

> Mr. Reynolds bought his daughter a speaker pillow for $12.19 with tax. If the tax was 74¢, what was the price of the pillow before tax? Make sure your answer is in dollars.

The $12.19 that Mr. Reynolds paid included the tax, but we need to know the price of the pillow *before* the tax was added. To find that we'll have to subtract the tax from what he paid, but first, we have to change 74¢ into dollars by moving the decimal point. Then we can subtract the columns.

$$
\begin{array}{r}
\overset{1}{}\ \overset{11}{}\ \\
12.\cancel{1}9 \\
-\ 0.74 \\
\hline
\$11.45
\end{array}
\qquad
\begin{array}{l}
\text{Change cents to} \\
\text{dollars, then just} \\
\text{subtract the columns.}
\end{array}
$$

After subtracting the columns, we put in the decimal point and dollar sign to get $11.45. That means that the pillow cost $11.45 before tax.

Practice 61

a. Subtract $\begin{array}{r} 6,005 \\ -\,3,268 \\ \hline \end{array}$

b. Write $\dfrac{41}{1,000}$ as a decimal. _____

c. Write 0.013 as a fraction. _____

Solve each word problem below.

d. Timothy wants to buy a new shirt. The price on the shirt says $18.35, but that doesn't include the tax. If the tax is 91¢, what will Timothy have to pay in dollars? _____

e. Joy bought a new CD at the music store for $15.71 with tax. If the tax was 96¢, what was the price of the CD before tax? Make sure your answer is in dollars. _____

Problem Set 61

Tell whether each sentence below is True or False.

1. Before adding dollars and cents, you should always change cents into dollar form. _____

2. It's okay to subtract an amount that's written with a cent symbol from an amount that's written in dollars. _____

Tell what each of the highlighted digits stands for in the numbers below.

3. 564.372

    A. thousandths   B. hundredths   C. tenths
    D. ones   E. tens   F. hundreds

4.   628.43**7**

   A. thousandths   B. hundredths   C. tenths

   D. ones   E. tens   F. hundreds

Answer each question below.

5.   Write four cents using a dollar sign and decimal point. _____

6.   Write the sum of 87¢ and 45¢ in dollar form.

   +_____

7.   If one penny is $\frac{1}{100}$ of a dollar, 63 pennies is what fraction of a dollar? _____

Tell whether a <, >, or = should go between each pair of decimals below.

8.   92.537 _____ 92.53   9.   5.173 _____ 5.175

Answer each question below.

10.   Write 0 tenths + 7 hundredths + 4 thousandths using digits. _____

11.   Write 2 tenths + 0 hundredths + 6 thousandths using digits. _____

Add or subtract (as required) each pair of decimals below.

12. $\begin{array}{r} 75.23 \\ -14.86 \\ \hline \end{array}$ 13. $56 + 21.34$

   +_____

14. $65 - 32.14$

$$- \underline{\hspace{3cm}}$$

Subtract each pair of numbers below.

15.
$$\begin{array}{r} 8,604 \\ -\ 3,527 \\ \hline \end{array}$$

(a) 16.
$$\begin{array}{r} 9,007 \\ -\ 6,849 \\ \hline \end{array}$$

Write each fraction below as a decimal.

17. $\dfrac{713}{1,000}$ _____

(b) 18. $\dfrac{29}{1,000}$ _____

Write each decimal below as a fraction.

19. 0.301 _____

(c) 20. 0.091 _____

Solve each word problem below.

(d) 21. Heather wants to buy a new box of sidewalk chalk. The price on the box says $10.25, but that doesn't include the tax. If the tax is 82¢, what will Heather have to pay in dollars? _____

(e) 22. Annabel bought a trick rope for $9.92 with tax. If the tax was 67¢, what was the price of the rope before tax? Make sure your answer is in dollars. _____

Lesson 62—The Meaning of Division

Multiplication is a short way to add the same number over and over, and **division** is just the reverse of multiplication. In division, we start with a number and break it down into equal groups. Here's an example.

Dividing 15 by 5 is the same as separating 15 coins into groups of 5 and then counting the number of groups. Since there are 3 groups, that means $15 \div 5$ is 3.

There are several ways to show division.

Four ways to show division:

$$56 \div 7 \qquad 7\overline{)56} \qquad \frac{7}{56} \qquad 56/7$$

The first way uses a symbol called the **division sign**. The way next to it uses what's called the **division box**. These are probably the two most common ways to show division. The third way is with a fraction bar, and the last way is with a slash. The slash isn't used very much, except when people are typing on a computer. All four of these ways mean the same thing, though. They all mean 56 divided by 7.

You should know your division facts so that you can answer simple division problems like $16 \div 2$ or $45 \div 9$, but if you do forget a fact, you can look up the answer in the multiplication table. For example, you could find the answer to $21 \div 3$ by finding the row that starts with 3 and looking across it until you see 21. This works well, but it takes awhile, and you won't always have a multiplication table available. An even better way to find the answer to a division problem is to just use the multiplication facts that you should have memorized. For example, if you forget what $54 \div 6$ is, just ask yourself "What whole number times 6 is 54?" The answer to that question is the answer to the problem.

You can actually use multiplication to check division as well. For example, if someone told you that $24 \div 4$ is equal to 6, you could check by seeing if 6×4 is 24. Since it works out, that means the answer is right.

Practice 62

a. How many groups of 6 can you make out of these 18 coins? _____

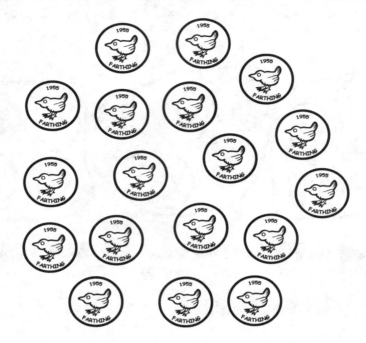

b. Tell which of these division problems means 12 divided by 2.

A. 2/12   B. $\dfrac{2}{12}$

C. $2\overline{)12}$ D. $2 \div 12$

E. none of the above

c. Divide $28 \div 4$ _____

Solve each word problem below.

d. Terry bought a new cage for his pet hamster, Vincent. If the total bill was $24.65 and he gave the cashier $30, how much should he have received in change? _____

e. Pattie wants to buy a new hat. The price on the hat says $15.25, but that doesn't include the tax. If the tax is 84¢, what will Pattie have to pay in dollars? _____

Problem Set 62

Tell whether each sentence below is True or False.

1. Dividing means breaking a number down into equal groups. _____

2. You cannot show division using a fraction bar. _____

Tell whether a <, >, or = should go between each pair of decimals below.

3. 34.671 _____ 34.67

4. 719.89 _____ 719.82

Add or subtract (as required) each pair of decimals below.

5.
$$\begin{array}{r} 83.56 \\ -\ 45.97 \\ \hline \end{array}$$

6.
$$\begin{array}{r} 57.63 \\ +\ 34.89 \\ \hline \end{array}$$

7. $83 - 61.54$

$$\begin{array}{r} - \\ \hline \end{array}$$

Subtract each pair of numbers below.

8.
$$\begin{array}{r} 7,251 \\ -\ 3,476 \\ \hline \end{array}$$

9.
$$\begin{array}{r} 7,001 \\ -\ 2,543 \\ \hline \end{array}$$

Write each fraction below as a decimal.

10. $\dfrac{913}{1,000}$ _____

11. $\dfrac{71}{1,000}$ _____

Write each decimal below as a fraction.

12. 0.847 _____

13. 0.013 _____

Answer each question below.

(a) 14. How many groups of 4 can you make out of these 12 jacks? _____

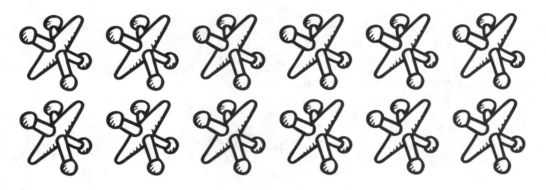

15. How many groups of 8 can you make out of these 16 rubber spiders? _____

(b) 16. Tell which of these division problems means 27 divided by 3.

    A. $27\overline{)3}$ B. $27 \div 3$

    C. $\dfrac{3}{27}$ D. $3/27$

    E. none of the above

17. Tell which of these division problems means 36 divided by 9.

    A. $9 \div 36$ B. $36\overline{)9}$

    C. $9/36$ D. $\dfrac{36}{9}$

    E. none of the above

Divide each pair of numbers below.

(c) 18. $24 \div 3$ _____   **19.** $\dfrac{40}{8}$ _____

20. $6\overline{)42}$ _____

Solve each word problem below.

(d) 21. Joe bought a new dog house for his dog, Barkley. If the total bill was $54.45 and he gave the cashier $60, how much should he have received in change? _____

(e) 22. Harvey wants to buy some meat at the meat market. The price on the meat says $11.75, but that doesn't include the tax. If the tax is 76¢, what will Harvey have to pay in dollars? _____

Lesson 63—Division Rules and Definitions

There are some important definitions to know when talking about division. For example, the number that is being divided is called the **dividend**, the number that you're dividing by is called the **divisor**, and the answer to a division problem is called the **quotient**. Here's an example.

$$\underset{\text{dividend}}{28} \div \underset{\text{divisor}}{7} = \underset{\text{quotient}}{4}$$

In this problem, 28 is the dividend and 7 is the divisor. The answer is 4, so 4 is the quotient. Notice that the dividend is the first number shown, and the divisor is the second. That's a fast way to tell the two apart if the problem uses the division sign.

When a problem is shown using the division box, the number underneath the box is always the dividend, and the number outside the box is the divisor. The quotient goes on top.

$$\underset{\text{divisor}}{5} \overline{\smash{)}\underset{\text{dividend}}{45}} \;\; \overset{\text{quotient}}{9}$$

The third way to show division is with the fraction bar. When division is shown this way, the number on top is always the dividend, and the number on bottom is the divisor.

$$\frac{\overset{\text{dividend}}{45}}{\underset{\text{divisor}}{5}}$$

Finally, there are also some important division rules to know. The first rule is that any number divided by 1 is equal to the number itself, no matter how big a number we divide.

$$98 \div 1 = 98$$
$$\frac{67}{1} = 67$$

Any number divided by 1 is equal to itself.

The second rule says that zero divided by any number (except 0) is always 0, no matter how big the number is.

$$0 \div 7 = 0$$
$$\frac{0}{11} = 0$$

Zero divided by any number is 0.

Sometimes people get confused and think that the second rule means $8 \div 0 = 0$, but this is wrong because the third rule actually says that you cannot divide another number by 0. Zero can be divided by something, but you can't divide *by* zero. This means that 0 can never be the second number in a division problem that uses the division sign or be outside the division box or in the bottom of a fraction.

$$8 \div 0 \quad 0\overline{)8} \quad \frac{8}{0}$$

None of these are allowed because you can't divide by 0.

Practice 63

a. Tell which number is the divisor in $42 \div 7$. _____

b. Divide $\dfrac{64}{1}$ _____   c. Divide $0 \div 49$ _____

Solve each word problem below.

d. Ruby bought a multicolored lamp for $21.15 and a soft chair for $52. How much did she spend in all? _____

e. Farley wants to buy a super bounce football. The price on the package says $9.75, but that doesn't include the tax. If the tax is 63¢, what will Farley have to pay in dollars?
    _____

Problem Set 63

Tell whether each sentence below is True or False.

1. In a division problem, the number that's being divided is always called the divisor.
    _____

2. In a division problem, the number that you're dividing by is always called the dividend.
    _____

For each problem below, choose the word that belongs in the blank.

3. When we show division with a fraction bar, the number on the _____ is the divisor.

   A. bottom   B. top   C. left

   D. right   E. side

4. When we show division with a division box, the number underneath the box is the _____.

   A. divisor   B. difference   C. quotient

   D. sum   E. dividend

Tell whether a <, >, or = should go between each pair of decimals below.

5. 75.816 _____ 75.81   6. 35.217 _____ 35.219

Subtract each pair of numbers below.

7.   64.38
   − 15.79
   _____

8. 56 − 27.81

   −
   _____

9.   8,106
   − 3,547
   _____

10.   4,003
    − 2,985
    _____

Answer each question below.

11. Write $\dfrac{43}{1,000}$ as a decimal. _____

12. Write 0.293 as a fraction. _____

13. Tell which of these division problems means 63 divided by 7.

    A. $63\overline{)7}$ B. $7 \div 63$

    C. $\dfrac{63}{7}$ D. $7/63$

    E. none of the above

(a) 14. Tell which number is the divisor in $72 \div 8$. _____

15. Tell which number is the dividend in $4\overline{)36}$ with quotient 9. _____

Do each problem below using the division rules for 1 and 0.

(b) 16. $\dfrac{56}{1}$ _____   **(c) 17.** $0 \div 24$ _____

Divide each pair of numbers below.

18. $18 \div 2$ _____   **19.** $\dfrac{35}{7}$ _____

20. $3\overline{)21}$ _____

Solve each word problem below.

(d) 21. Harley bought a helmet for $17.25 and knee pads for $34. How much did Harley spend in all? _____

(e) 22. Duchess wants to buy some pink slippers. The price on the box says $8.75, but that doesn't include the tax. If the tax is 67¢, what will Duchess have to pay in dollars?

_____

Quiz 9

Tell whether each sentence below is True or False.

1. Whenever you want to change a fraction with 1,000 in its bottom into a decimal, you need to put three places to the right of the decimal point. _____

2. In a division problem, the number that you're dividing by is always called the divisor. _____

Write each of the amounts below using a dollar sign and a decimal point.

3. 5¢ _____

4. thirty-two dollars and forty one cents _____

Tell whether a <, >, or = should go between each pair of decimals below.

5. 139.42 _____ 139.424

6. 241.35 _____ 241.37

Add or subtract (as required) each pair of numbers below.

7.
$$
\begin{array}{r}
92.17 \\
+\ 35.48 \\
\hline
\end{array}
$$

8. $81 + 59.74$

$$+\ \underline{}$$

9. $62 - 41.93$

10.
$$
\begin{array}{r}
7,005 \\
-\ 3,127 \\
\hline
\end{array}
$$

$$-\ \underline{}$$

Write each fraction below as a decimal.

11. $\dfrac{79}{1,000}$ _____

12. $\dfrac{3}{1,000}$ _____

Write each decimal below as a fraction.

13. 0.049 _____

14. 0.007 _____

Answer each question below.

15. When we show division with a division box, the number on top of the box is the _____.

   A. divisor   B. difference   C. quotient

   D. sum   E. dividend

16. Tell which of these division problems means 54 divided by 9.

   A. $\dfrac{54}{9}$ B. $9 \div 54$

   C. $54\overline{)9}$ D. 9/54

   E. none of the above

17. Tell which number is the divisor in $48 \div 6$. _____

18. Tell which number is the dividend in $2\overline{)14}^{\,7}$. _____

Do each problem below using the division rules for 1 and 0.

19. $\dfrac{40}{1}$ _____

20. $0 \div 10$ _____

Divide each pair of numbers below.

21. $15 \div 3$ _____

22. $5\overline{)40}$ _____

Solve each word problem below.

23. Tank bought an electric scooter so he could move around faster. If the total bill was $44.92 and he gave the cashier $50, how much should he have received in change?

_____

24. Bucky wants to buy a new slingshot at the store. The price on the box says $7.85, but that doesn't include the tax. If the tax is 59¢, what will Bucky have to pay in dollars?

_____

Lesson 64—Dividing with a Remainder

Some divisions don't have whole number answers. Here's an example.

$$13 \div 6$$

This problem is asking "what number times 6 equals 13?" Two won't work because 2 times 6 is 12. Three won't work either, because 3 times 6 is 18, which is too big. On problems like this, we have to use **long division**. Here's what that looks like.

$$6 \overline{)1\ 3}$$

Notice that long division uses the division box. Since 13 is the dividend—the number being divided—we put it inside the box, and then we put 6 outside the box because it's the divisor.

the answer ➡
$$
\begin{array}{r}
2 \\
6 \overline{)1\ 3} \\
-1\ 2 \\
\hline
1
\end{array}
$$
the remainder ➡   13 divided by 6.

Next, we thought of a whole number that when multiplied by 6 was just a little less than 13. The whole number 2 worked since 2 times 6 is 12. So we wrote a 2 above the 3. Next, we multiplied 6 by 2 and then wrote the answer below 13. Finally, we subtracted 12 from 13 to get 1. That means that 13 divided by 6 is 2 with 1 left over. The leftover part is called the remainder, and the remainder part of the answer is shown with an R.

2 R1   The R stands for remainder.

So when we try to divide 13 by 6, we're left with 2 groups of 6 and 1 left over. We can check this by looking at a picture of 13 strawberries. The picture shows that when we try to divide 13 into groups of 6, there is 1 left over.

This is the remainder.

Here's another example.

the answer ⟶ $\overset{6}{4)\overline{2\ 7}}$ 27 divided by 4.

$\dfrac{-2\ 4}{}$

the remainder ⟶ 3

First we thought of a number that when multiplied by 4 is a little less than 27. The answer was 6. We then multiplied 6 by 4 and wrote the 24 beneath the 27. Next, we subtracted to get an answer of 6 R3. It's possible to check this without drawing a picture. All we have to do is multiply the number on top by the number outside the division box. Then, just add back the remainder.

$6 \times 4 = 24$
$24 + 3 = 27$

To check, multiply the number on top by the divisor, and then add the remainder.

Since the answer after adding the remainder is the same as the dividend from the original division problem, the answer checks out.

Practice 64

a. Tell which number is the divisor in $9)\overset{5}{\overline{45}}$. _____

Divide each pair of numbers below. Check your work, and write any remainders next to your answer.

b. $6)\overline{25}$ c. $7)\overline{17}$

Solve each word problem below.

d. Checkers bought some bongo drums for $25.95 and a triangle for $14. How much did he spend in all?_____

e. Maya bought a new recipe book at the store. If the total bill was $21.37 and she gave the cashier $30, how much should she have received in change? _____

Problem Set 64

Tell whether each sentence below is True or False.

1. The remainder in a division problem can never be bigger than 1. _____

2. To check the answer to a division problem that has a remainder, you multiply the quotient (without the remainder) by the divisor then add the remainder to that result. _____

Write each number below using digits.

3. seven hundred nineteen and four tenths. _____

4. six hundred forty-four and eighty-three hundredths. _____

Tell whether a <, >, or = should go between each pair of decimals below.

5. 471.59 _____ 471.58

6. 325.81 _____ 325.817

Answer each question below.

7. Write 0.061 as a fraction. _____

8. Write $\dfrac{259}{1,000}$ as a decimal. _____

Add or subtract (as required) each pair of numbers below.

9.
$$\begin{array}{r} 73.14 \\ + 46.57 \\ \hline \end{array}$$

10. $86 + 14.32$

$$\begin{array}{r} + \\ \hline \end{array}$$

11. $96 - 31.54$

12.
$$\begin{array}{r} 6,013 \\ -\ 2,745 \\ \hline \end{array}$$

$$\underline{-}$$

13. Tell which of these division problems means 56 divided by 8.

    A. $8/56$ B. $56\overline{)8}$

    C. $56 \div 8$ D. $\dfrac{8}{56}$

    E. none of the above

(a) 14. Tell which number is the divisor in $3\overline{)24}$ with 8 above. _____

15. Tell which number is the dividend in $16 \div 4$. _____

Do each problem below using the division rules for 1 and 0.

16. $30 \div 1$ _____   **17.** $\dfrac{0}{32}$ _____

Divide each pair of numbers below. Check your work, and write any remainders next to your answer.

18. $4\overline{)28}$ **(b) 19.** $3\overline{)22}$

(c) 20. $4\overline{)26}$

Solve each word problem below.

(d) 21.   Hector bought a plastic sword for $34.25 and a shield for $15. How much did Hector spend in all? _____

(e) 22.   Milo bought a set of old bagpipes at the flea market. If the total bill was $15.81 and he gave the cashier $20, how much should he have received in change? _____

Lesson 65—Division with a Two-Digit Answer – Part 1

Some long division problems are tough because instead of trying to do the whole problem at once, we have to divide one digit at a time. Here's an example.

$$
\begin{array}{r}
\text{the answer} \longrightarrow \quad 1\ 3 \\
6\overline{\smash{)}7\ 8} \qquad \text{78 divided by 6.} \\
-6 \\
\overline{1\ 8} \\
-1\ 8 \\
\text{no remainder} \longrightarrow \overline{0}
\end{array}
$$

First we found the number that when multiplied by 6 was a little less than 7. It was 1. Next, we multiplied 1 by 6, wrote it underneath the 7, and subtracted. Then we had to bring down the next digit in 78, which was 8. That changed the 1 into an 18. Next, we had to figure out how many times 6 went into 18, so we put a 3 on top, multiplied, and subtracted again. Since there were no more digits to bring down in 78, the problem was finished. So the answer was 13 with no remainder.

Notice that there were four steps to the long division process: first we divide, then multiply, then subtract, and then bring down the next digit. Next, we just repeat those steps until there are no other numbers left to bring down. The answer to the last subtraction is always the remainder. Here are the four steps listed in a table.

The Four Steps of Long Division

1.	Divide.
2.	Multiply.
3.	Subtract.
4.	Bring down the next number and repeat.

Practice 65

a. Tell which number is the dividend in $\dfrac{40}{8}$. _____

Divide each pair of numbers below. Check your work, and write any remainders next to your answer.

b. $6\overline{)96}$ **c.** $8\overline{)92}$

Solve each word problem below.

d. Maverick bought a leather whip for $16.32. If he gave the cashier $20, how much should he have received in change? _____

e. Gabby wants to buy a pink glitter lamp at the store. The price tag says $12.25, but that doesn't include the tax. If the tax is 92¢, what will she have to pay in dollars? _____

Problem Set 65

Tell whether each sentence below is True or False.

1. The method we use to solve division problems is to divide, multiply, subtract, and bring down. _____

2. The answer to the last subtraction in a division problem is always the remainder. _____

Tell whether a <, >, or = should go between each pair of decimals below.

3. 291.34 _____ 291.348   **4.** 62.124 _____ 62.123

Answer each question below.

5. Write nine cents using a dollar sign and decimal point._____

6. If it takes 10 dimes to make $1, how many dimes does it take to make $4? _____

7. Write $\dfrac{23}{1,000}$ as a decimal. _____

8. Write 0.041 as a fraction. _____

Add or subtract (as required) each pair of numbers below.

9.
$$
\begin{array}{r}
82.41 \\
+\,37.65 \\
\hline
\end{array}
$$

10. $73 + 21.64$

$$
\begin{array}{r}
+ \\
\hline
\end{array}
$$

11.
$$
\begin{array}{r}
5,003 \\
-\,2,647 \\
\hline
\end{array}
$$

12. $94 - 12.59$

$$
\begin{array}{r}
- \\
\hline
\end{array}
$$

13. Tell which of these division problems means 24 divided by 4.

    A. 4/24   B. $\dfrac{4}{24}$

    C. $4 \div 24$ D. $4\overline{)24}$

    E. none of the above

(a) 14. Tell which number is the dividend in $\dfrac{36}{9}$. _____

15. Tell which number is the divisor in $8\overline{)72}$. _____

Divide each pair of numbers below. Check your work, and write any remainders next to your answer.

16. $9\overline{)22}$

(b) 17. $5\overline{)75}$

18. $3\overline{)48}$

(c) 19. $4\overline{)94}$

20. $8\overline{)89}$

Solve each word problem below.

(d) 21. Lilly bought a new pair of frilly socks for $11.32. If she gave the cashier $20, how much should she have received in change? _____

(e) 22. Alonzo wants to buy some sheep's clothing at the costume store. The price tag says $18.75, but that doesn't include the tax. If the tax is 94¢, what will he have to pay in dollars? _____

Lesson 66—Division Word Problems

Division can be very useful in the real world. Here's an example of a real-world division problem.

Henry has to unload 32 crates. If he can only carry 4 crates on his dolly, how many trips will it take him?

This is just asking us how many groups of 4 it will take to make 32, so we know it has to be a division problem.

$$32 \div 4 = 8$$

After realizing this is a division problem, the rest can actually be done in your head, because to divide 32 by 4, you just need to know what number times 4 equals 32. The answer to that is 8, so it's going to take Henry 8 trips to unload all the crates. Here's another example.

Each table had 7 chairs around it, if there were 42 chairs in total, how many tables were there?

This is also a division problem because it's asking how many groups of 7 it will take to make 42. The answer is 6 tables since 6 is the number that when multiplied by 7 gives 42.

$$42 \div 7 = 6$$

Here's one last problem.

The caterer served a total of 49 crab cakes on 7 different platters. If she put the same number of cakes on each platter, how many were on each platter?

This problem is asking us to break 49 into 7 equal groups, and then count how many are in each group. We can do that by dividing 49 by 7 to get 7 crab cakes on each platter.

.

$$49 \div 7 = 7$$

Notice that in all of these division problems we're always given a total and then asked "how many were on *each*." Phrases like "how many were on each" or "what was the number in each" or "how many groups were there" are clues that we're supposed to divide.

The main point of this lesson is that we can use division to solve lots of different real-world problems. The hard part is just figuring out whether we're supposed to divide or multiply.

Practice 66

    a.   Tell which number is the divisor in $16 \div 2$. _____

Divide each pair of numbers below. Check your work, and write any remainders next to your answer.

    b. $3\overline{)51}$ **c.** $4\overline{)67}$

Solve each word problem below.

    d.   Esmeralda needs to move 28 dishes into the cabinet. If she can carry 4 dishes at a time, how many trips will it take her to move them all? _____

    e.   Pookie separated the flowers into 8 groups with the same number in each group. If there are 48 flowers in total, how many are in each group? _____

Problem Set 66

Tell whether each sentence below is True or False.

    1.   Multiplying means adding something over and over and dividing means breaking something down into equal groups. _____

    2.   Phrases like "how many were on each" or "what was the number in each" or "how many groups were there" are clues that you're supposed to multiply. _____

For the problem below, choose the group of words that belong in the blank.

    3. $62.38   Sixty-two dollars _____.

         A. thirty-eight cents   B. and thirty-eight hundredths
         C. and thirty eight cents   D. and thirty-eight cents
         E. and thirty eight hundredths

Answer each question below.

4. Write $\dfrac{67}{1,000}$ as a decimal. _____

5. Write 0.827 as a fraction. _____

Tell whether a <, >, or = should go between each pair of decimals below.

6. 487.162 _____ 487.16   **7.** 27.264 _____ 27.261

Add or subtract (as required) each pair of numbers below.

8. $\begin{array}{r} 78.52 \\ + 48.67 \\ \hline \end{array}$ **9.** $68 + 32.54$

$\begin{array}{r} + \\ \hline \end{array}$

10. $\begin{array}{r} 8,306 \\ - 4,679 \\ \hline \end{array}$ **11.** $\begin{array}{r} 9,006 \\ - 3,827 \\ \hline \end{array}$

Answer each question below.

12. Tell which of these division problems means 15 divided by 3.

A. $3 \div 15$ B. $15\overline{)3}$

C. $3/15$ D. $\dfrac{15}{3}$

E. none of the above

(a) 13. Tell which number is the divisor in $63 \div 7$. _____

14. Tell which number is the dividend in $6\overline{)42}$ with quotient 7. _____

Divide each pair of numbers below. Check your work, and write any remainders next to your answer.

15. $24 \div 8$ _____

16. $7\overline{)37}$

(b) 17. $4\overline{)72}$

18. $2\overline{)84}$

(c) 19. $5\overline{)68}$

20. $3\overline{)95}$

Solve each word problem below.

(d) 21. Kip needs to move 30 blankets into the barracks. If he can carry 6 blankets at a time, how many trips will it take him to move them all? _____

(e) 22. Mr. Blue put his tomatoes into 6 buckets with the same number in each bucket. If there are 54 tomatoes in total, how many are in each bucket? _____

Lesson 67—Circles

Circles are a really important part of geometry. The point in the middle of a circle is called the circle's center, and the letter that names the center is also used to name the entire circle. For example, the center of circle M is point M.

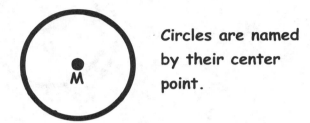

Circles are named by their center point.

Another important thing about circles is that the distance from the center to the edge is the same all the way around. That means that line segment MN is equal to line segment MO, since both segments go from the center to the edge.

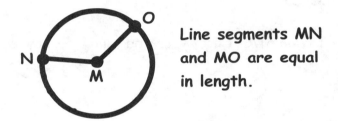

Line segments MN and MO are equal in length.

The distance from the center to the edge is called the **radius** of the circle, so segments MN and segment MO are both radiuses (radii) of circle M.

Another important word is **diameter**, which is just the line segment that starts from one edge of a circle then travels through the center point all the way to the other edge. Here's an example.

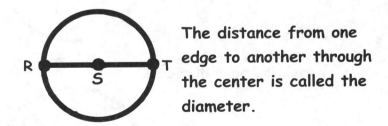

The distance from one edge to another through the center is called the diameter.

Line segment RT is the diameter of this circle. The diameter of a circle is always twice the length of the radius.

The last thing to know about a circle is that sometimes we have to calculate the distance around it. Remember, the distance around a polygon is called the perimeter, but the distance around a circle is actually called the **circumference**.

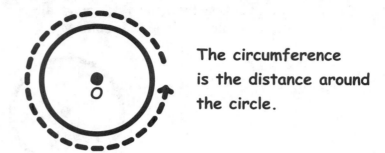

The circumference is the distance around the circle.

There are times when knowing the distance around a circle is pretty important. For example, if you were building a fence shaped like a circle, you'd need to know the distance all the way around it in order to know how much lumber would be required.

Practice 67

a. Divide $6\overline{)76}$. Check your work, and write any remainders next to your answer.

b. What is the diameter of circle *P*? _____

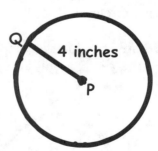

4 inches

c. What is the radius of circle *S*? _____

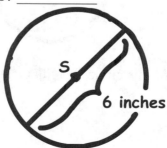

6 inches

Solve each word problem below.

d. Dottie wants to buy a harmonica. The price tag says $11.25, but that doesn't include the tax. If the tax is 97¢, what will she have to pay in dollars? _____

e. Coach Meriwether separated the otters who were trying out for the diving team into 9 equal groups. If 18 otters were trying out in total, how many were in each group? _____

Problem Set 67

Tell whether each sentence below is True or False.

1. The letter that is used to name the center point of a circle is also used to name the entire circle. _____

2. In a circle, the distance from the center to the edge is called a radius. _____

3. The distance all the way around a circle is called the perimeter. _____

For each problem below, choose the word that belongs in the blank.

4. The _____ is the distance all the way across the circle through the center.

    A. diameter   B. perimeter   C. radius
    D. center   E. circumference

5. The diameter of a circle is always twice as big as the _____.

    A. diameter   B. perimeter   C. radius
    D. center   E. circumference

Tell whether a $<$, $>$, or $=$ should go between each pair of decimals below.

6. 921.43 ____ 912.437   **7.** 36.154 ____ 36.156

Add or subtract (as required) each pair of numbers below.

8.
$$\begin{array}{r} 82.63 \\ + 12.84 \\ \hline \end{array}$$

9. $57 + 23.63$

$$\begin{array}{r} + \\ \hline \end{array}$$

10.
$$\begin{array}{r} 8,004 \\ - 1,539 \\ \hline \end{array}$$

11. $70 - 25.68$

$$\begin{array}{r} - \\ \hline \end{array}$$

Answer each question below.

12. Write $\dfrac{55}{1,000}$ as a decimal. _____

13. Write 0.003 as a fraction. _____

14. Tell which number is the dividend in $\dfrac{32}{8}$. _____

Divide each pair of numbers below. Check your work, and write any remainders next to your answer.

15. $3\overline{)45}$

16. $5\overline{)85}$

(a) 17.   4⟌63   18.   7⟌79

Answer each question below.

(b) 19.   What is the diameter of circle *A*? _____

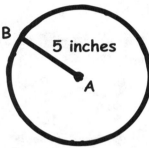

(c) 20.   What is the radius of circle *O*? _____

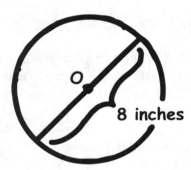

Solve each word problem below.

(d) 21.   Skipper wants to buy a new CD at the music store. The price tag says $10.65, but that doesn't include the tax. If the tax is 83¢, what will he have to pay in dollars?
_____

(e) 22.   Coach Franklin separated the players who were trying out for the baseball team into 8 equal groups. If 56 players were trying out in total, how many were in each group?
_____

Lesson 68—Types of Quadrilaterals

Remember, a quadrilateral is just a polygon that has four sides and four angles, such as a square or a rectangle, but there are actually more types of quadrilaterals than just squares and rectangles. Some quadrilaterals aren't special in any way; they just have four sides and four angles but no parallel sides.

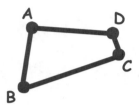

Quadrilaterals with no parallel sides are called plain quadrilaterals.

Another kind of quadrilateral is a **trapezoid**. It has one pair of parallel sides.

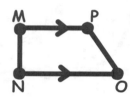

A trapezoid has one pair of parallel sides.

The little arrows in the diagram mean that MP and NO are parallel to each other.

The next kind of quadrilateral is called a **parallelogram**. In a parallelogram, both pairs of opposites are parallel. For example, in the parallelogram below, the sides with the single arrows are parallel to each other, and the sides with the double arrows are parallel to each other.

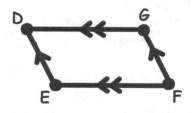

In parallelograms, both pairs of opposites sides are parallel.

There's another kind of quadrilateral called a **rhombus**. All four sides of a rhombus have the same length, but the angles don't have to be equal. For example, in the rhombus below, angle S is bigger than angle T, even though the sides are all equal to 3.

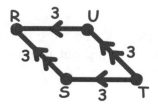

The sides of a rhombus are all the same length.

The next type of quadrilateral is the **rectangle**. The rectangle is like a parallelogram, since both pairs of opposite sides are parallel. The thing that makes the rectangle different, though, is that every one of its angles is a right angle.

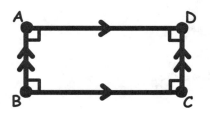

A rectangle is a parallelogram with all right angles.

Finally, there's the **square**. In a square, all four sides are equal and all four angles are right angles. So a square is really just a special kind of rhombus—one that has four right angles. A square is also a special kind of rectangle—one with four equal sides.

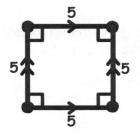

The sides of a square are all equal and the angles are all right angles.

Practice 68

Tell whether each quadrilateral below is a plain quadrilateral, trapezoid, parallelogram, rhombus, rectangle, or a square.

a. _____

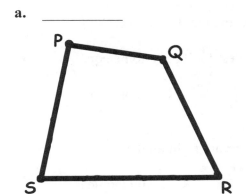

b. _____

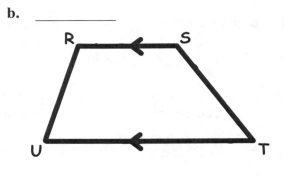

c. _____

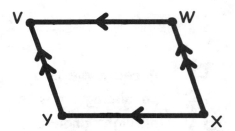

Solve each word problem below.

d. Frisco bought some new spurs for $11.79. If he gave the cashier $20, how much should he have received in change? _____

e. Blossom needs to carry 35 ears of corn into the barn. If she can carry 7 ears of corn at a time, how many trips will it take her to move them all? _____

Problem Set 68

Tell whether each sentence below is True or False.

1. A trapezoid is a quadrilateral with one pair of parallel sides. _____

2. The four sides of a rectangle always have the same length. _____

For each problem below, choose the word that belongs in the blank.

3. A _____ has four equal sides, but the angles don't have to be equal.

   A. square   B. rectangle   C. trapezoid
   D. rhombus   E. parallelogram

4. A _____ is a quadrilateral where all angles are right angles.

   A. trapezoid   B. rhombus   C. rectangle
   D. plain quadrilateral E. parallelogram

5. In a _____, all four sides have the same length and all four angles are right angles.

    A. square   B. parallelogram   C. rhombus

    D. trapezoid   E. plain quadrilateral

Tell whether a <, >, or = should go between each pair of decimals below.

6. 42.375 _____ 41.376   **7.** 163.572 _____ 163.57

Subtract each pair of numbers below.

8. $48 - 35.18$

9.
$$\begin{array}{r} 7{,}007 \\ -\,4{,}529 \\ \hline \end{array}$$

Answer each question below.

10. Write $\dfrac{89}{1{,}000}$ as a decimal. _____

11. Write 0.009 as a fraction. _____

Divide each pair of numbers below. Check your work, and write any remainders next to your answer.

12. $3\overline{)54}$ **13.** $4\overline{)84}$

14. 5)‾97

15. 8)‾99

Answer each question below.

16. What is the diameter of circle T? _____

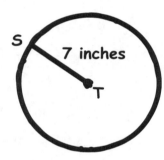

17. What is the radius of circle P? _____

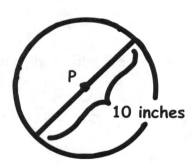

Tell whether each quadrilateral below is a plain quadrilateral, trapezoid, parallelogram, rhombus, rectangle, or a square.

(a) 18. _____   **(b) 19.** _____

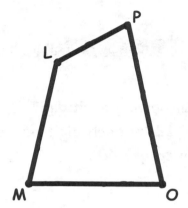
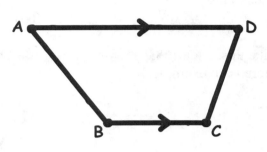

(c) 20. _____

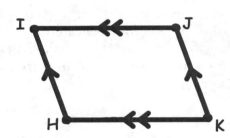

Solve each word problem below.

(d) 21.   Barnaby bought a model sailboat for $12.84. If he gave the cashier $20, how much should he have received in change? _____

(e) 22.   Maximus needs to move 45 jars of pickles into the cellar. If he can carry 5 jars at a time, how many trips will it take him to move them all? _____

Lesson 69—Multiplying Two 2-Digit Numbers

Sometimes it's necessary to multiply a two-digit number by another two-digit number. Here's an example.

$$34 \times 12$$

In cases like this, we just have to multiply each of the digits in the bottom by each of the digits in the top. Here is an example.

```
      3 4
    × 1 2
    ─────
    1 6 8
    3 4 0
    ─────
    4 0 8
```

Multiplying each digit of 12 by each digit of 34 to get 408.

First, we multiplied 2 by each of the numbers on top, which gave us 68. Next, we multiplied 1 by each of the top digits, but we had to write the results on a second row, beneath the 68. We also started the second row with a 0, which is very important. The last step was to add the two rows, starting with the ones column. In the next column, $6 + 4$ is 10, so we had to carry a 1. After adding both rows, we were left with 408. Here's another example.

```
      4 2
    × 2 3
    ─────
    1 2 6
    8 4 0
    ─────
    9 6 6
```

Multiplying each digit of 23 by each digit of 42 to get 966.

Notice that once again, we just multiplied each digit of the bottom number by each digit of the top number, and we also started the second row with a zero. After adding the two rows, we found out that 966 is the product.

Practice 69

a. Tell whether the quadrilateral below is a plain quadrilateral, trapezoid, parallelogram, rhombus, rectangle, or a square. _____

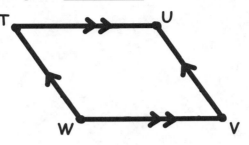

b. Multiply $\begin{array}{r} 23 \\ \times\ 13 \\ \hline \end{array}$

c. Multiply $\begin{array}{r} 32 \\ \times\ 14 \\ \hline \end{array}$

Solve each word problem below.

d. LuLu wants to buy a new hat. The price tag says $8.45, but that doesn't include the tax. If the tax is 63¢, what will Lulu have to pay in dollars? _____

e. Tucker bought 14 boxes of golf balls for the tournament. If each box has 3 golf balls, how many golf balls did he buy in all? _____

Problem Set 69

Tell whether each sentence below is True or False.

1. To multiply 2 two-digit numbers, just multiply each of the digits on bottom by each of the digits on top. _____

2. To multiply 2 two-digit numbers, you need to start the second row with a 0 before multiplying the tens digit by the digits on top. _____

Tell whether a <, >, or = should go between each pair of decimals below.

3. 257.419____275.411

4. 35.165____35.164

Subtract each pair of numbers below.

5. 85 – 14.27

6.
$$\begin{array}{r} 8,005 \\ -\ 6,437 \\ \hline \end{array}$$

_____

Answer each question below.

7. Write $\dfrac{15}{1,000}$ as a decimal. _____

8. Write 0.099 as a fraction. _____

Divide each pair of numbers below. Check your work, and write any remainders next to your answer.

9. $7\overline{)98}$

10. $4\overline{)68}$

11. $6\overline{)89}$

12. $5\overline{)76}$

Answer each question below.

13. What is the diameter of circle C? _____

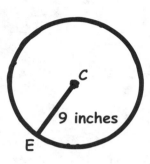

14. What is the radius of circle R? _____

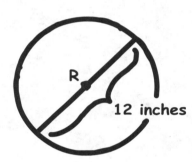

Tell whether each quadrilateral below is a plain quadrilateral, trapezoid, parallelogram, rhombus, rectangle, or a square.

(a) 15. _____   **16.** _____

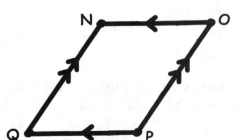   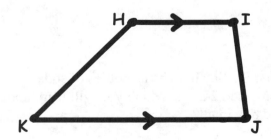

Multiply each pair of numbers below.

(b) 17.
$$\begin{array}{r} 24 \\ \times\,21 \\ \hline \end{array}$$

(c) 18.
$$\begin{array}{r} 33 \\ \times\,22 \\ \hline \end{array}$$

19.
$$\begin{array}{r} 41 \\ \times\,32 \\ \hline \end{array}$$

20.
$$\begin{array}{r} 52 \\ \times\,13 \\ \hline \end{array}$$

Solve each word problem below.

(d) 21. Winston wants to buy a premium dog bone, that means one that came from a really good piece of steak. The bone costs $7.95, but that doesn't include the tax. If the tax is 68¢, what will Winston have to pay in dollars? _____

(e) 22. Mrs. Shelley bought 17 bottles of soda for the soccer team's victory party. If each bottle contained 2 liters, which you will learn about a later lesson, how many liters of soda did she buy in all? _____

Lesson 70—Rounding and Estimating When Multiplying with Two-Digit Numbers

Multiplying two digit numbers can take awhile, but sometimes we only need an estimate, and that can even be done in your head. Here's an example.

$$63 \times 42$$
$$\downarrow \quad \downarrow$$
$$60 \times 40$$

Rounding to the nearest ten.

After we round 63 and 42 to the nearest ten, we just need to multiply the rounded numbers to get an estimate. The method is similar to multiplying numbers like 20 and 9. Here's how it works.

f

$$\overset{1}{6}\overset{1}{0} \times \overset{}{4}\overset{}{0} = 2,\overset{2}{4}\overset{}{00}$$
$$6 \times 4 = 24$$

Multiply the non-zero digits, then count the zeros and add them to the end.

The first step was to multiply 6 and 4 to get 24. Then, we put two zeros after the 24 because 60 and 40 both have a 0 and we're supposed to count up all the zeros and add them to the end. So an estimate of 63×42 is 2,400. Here's another example.

$$89 \times 75$$
$$\downarrow \quad \downarrow$$
$$90 \times 80 = 7,200$$
$$9 \times 8 = 72$$

Round the numbers, multiply the non-zero digits, and add all the zeros to the end.

Once again, we first rounded each number to the nearest ten. Then we multiplied the 9 and 8 to get 72. Next, we put two 0s after 72, since both 80 and 90 have a 0, and one 0 plus one 0 is two 0s. That left us with 7,200 as an estimate of 89×75.

335

Practice 70

a. Multiply $\begin{array}{r} 72 \\ \times\, 14 \\ \hline \end{array}$

Find estimates for each problem below by rounding each of the numbers to the nearest ten and then multiplying in your head.

b. 61×53 _____

c. 48×25 _____

Solve each word problem below.

d. Dingo bought some new rollerblades at the store. If the total bill was $24.98 and he gave the cashier $40, how much should he have received in change? _____

e. Zoe's coach told her that she needs to practice her gymnastics routine for a total of 24 hours. If she can practice 4 hours each day, how many days will it take her to finish practicing? _____

Problem Set 70

Tell whether each sentence below is True or False.

1. On some two-by-two multiplication problems, we only need an estimate. _____

2. When multiplying two numbers that end in zero, we first multiply the numbers that aren't zeros; then we add however many zeros there are in the problem to that result. _____

Subtract each pair of numbers below.

3.
$$\begin{array}{r} 7,008 \\ -\ 4,369 \\ \hline \end{array}$$

4. $35 - 21.83$

$$\begin{array}{r} - \\ \hline \end{array}$$

Write each number below using digits.

5. thirty-nine and seven tenths. _____

6. three hundred sixty and eighty-two hundredths. _____

Divide each pair of numbers below. Check your work, and write any remainders next to your answer.

7. $2\overline{)92}$

8. $5\overline{)96}$

9. $7\overline{)79}$

Answer each question below.

10. What is the diameter of circle *G*? _____

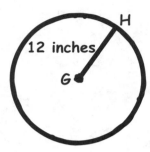

11. What is the radius of circle *S*? _____

Tell which definition best describes each quadrilateral below: plain quadrilateral, trapezoid, parallelogram, rhombus, rectangle, or a square.

12. _____

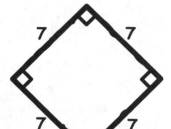

13. _____

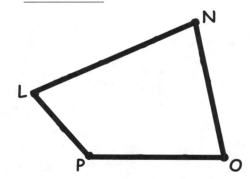

Multiply each pair of numbers below.

(a) 14.
$$\begin{array}{r} 44 \\ \times\ 12 \\ \hline \end{array}$$

15.
$$\begin{array}{r} 32 \\ \times\ 14 \\ \hline \end{array}$$

16.
$$\begin{array}{r} 61 \\ \times\ 24 \\ \hline \end{array}$$

17.
$$\begin{array}{r} 33 \\ \times\ 31 \\ \hline \end{array}$$

Find estimates for each problem below by rounding each of the numbers to the nearest ten and then multiplying in your head.

(b) 18. 52×41 _____

19. 87×29 _____

(c) 20. 78×45 _____

Solve each word problem below.

(d) 21. Maximus bought a new pair of boxing gloves. If the total bill was $34.74 and he gave the cashier $50, how much should he have received in change? _____

(e) 22. Meredith's music teacher says needs to practice her clarinet for a total of 15 hours if she wants to really master the piece. If Meredith can practice 3 hours each day, how many days will it take her to finish practicing? _____

Quiz 10

Tell whether each sentence below is True or False.

1. In a circle, the distance from the center to the edge is called a diameter. _____

2. When multiplying 2 two-digit numbers, you need to start the second row with a 0 before multiplying the tens digit by the digits on top. _____

Write each of the amounts below using a dollar sign and a decimal point.

3. six cents _____

4. forty dollars and twenty-one cents _____

Subtract each pair of numbers below.

5. $\begin{array}{r} 8,004 \\ -\,5,285 \\ \hline \end{array}$

6. $74 - 42.16$

_____

Answer each question below.

7. Write $\dfrac{127}{1,000}$ as a decimal. _____

8. Write 0.611 as a fraction. _____

Divide each pair of numbers below. Check your work, and write any remainders next to your answer.

9. $4\overline{)68}$

10. $3\overline{)74}$

11. $8\overline{)89}$

Answer each question below.

12. What is the diameter of circle *M*? _____

13. What is the radius of circle *U*? _____

Tell which definition best describes each quadrilateral below: plain quadrilateral, trapezoid, parallelogram, rhombus, rectangle, or a square.

14.  _____

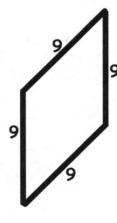

15.  _____

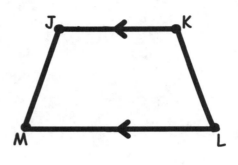

Multiply each pair of numbers below.

16.   43
    × 32
    ____

17.   31
    × 16
    ____

18.   51
    × 34
    ____

19.   73
    × 23
    ____

Find estimates for each of the problems below by rounding each of the numbers to the nearest ten and then multiplying in your head.

20. 41×33 _____

21. 87×62 _____

22. 75×28 _____

Solve each word problem below.

23. Nitro wants to buy some new grips for his handlebars. The price tag says $10.25, but that doesn't include the tax. If the tax is 87¢, what will Nitro have to pay in dollars? _____

24. Pookie separated the muffins into 7 groups with the same number in each group. If there are 21 muffins in total, how many are in each group? _____

Lesson 71—More Multiplying with Carrying

Sometimes it's necessary to carry when multiplying two-digit numbers. Here's an example.

Multiplying each digit of 15 by each digit of 47 to get 705.

When we multiplied the 5 in 15 by the 7 in 47, we had to carry a 3 to the tens column. However, when we went to the second row, we had to cross out the 3 so it wouldn't get added again. After adding the two rows, we found that the final answer was 705. Here's another example.

Multiplying each digit of 32 by each digit of 58 to get 1,856.

In this problem, we had to carry when calculating both the first and second rows. Also, notice that we crossed out the number that was carried first, just as before, and since the final answer, 1,856, had four digits, we put in a comma.

The main thing to remember is that when multiplying by two-digit numbers, be sure to cross out any digits you've carried so you don't mistakenly add them again.

Practice 71

a. Multiply
$$\begin{array}{r} 63 \\ \times\ 26 \\ \hline \end{array}$$

b. Multiply
$$\begin{array}{r} 58 \\ \times\ 34 \\ \hline \end{array}$$

c. Find an estimate for 91×15 by rounding each of the numbers to the nearest ten and then multiplying in your head. _____

Solve each word problem below.

d. Gizmo bought some metal polish for $16.75 and some red blinking bulbs for $14. How much did he spend in all?_____

e. Callie needs to memorize the names of 40 presidents for her test. If she plans to memorize 5 names each day, how many days will it take her to memorize them all? _____

Problem Set 71

Tell whether each sentence below is True or False.

1. In the problem $\begin{array}{r} 39 \\ \times\ 15 \\ \hline \end{array}$, when we multiply the 1 by the 9, we're really multiplying by 10. _____

2. After you're finished with a digit that has been carried, you should probably mark it out so you don't end up adding it to a number you're not supposed to. _____

Subtract each pair of numbers below.

3. $42 - 30.84$

4.
$$\begin{array}{r} 6,002 \\ -\ 1,425 \\ \hline \end{array}$$

$$\underline{}$$

Answer each question below.

5. Write $\dfrac{923}{1,000}$ as a decimal. _____

6. Write 0.109 as a fraction. _____

Write each number below using digits.

7. nine hundred seven and fifty-one hundredths. _____

8. two hundred sixty and four hundredths. _____

Divide each pair of numbers below. Check your work, and write any remainders next to your answer.

9. $4\overline{)56}$

10. $3\overline{)53}$

11. $6\overline{)75}$

Answer each question below.

12. What is the radius of circle *D*? _____

13. Tell which definition best describes each quadrilateral below: plain quadrilateral, trapezoid, parallelogram, rhombus, rectangle, or a square. _____

Multiply each pair of numbers below.

14. $\begin{array}{r} 81 \\ \times\,34 \\ \hline \end{array}$

(a) 15. $\begin{array}{r} 42 \\ \times\,27 \\ \hline \end{array}$

(b) 16. $\begin{array}{r} 75 \\ \times\,43 \\ \hline \end{array}$

17. $\begin{array}{r} 86 \\ \times\,39 \\ \hline \end{array}$

Find estimates for each problem below by rounding each of the numbers to the nearest ten and then multiplying in your head.

18. 32×13 _____   **19.** 52×38 _____

(c) 20. 81×25 _____

Solve each word problem below.

(d) 21. Duchess bought a play castle for $24.65 and a princess training manual for $12. How much did she spend in all? _____

(e) 22. Major Howell has been given a total of 36 missiles. If he plans to put 4 missiles on each of his fighter jets, how many jets does he have? _____

Lesson 72—Multiplying Two Big Numbers

Multiplying three-digit numbers works basically the same as multiplying two 2-digit numbers, but the problems take a little longer. Here's an example.

Follow the same pattern.

```
        3   2   1
    ×   1   3   2
    _____
        6   4   2
    1
        9   6   3   0  ←—— Skip 1 place here.
    1
    3   2   1   0   0  ←—— Skip 2 places here.
    _____
    4   2 , 3   7   2
```

We just multiplied each of the digits in the bottom number by each of the digits in the top number, starting with the ones digit in the bottom number. After multiplying the 2 by each digit in 321, we created a second row and filled in the first spot with a zero. Then, we multiplied the 3 by each of the digits in 321. After that, we had to multiply the 1 in 132 by each of the digits of 321 and write the results on a third row, underneath the 9-6-3-0. However, notice that we had to begin the third row with two 0s. That's because the 1 in 132 really stands for 100, so the results of the third row had to start in the hundreds place. The last step was to add the three rows, and that left us with 42,372.

The main point of this lesson is that to multiply two 3-digit numbers, you need to multiply each of the digits on the bottom by each of the digits on the top, which means you'll end up with three rows instead of two. Also, the third row should start with two 0s before multiplying.

Practice 72

a. Multiply
$$\begin{array}{r} 89 \\ \times\, 35 \\ \hline \end{array}$$

b. Multiply
$$\begin{array}{r} 321 \\ \times\, 312 \\ \hline \end{array}$$

c. Find an estimate for 81×65 by rounding each of the numbers to the nearest ten and then multiplying in your head. _____

Solve each word problem below.

d. Maggie wants to buy a chocolate cake at the bakery. The price tag on the cake says $12.55, but that doesn't include the tax. If the tax is 79¢, what will Maggie have to pay in dollars? _____

e. The landscaper bought 9 identical flower pots and then planted the same number of flowers in each pot. If he planted 81 flowers in total, how many did he plant in each pot? _____

Problem Set 72

Tell whether each sentence below is True or False.

1. Multiplying 2 three-digit numbers is basically the same as multiplying 2 two-digit numbers. _____

2. When multiplying 2 three-digit numbers, we always start the third row with two 0s. _____

For each problem below, choose the group of words that belong in the blank.

3. $72.41   Seventy-two dollars _____.

    A. forty-one cents   B. and forty-one hundredths
    C. and forty one cents   D. and forty-one cents
    E. and forty one hundredths

4. $18.03   Eighteen dollars_____.

    A. three cents   B. and three hundredths
    C. and three cents   D. and zero three cents
    E. three hundredths

Add or subtract (as required) each pair of numbers below.

5.
$$
\begin{array}{r}
4,091 \\
+\,2,119 \\
\hline
\end{array}
$$

6. $62 - 31.27$

$$\underline{}$$

Answer each question below.

7. Write $\dfrac{57}{1,000}$ as a decimal. _____

8. Write 0.007 as a fraction. _____

Divide each pair of numbers below. Check your work, and write any remainders next to your answer.

9. $2\overline{)54}$

10. $4\overline{)57}$

11. $5\overline{)97}$

Answer each question below.

12. What is the diameter of circle *K*? _____

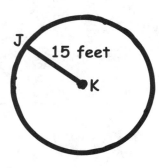

13. Tell whether the quadrilateral below is a plain quadrilateral, trapezoid, parallelogram, rhombus, rectangle, or a square. _____

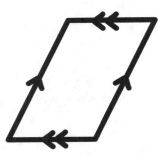

Multiply each pair of numbers below.

14.
$$\begin{array}{r} 85 \\ \times\, 43 \\ \hline \end{array}$$

(a) 15.
$$\begin{array}{r} 96 \\ \times\, 26 \\ \hline \end{array}$$

(b) 16.
$$\begin{array}{r} 213 \\ \times\, 123 \\ \hline \end{array}$$

17.
$$\begin{array}{r} 432 \\ \times\, 321 \\ \hline \end{array}$$

Find estimates for each problem below by rounding each of the numbers to the nearest ten and then multiplying in your head.

18. 49×17 _____

19. 63×21 _____

(c) 20. 92×45 _____

Solve each word problem below.

(d) 21. Hoss wants to buy some string for his weed cutter. The price tag says $11.75, but that doesn't include the tax. If the tax is 88¢, what will Hoss have to pay in dollars? _____

(e) 22. Skipper bought a bookcase with 6 shelves and then he placed an equal number of books on each shelf. If the case now contains 42 books, how many books did he put on each shelf? _____

Lesson 73—Carrying When Multiplying Two Big Numbers

It's often necessary to carry when multiplying two 3-digit numbers. Here's an example.

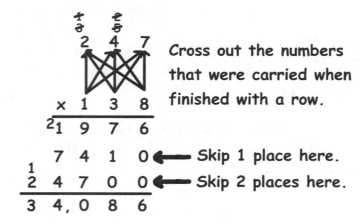

Cross out the numbers that were carried when finished with a row.

Skip 1 place here.

Skip 2 places here.

Notice that we handled this problem the same way we've handled previous problems. We just multiplied each of the digits in 138 by each of the digits in 247. However, when we multiplied the 8 by each of the digits in 247, we had to carry twice. Then, when we moved to the second row, we crossed those digits out so we didn't accidentally add them again. We also had to carry when multiplying the 3 in 138 by each digit of 247, and again, we crossed out the carried digits before moving to the third row. After adding all of the digits and putting in the comma, we ended up with a final answer of 34,086.

The only difference between the problem in this lesson and the other three-by-three multiplication problems from before is that it was messier because of all the carrying. However, the steps to get the answer are exactly the same.

Practice 73

a. Multiply $\begin{array}{r} 73 \\ \times\, 57 \end{array}$

b. Multiply $\begin{array}{r} 413 \\ \times\, 312 \end{array}$

c. Multiply $\begin{array}{r} 624 \\ \times\, 178 \\ \hline \end{array}$

Solve each word problem below.

d. Austin is a punter, and he recently bought a new pair of cleats for $26.93. If he gave the cashier $40, how much should he have received in change? _____

e. Millie baked a total of 48 cupcakes. If she used 8 identical cupcake pans, how many cupcakes did she bake in each pan? _____

Problem Set 73

Tell whether each sentence below is True or False.

1. You never have to carry when multiplying two three-digit numbers. _____

2. You cannot carry more than two times in the same problem. _____

Add or subtract (as required) each pair of numbers below.

3. $57 + 24.36$

$$+\; \underline{\hspace{3cm}}$$

4. $\begin{array}{r} 3,167 \\ -\, 1,948 \\ \hline \end{array}$

Answer each question below.

5. Write $\dfrac{2}{1,000}$ as a decimal. _____

6. Write 0.089 as a fraction. _____

7. If it takes 4 quarters to make $1, how many quarters does it take to make $9?

_____

Divide each pair of numbers below. Check your work, and write any remainders next to your answer.

8. 3)66̄

9. 5)62̄

10. 6)93̄

11. What is the radius of circle *O*? _____

Tell which definition best describes each quadrilateral below: plain quadrilateral, trapezoid, parallelogram, rhombus, rectangle, or a square.

12. _____

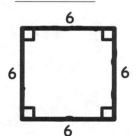

13. _____

Multiply each pair of numbers below.

14.
$$\begin{array}{r} 49 \\ \times\, 31 \\ \hline \end{array}$$

15.
$$\begin{array}{r} 65 \\ \times\, 18 \\ \hline \end{array}$$

(a) 16.
$$\begin{array}{r} 79 \\ \times\, 46 \\ \hline \end{array}$$

(b) 17.
$$\begin{array}{r} 423 \\ \times\, 213 \\ \hline \end{array}$$

(c) 18.
$$\begin{array}{r} 583 \\ \times\, 146 \\ \hline \end{array}$$

Find estimates for each of the problems below by rounding each of the numbers to the nearest ten and then multiplying in your head.

19. 39×31 _____

20. 72×48 _____

Solve each word problem below.

(d) 21. Chad bought a badminton set for $24.76. If he gave the cashier $40, how much should he have received in change? _____

(e) 22. Lizzie put all of the 32 doggy treats that she made in bags. If she put the same number of treats in each bag and she used 4 bags, how many treats were in each bag?

_____

Lesson 74—Small Units of Time

Hours, **minutes**, and **seconds** are called **units of time** in math. Hours are the longest, then come minutes and then seconds. There are 24 hours in each day, sixty minutes in each hour, and 60 seconds in each minute.

$$1 \text{ day} = 24 \text{ hours}$$

$$1 \text{ hour} = 60 \text{ minutes}$$

$$1 \text{ minute} = 60 \text{ seconds}$$

To measure something long, such as the time it takes to go on a cross-country vacation, you would need to use hours. For shorter times, you'd use minutes, and for something really short, such as how long it takes a ball to fall to the ground, you would use seconds.

Sometimes it's actually necessary to change hours into minutes or minutes into seconds. These are called **unit conversions**. Here's an example.

Lisa took a 3 hour nap on Saturday afternoon. How many minutes did she nap?

Since there are 60 minutes in an hour, we just have to add 60 to itself 3 times, which is the same as 60×3. You can multiply that in your head to get 180 minutes. Here's another example.

It took Chad 8 minutes to solve the puzzle. How many seconds did it take him?

To solve this problem, we have to multiply 60 times 8 because one minute is 60 seconds. That means Chad took 480 seconds to solve the puzzle.

There are a few other things to know about time. Each new day begins at **midnight**, which is 12 o'clock. The first hour after that is called 1 o'clock. Then there's 2 o'clock, 3 o'clock, and it keeps going all the way until 12 o'clock, which is called **noon**. After noon, the numbers start all over again with 1 o'clock, 2 o'clock, 3 o'clock, and on up to 12 o'clock again, which is a new midnight and the start of another day. That means that there are two of each of the o'clocks in a day.

To write a time between hours, use hours and minutes, and separate the hours from minutes with a colon. Here's an example.

three forty-five A.M.
3:45 A.M.

The A.M. means that the time is 3 hours and forty-five minutes after midnight, so 3:45 A.M. is the first 3:45 in the day. The second three forty-give is written with a P.M. after it. The P.M. means that the time is after noon, so 3:45 P.M. is three hours and forty-five minutes after noon. Any time with A.M. after it is in the first 12 hours of the day, and any time with P.M. after it is in the afternoon or evening.

Most people measure time with either a watch or a clock. Digital watches and clocks show the time with numbers. So on a digital clock 8:43 in the morning looks like this.

There are also old-fashioned watches and clocks that show the time with "hands." The little hand points to the hour and the big hand points to the minute. The face of a clock or watch usually shows the numbers 1 through 12. These represent hours, and then in between each number, there are 5 little marks, and that adds up to 60 little marks in all. In one hour's time, the big hand will go around the clock exactly once, which is 60 minutes, but the little hand—the hours hand—will just move from one number to the number after it. Here's a picture of a clock at 8:10.

Practice 74

    a.   How many minutes are in 5 hours? _____

    b.   Write the time that is 32 minutes after 9 in the morning. _____

c. Write the time on the watch below. Assume it's in the morning. _____

Solve each word problem below.

d. Bella would like to buy a movie pass that includes a soda and popcorn. The price of the pass is $10.75, but that doesn't include the tax. If the tax is 82¢, what will Bella have to pay in dollars? _____

e. Otis and his dad bought 3 identical boxes of nails. If there were 28 nails in each box, how many nails did they buy in total? _____

Problem Set 74

Tell whether each sentence below is True or False.

1. When we change hours into minutes, that's called a unit conversion. _____

2. Each new day begins at midnight. _____

3. The time 2:38 A.M. means 2 hours and 38 minutes after midnight. _____

Write each of the amounts below using a dollar sign and a decimal point.

4. eighty-six cents _____

5. seven cents _____

Divide each pair of numbers below. Check your work, and write any remainders next to your answer.

6. $4\overline{)55}$ 7. $5\overline{)82}$

8. What is the diameter of circle Q? _____

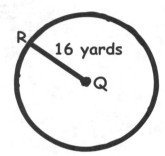

9. Tell whether the quadrilateral below is a plain quadrilateral, trapezoid, parallelogram, rhombus, rectangle, or a square. _____

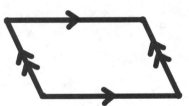

Answer each question below.

(a) 10. How many minutes are in 6 hours? _____

11. How many seconds are in 24 minutes? _____

(b) 12. Write the time that is 21 minutes after 8 in the morning. _____

13. Write the time that is 3 hours and 42 minutes after noon. _____

Write the time on each watch below. Assume it's in the morning for the first watch and evening for the second watch.

(c) 14. _____

15. _____

Multiply each pair of numbers below.

16.   86
     × 64

17.   53
     × 46

18.   734
     × 127

Find estimates for each problem below by rounding each of the numbers to the nearest ten and then multiplying in your head.

19. 58×47 _____

20. 81×29 _____

Solve each word problem below.

(d) 21. Trixie wants to buy a new purse. The price tag says $15.25, but that doesn't include the tax. If the tax is 88¢, what will Trixie have to pay in dollars? _____

(e) 22. Magenta bought 5 cases of mineral water. If there were 24 bottles in each case, how many bottles did she buy in total? _____

Lesson 75—Division with a Two-Digit Answer – Part 2

There are four steps to long division: divide, multiply, subtract, and bring down. However, some long division problems are a little more complicated. Here's the first example.

the answer ➡

$$
\begin{array}{r}
5\ 2 \\
7\overline{)3\ 6\ 4} \\
-3\ 5 \\
\hline
1\ 4 \\
-1\ 4 \\
\hline
0
\end{array}
$$

no remainder ➡ 0

7 won't go into 3,
so divide 7 into 36.

First, we tried to divide 7 into 3, but 7 wouldn't go into 3, so we had to divide 7 into 36 instead. Since 7 goes into 36 five times, we wrote a 5 above the 6 and multiplied it by 7 to get 35, which we wrote underneath. The next step was to subtract and then bring down the 4, giving us 14. Seven goes into 14 two times, and after multiplying and subtracting, we were finished with the problem. So 364 divided by 7 is 52, and there's no remainder. Here's another example.

the answer ➡

$$
\begin{array}{r}
4\ 7 \\
3\overline{)1\ 4\ 2} \\
-1\ 2 \\
\hline
2\ 2 \\
-2\ 1 \\
\hline
1
\end{array}
$$

remainder ➡ 1

3 won't go into 1,
so divide it into 14.

Three wouldn't go into 1, so we had to divide it into 14. After multiplying 4 by 3, we wrote the 12 underneath the 14 and subtracted. The next step was to bring down the 2 and then see how many times 3 would go into 22. Then we just repeated the steps of long division to get a final answer of 47 R1. We could check the answer by multiplying 47 by 3, which would give us 141. After adding the remainder of 1 back, we'd get 142, which is the original dividend. That means the answer checks out.

Practice 75

a. Write the time on the watch below. Assume it's in the morning. _____

Divide each pair of numbers below. Check your work, and write any remainders next to your answer.

b. 2)‾1‾5‾2‾

c. 5)‾3‾7‾8‾

Solve each word problem below.

d. Lucinda recently bought some cool gardening clogs. If the total bill was $21.95 and she gave the cashier $50, how much did she receive in change? _____

e. The students only have 56 crayons to use for coloring. If there are 7 students, and the Sunday School teacher wants each to get the same amount of crayons, how many crayons should each receive? _____

Problem Set 75

Tell whether each sentence below is True or False.

1. Sometimes the divisor, which is the number outside the division box, will not go into the first number in the dividend. _____

2. Division problems with two digits in the answer can sometimes have a remainder. _____

Subtract each pair of numbers below.

3.
$$\begin{array}{r} 8,742 \\ -\,6,217 \\ \hline \end{array}$$

4. $74 - 23.92$

_____

5. What is the radius of circle *M*? _____

6. Tell whether the quadrilateral below is a plain quadrilateral, trapezoid, parallelogram, rhombus, rectangle, or a square. _____

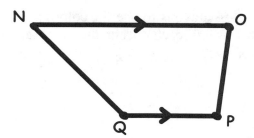

Answer each question below.

7. How many minutes are in 7 hours? _____

8. How many seconds are in 14 minutes? _____

9. Write the time that is 35 minutes after 9 at night. _____

10. Write the time that is 6 hours and 43 minutes after midnight. _____

Write the time on each watch below. Assume it's in the morning for the first watch and the evening for the second watch.

(a) 11. _____   12. _____

Multiply each pair of numbers below.

13. $\begin{array}{r} 38 \\ \times\,29 \\ \hline \end{array}$ 14. $\begin{array}{r} 95 \\ \times\,41 \\ \hline \end{array}$ 15. $\begin{array}{r} 823 \\ \times\,183 \\ \hline \end{array}$

Find estimates for each problem below by rounding each of the numbers to the nearest ten and then multiplying in your head.

16. 31×19 _____

17. 48×27 _____

Divide each pair of numbers below. Check your work, and write any remainders next to your answer.

18. $3\overline{)74}$

(b) 19. $4\overline{)388}$

(c) 20. $6\overline{)253}$

Solve each word problem below.

(d) 21. Blossom bought a wheelbarrow at the store. If the total bill was $32.38 and she gave the cashier $40, how much did she receive in change? _____

(e) 22. Gizmo is cooking 16 hot dogs for a small outdoor party. If there are 8 people present, and they plan to share the hot dogs equally, how many should each receive? _____

Lesson 76—Dividing with Three-Digit Answers

Some division problems have three-digit answers. Here's an example.

$$
\begin{array}{r}
\text{the answer} \rightarrow\ 3\ 2\ 4 \\
2\overline{)6\ 4\ 8} \\
-6 \\
\hline
0\ 4 \\
-4 \\
\hline
0\ 8 \\
-8 \\
\hline
\text{no remainder} \rightarrow\ 0
\end{array}
$$

A division problem with a three-digit answer.

The first thing we did in this problem was to divide 6 by 2, which gave us 3. We then followed the steps of long division by multiplying, subtracting, and bringing down the next number. Two goes into 4 two times, so we wrote a 2 on top, then multiplied, subtracted, and brought down the last number, 8. Finally, since 2 goes into 8 four times, we wrote the 4 on top, multiplied, and subtracted, which gave us no remainder. So the answer was 324. Here's another example.

$$
\begin{array}{r}
\text{the answer} \rightarrow\ 1\ 2\ 7 \\
5\overline{)6\ 3\ 6} \\
-5 \\
\hline
1\ 3 \\
-1\ 0 \\
\hline
3\ 6 \\
-3\ 5 \\
\hline
\text{remainder} \rightarrow\ 1
\end{array}
$$

A division problem with a three-digit answer and a remainder.

We started by dividing 6 by 5, which gave us a 1 on top. Then we wrote the product of 1 and 5, which is 5, below, and subtracted to get 1. Next, we brought down the 3 and continued doing the steps of long division until there were no numbers left to bring down. So the answer came out to be 127 R1.

The main point of the lesson is that division problems that have three-digit answers are solved using the divide, multiply, subtract, and bring-down method.

Practice 76

Divide each pair of numbers below. Check your work, and write any remainders next to your answer.

    a. $3\overline{)284}$ **b.** $2\overline{)638}$

    c. $5\overline{)843}$

Solve each word problem below.

    d. Camo would like to buy a new canteen. The price tag says $17.25, but that doesn't include the tax. If the tax is 86¢, what will Camo have to pay in dollars? _____

    e. Jade separated the candy she bought into 6 groups with the same number in each group. If there are 24 pieces of candy in total, how many are in each group? _____

Problem Set 76

Tell whether each sentence below is True or False.

    1. You can divide a three-digit number by a one-digit number and get a three-digit answer. _____

    2. When dividing a one-digit divisor into a three-digit dividend, the first step is to see if the divisor will go into the first digit of the dividend. _____

Write each of the amounts below using a dollar sign and a decimal point.

3. ten dollars and thirty-nine cents _____

4. four cents _____

Answer each question below.

5. How many minutes are in 9 hours? _____

6. How many seconds are in 16 minutes? _____

7. Write the time that is 27 minutes after 10 in the morning. _____

8. Write the time that is 5 hours and 33 minutes after noon. _____

Write the time on each watch below. Assume it's in the morning for the first watch and afternoon for the second watch.

9. _____

10. _____

Multiply each pair of numbers below.

11.
$$\begin{array}{r} 93 \\ \times\ 47 \\ \hline \end{array}$$

12.
$$\begin{array}{r} 84 \\ \times\ 56 \\ \hline \end{array}$$

13.
$$632$$
$$\times\,121$$

Find estimates for each problem below by rounding each of the numbers to the nearest ten and then multiplying in your head.

14. 59×17 _____

15. 93×36 _____

Divide each pair of numbers below. Check your work, and write any remainders next to your answer.

16. $7\overline{)448}$

(a) 17. $4\overline{)175}$

(b) 18. $2\overline{)856}$

19. $3\overline{)765}$

(c) 20. $4\overline{)637}$

Solve each word problem below.

(d) 21. The Commodore would like to buy a new telescope. The price tag says $14.75, but that doesn't include the tax. If the tax is 89¢, what will The Commodore have to pay in dollars? _____

(e) 22. Winnie separated the wildflowers she picked into 5 groups with the same number in each group. If there are 25 wildflowers in total, how many are in each group? _____

Lesson 77—Dividing with a Two-Digit Divisor

Sometimes the divisor, the number outside the division box, has two digits. Here's an example.

the answer ➡ 1 1
13)1 4 3
       −1 3
          1 3
        −1 3
no remainder ➡ 0

Sometimes the
divisor has two
digits.

Since 13 is too big to go into 1, we first divided 13 into 14. Thirteen would only go into 14 once, so we wrote a 1 above the 4, multiplied, subtracted, and brought down the next number. The next step was to figure out how many times 13 would go into 13, and that was just 1 with no remainder. So the answer to 143÷13 was 11 with no remainder. See, there's really nothing different about dividing by a two-digit number; it's just harder to figure out each division step because we're dealing with a bigger number. Here's another example.

the answer ➡ 1 1
16)1 7 9
       −1 6
          1 9
        −1 6
remainder ➡ 3

A problem with
a two-digit divisor
and a remainder.

Once again we just followed the four steps of long division by dividing, multiplying, subtracting, and bringing down the next number. After bringing down the last number, we got an answer of 11 with a remainder of 3.

Practice 77

Divide each pair of numbers below. Check your work, and write any remainders next to your answer.

   a.   4)848   **b.**   5)782

c. $13\overline{)144}$

Solve each word problem below.

d. Julius bought some new headphones for $21.58. If he gave the cashier $40, how much did he receive in change? _____

e. The tennis coach bought 15 tennis balls for the competition. If there were 3 balls in each can, how many cans of tennis balls did he buy? _____

Problem Set 77

Tell whether each sentence below is True or False.

1. The divide, multiply, subtract and bring down method won't work when you're dividing by a two-digit number. _____

2. When dividing by a two-digit number, you need to try to divide the divisor into the first two digits of the dividend. _____

Answer each question below.

3. Write $\dfrac{211}{1,000}$ as a decimal. _____

4. Write 0.107 as a fraction. _____

Subtract each pair of numbers below.

5.
$$\begin{array}{r} 4,549 \\ -\ 1,728 \\ \hline \end{array}$$

6.
$$\begin{array}{r} 62.91 \\ -\ 11.82 \\ \hline \end{array}$$

375

Answer each question below.

7. How many minutes are in 8 hours? _____

8. Write the time that is 9 hours and 41 minutes after midnight. _____

Write the time on each watch below. Assume it's in the morning for the first watch and evening for the second watch.

9. _____

10. _____

Multiply each pair of numbers below.

11.
$$\begin{array}{r} 65 \\ \times\ 32 \\ \hline \end{array}$$

12.
$$\begin{array}{r} 73 \\ \times\ 36 \\ \hline \end{array}$$

13.
$$\begin{array}{r} 734 \\ \times\ 412 \\ \hline \end{array}$$

Find estimates for each problem below by rounding each of the numbers to the nearest ten and then multiplying in your head.

14. 61×77 _____

15. 21×18 _____

Divide each pair of numbers below. Check your work, and write any remainders next to your answer.

16. $3\overline{)216}$

(a) 17. $3\overline{)693}$

(b) 18. $6\overline{)897}$

19. $6\overline{)194}$

(c) 20. $14\overline{)154}$

Solve each word problem below.

(d) 21. Duke bought a new set of ski poles for $43.18. If he gave the cashier $50, how much did he receive in change? _____

(e) 22. Genevieve invited a total of 36 guests to her party. If there were 6 guests at each table, how many tables were there? _____

Quiz 11

Tell whether each sentence below is True or False.

1. When multiplying 2 three-digit numbers, we always start the third row with two 0s. _____

2. Each new day begins at midnight. _____

Write each number below using digits.

3. seven hundred forty and ninety-one hundredths. _____

4. two hundred nine and eight hundredths. _____

Answer each question below.

5. Write seventeen dollars and two cents using a dollar sign and decimal point. _____

6. If it takes 20 nickels to make $1, how many nickels does it take to make $5? _____

Subtract each pair of numbers below.

7.
$$\begin{array}{r} 7,021 \\ -\ 4,586 \\ \hline \end{array}$$

8. $83 - 52.46$

_____

Answer each question below.

9. How many seconds are in 25 minutes? _____

10. Write the time that is 1 hour and 19 minutes after noon. _____

Write the time on each watch below. Assume it's in the morning for the first watch and afternoon for the second watch.

11. _____

12. _____

Multiply each pair of numbers below.

13.
$$58 \\ \times 43$$

14.
$$85 \\ \times 64$$

15.
$$631 \\ \times 139$$

Find estimates for each problem below by rounding each of the numbers to the nearest ten and then multiplying in your head.

16. 51×93 _____

17. 38×49 _____

Divide each pair of numbers below. Check your work, and write any remainders next to your answer.

18. $6\overline{)254}$ **19.** $5\overline{)585}$

20. $3\overline{)539}$ **21.** $11\overline{)123}$

22. $15\overline{)168}$

Solve each word problem below.

23. Matilda bought a birthday card for her friend. If the total bill was $4.48 and she gave the cashier $20, how much did she receive in change? _____

24. The pecan grove has 9 rows of pecan trees. If there are 12 trees in each row, how many pecan trees are there altogether? _____

Lesson 78—Dividing Numbers that End in Zero in Your Head

It's possible to divide two numbers that end in zero in your head. Here's an example.

$$\overset{1 \ - \ 1 \ = \ \text{zero 0s}}{60 \div 20 = 3}$$

$$6 \div 2 = 3$$

Divide the non-zero numbers and subtract the zeros.

The first step was to divide the digits that aren't zero. Then, instead of adding up the zeros in both numbers, we subtracted them. Since 60 has one 0 and 20 has one 0, and $1-1$ is 0, the answer shouldn't have any 0s. Here's another example.

$$\overset{2 \ - \ 1 \ = \ 1 \ \text{zero}}{800 \div 20 = 40}$$

$$8 \div 2 = 4$$

Two 0s minus one 0 leaves us with one 0 in the answer.

First we divided the non-zero numbers, 8 and 4, to get 2. Then, since 800 has two 0s and 40 has one 0, and $2-1$ is 1, the answer should have one 0. Here's one last example.

$$\overset{2 \ - \ 0 \ = \ \text{two 0s}}{900 \div 3 = 300}$$

$$9 \div 3 = 3$$

Two 0s minus no 0s gives us two 0s in the answer.

At first, you might think this one can't be done in your head because the second number doesn't end in zero, but actually it can. All we had to do was divide 9 by 3. Then, we subtracted the zeros. Since there are two 0s in 900 and no zeros in 3, there should be two 0s in the answer. That means that 900 divided by 3 is 300.

The main point of this lesson is that dividing numbers that end in zeros in your head is pretty basic. Simply divide the digits that aren't zero first. Then, count the zeros in both numbers and subtract those. That's how many zeros should go after the answer you got when you divided the non-zero digits.

Practice 78

    a. Divide $18\overline{)199}$

Divide each pair of numbers below in your head.

    b. $90 \div 30$ _____

    c. $800 \div 2$ _____

Solve each word problem below.

    d. Bianca would like to buy a new bracelet. The price tag says $13.25, but that doesn't include the tax. If the tax is 86¢, what will Bianca have to pay in dollars? _____

    e. Baby Blue separated his collection of model airplanes into 9 groups with the same number in each group. If there are 54 model airplanes in total, how many are in each group? _____

Problem Set 78

Tell whether each sentence below is True or False.

    1. To divide two numbers that end in zero in your head, just divide the digits that aren't zeros and then add the all the zeros in the problem to that result. _____

    2. You should not divide 400 by 4 in your head because the 4 doesn't end in zero. _____

Answer each question below.

    3. Write $\dfrac{27}{1,000}$ as a decimal. _____

    4. Write 0.409 as a fraction. _____

5. How many seconds are in 15 minutes? _____

6. Write the time that is 7 hours and 12 minutes after noon. _____

Write the time on each watch below. Assume it's in the morning for the first watch and evening for the second watch.

7. _____

8. _____

Multiply each pair of numbers below.

9.
$$95 \times 48$$

10.
$$78 \times 32$$

11.
$$532 \times 123$$

Find estimates for each problem below by rounding each of the numbers to the nearest ten and then multiplying in your head.

12. 59×82 _____

13. 46×67 _____

Divide each pair of numbers below. Check your work, and write any remainders next to your answer.

14. $5\overline{)329}$

15. $4\overline{)864}$

16. $7\overline{)927}$

(a) 17. $12\overline{)134}$

Divide each pair of numbers below in your head.

(b) 18. $80 \div 20$ _____

19. $600 \div 30$ _____

(c) 20. $400 \div 2$ _____

Solve each word problem below.

(d) 21. Peaches would like to buy a new headband. The price tag says \$7.65, but that doesn't include the tax. If the tax is 73¢, what will Peaches have to pay in dollars? _____

(e) 22. Garth separated the fishing lures into 7 groups with the same number in each group. If there are 42 lures in total, how many are in each group? _____

Lesson 79—Harder Two-Digit Divisor Problems

Sometimes dividing by two digits is more difficult because the divisor is a larger number. Here's an example.

$$21 \overline{)4\ 4\ 1}$$

It's hard to tell how many times 21 will go into 44 because they are both big numbers. One way to figure it out is to just guess until we find the right number, but it's better to use a rounding and estimating method. The first step is to round 21 and 44 to the nearest ten.

$$44 \div 21$$
$$\downarrow \quad \downarrow$$
$$40 \div 20$$

Rounding to the nearest ten.

Now, instead of dividing 44 by 21, we imagine we're dividing 40 by 20, which is just 2.

$$40 \div 20 = 2$$

Next, we need to go back to the problem and write a 2 above. Then we multiply 2 by 21. Since 2 times 21 is 42, and 42 is close to 44 without going over, the method worked. So now we write 42 beneath the 44. Then we subtract and bring the 1 down.

$$
\begin{array}{r}
2 \\
21 \overline{)4\ 4\ 1} \\
-4\ 2 \\
\hline
2\ 1
\end{array}
$$

Next, we need to divide 21 into 21, and since any number divided by itself is just 1, we write a 1 on top. Then we multiply the 1 by 21 and subtract.

the answer ➡
$$
\begin{array}{r}
2\ 1 \\
21 \overline{)4\ 4\ 1} \\
-4\ 2 \\
\hline
2\ 1 \\
-2\ 1 \\
\hline
\end{array}
$$
no remainder ➡ 0

So the answer is 21 with no remainder.

Here's another example.

```
    the answer ➝    3 2
                28 )8 9 7
                   -8 4
                    ___
                     5 7
                    -5 6
                    ___
    remainder ➝      1
```

Once again, we rounded the numbers to the nearest ten and then divided. Since 89 rounded to the nearest 10 is 90 and 28 rounded to the nearest ten is 30, we divided 30 into 90 to get 3. The next step was to multiply 3 by 28. Since 3 times 28 is 84, and 84 is as close as we can get to 89 without going over, we wrote 84 below, subtracted, and brought down the next number. Then, we had to round again, but this time we thought about how many times 30 would go into 60. Since 30 will go 2 times, we multiplied 28 by 2 and subtracted. After that, there were no more numbers to bring down, so the final answer had to be 32 R1.

The main point is that with some two-digit divisor problems, rounding and estimating can help you see how many times one number will go into another.

Practice 79

a. Divide $8,000 \div 4$ in your head. _____

b. Divide $16 \overline{)178}$

c. Divide $26 \overline{)613}$

Solve each word problem below.

d. Don Miguel bought a new ukulele for $32.45. If he gave the cashier $50, how much did he receive in change? _____

e. Everyday, Ally reads 25 pages in her favorite novel. How many pages will she read after 6 days? _____

Problem Set 79

Tell whether each sentence below is True or False.

1. With some two-digit divisor problems, it's faster to round and estimate when trying to figure out how many times one number will go into another. _____

2. Whenever you divide by a two-digit number, you can never have a remainder. _____

Answer each question below.

3. If it takes 4 quarters to make $1, how many quarters does it take to make $11? _____

4. What is the radius of circle *T*? _____

Add each pair of numbers below.

5. $\begin{array}{r} 96.07 \\ +\ 35.48 \\ \hline \end{array}$

6. $84 + 51.32$

    $\begin{array}{r} + \\ \hline \end{array}$

Answer each question below.

7. How many minutes are in 17 hours? _____

8. Write the time that is 8 hours and 26 minutes after midnight. _____

Write the time on the watch below. Assume it's in the evening.

9. _____

Multiply each pair of numbers below.

10. $\begin{array}{r} 634 \\ \times\ 52 \\ \hline \end{array}$
         11. $\begin{array}{r} 934 \\ \times\ 132 \\ \hline \end{array}$

Find estimates for each problem below by rounding each of the numbers to the nearest ten and then multiplying in your head.

12. 94×32 _____
         13. 81×39 _____

Divide each pair of numbers below in your head.

14. $80 \div 2$ _____
         15. $9,000 \div 30$ _____

(a) 16. $2,000 \div 2$ _____

Divide each pair of numbers below. Check your work, and write any remainders next to your answer.

17. $6\overline{)449}$ **18.** $8\overline{)914}$

(b) 19. $17\overline{)189}$ **(c) 20.** $27\overline{)568}$

Solve each word problem below.

(d) 21. Sunny bought a new kite for \$21.78. If she gave the cashier \$40, how much did she receive in change? _____

(e) 22. Everyday, Jasper hits 75 golf balls for practice. How many golf balls will he hit after 7 days? _____

Lesson 80—Zeros in the Quotient

Sometimes dividing numbers with zeros in them is tricky. Here's an example.

$$\begin{array}{r} 6\,0 \\ 5\,\overline{)3\,0\,0} \\ -3\,0 \\ \overline{0\,0} \\ -0\,0 \\ \overline{0} \end{array}$$

Zero divided by
5 is just 0.

If you were to try to divide 300 by 5 in your head, you would find that 3 divided by 5 is not a whole number, so the best way to handle problems like this is to use long division, and since 5 wouldn't go into 3, we divided 5 into 30, which gave us a 6 on top. We then multiplied 6 by 5, subtracted, and brought down the next number. That gave us a 00, which looks weird, but actually 00 is the same as 0, and 0 divided by 5 is just 0. So the answer was 60 with no remainder. Here's a similar problem.

the answer ➡
$$\begin{array}{r} 2\,0\,9 \\ 4\,\overline{)8\,3\,6} \\ -8 \\ \overline{0\,3} \\ -0 \\ \overline{3\,6} \\ -3\,6 \\ \overline{0} \end{array}$$
remainder ➡ 0

It's okay to
have zeros
in the quotient.

First we divided 4 into 8, wrote a 2 on top, and then multiplied, subtracted, and brought down the next number. After bringing down the next number, we were left with 03, which is the same as 3. Since 4 won't go into 3, we put a 0 on top. We then multiplied 0 by 4, which is just 0, and subtracted to get 3. Next, we brought down the 6 and figured out how many times 4 went into 36. The last step was to multiply and subtract. Since there were no more numbers to bring down, the answer turned out to be 209 with no remainder.

The main point of this lesson is that some long division problems have a 0 in the answer, and that happens when the divisor is bigger than the number it's being divided into.

Practice 80

Divide each pair of numbers below. Check your work, and write any remainders next to your answer.

a. $26\overline{)576}$

b. $5\overline{)200}$

c. $7\overline{)763}$

Solve each word problem below.

d. Star Panda would like to buy an extra memory cartridge. The price tag says $14.75, but that doesn't include the tax. If the tax is 81¢, what will Star Panda have to pay in dollars? _____

e. Opal separated the spools of thread into 6 groups with the same number in each group. If there are 30 spools in total, how many are in each group? _____

Problem Set 80

Tell whether each sentence below is True or False.

1. You can calculate $400 \div 8$ in your head by first dividing 40 by 8 then adding a 0 to that result. _____

2. Seven will go into 2 zero times. _____

Answer each question below.

3. Write $\dfrac{83}{1,000}$ as a decimal. _____

4. Write 0.003 as a fraction. _____

Write each of the amounts below using a dollar sign and a decimal point.

5. six dollars and seventy-four cents _____

6. ninety-one cents _____

Answer each question below.

7. How many seconds are in 19 minutes? _____

8. Write the time that is 10 hours and 48 minutes after noon. _____

Multiply each pair of numbers below.

9.
$$\begin{array}{r} 63 \\ \times\, 19 \\ \hline \end{array}$$

10.
$$\begin{array}{r} 521 \\ \times\, 414 \\ \hline \end{array}$$

Find estimates for each problem below by rounding each of the numbers to the nearest ten and then multiplying in your head.

11. 52×67 _____

12. 19×23 _____

Divide each pair of numbers below in your head.

13. $80 \div 40$ _____

14. $6,000 \div 200$ _____

15. $8,000 \div 8$ _____

Divide each pair of numbers below. Check your work, and write any remainders next to your answer.

16. $7\overline{)899}$　　　　　　　　　　　　**17.** $8\overline{)187}$

(a) 18. $28\overline{)621}$　　　　　　　　　　**(b) 19.** $8\overline{)400}$

(c) 20. $3\overline{)612}$

Solve each word problem below.

(d) 21.　Benjamin would like to buy a new ping pong paddle. The price tag says $15.25, but that doesn't include the tax. If the tax is 92¢, what will Benjamin have to pay in dollars? _____

(e) 22.　Hattie separated the trinkets into 4 groups with the same number in each group. If there are 16 trinkets in total, how many are in each group? _____

Lesson 81—Longer Units of Time

In addition to hours, minutes, and seconds, there are larger units of time. The next largest unit after the hour is the **day**, and there are 24 hours in every day.

24 hours = 1 day

You can change days into hours by multiplying by 24. For instance, 2 times 24 is 48, so 2 days is the same as 48 hours. After days comes **weeks**, and there are 7 days in a week.

Days of the Week

Monday   Tuesday   Wednesday   Thursday   Friday   Saturday   Sunday

Since 7 days equal 1 week, you can change weeks to days by multiplying by 7. After weeks comes **months**, and there are 12 months in all.

Months of the Year

January	February	March	April
May	June	July	August
September	October	November	December

All 12 of these months make up a year, so there are 12 months in 1 year. You can change years into months by multiplying by 12.

A **calendar** is just a chart that shows all the days of the year, month, and week in order. This calendar is for the month of November.

♣ November ♣

S	M	T	W	T	F	S
				1	2	3
4	5	6	7	8	9	10
11	12	13	14	15	16	17
18	19	20	21	22 Thanksgiving	23	24
25	26	27	28	29	30	

The first S stands for Sunday, so Sunday is the first day of the week, and the last S stands for Saturday. There are also two Ts. The first T stands for Tuesday and the second stands for Thursday. Calendars also show when holidays are. The 22nd on this calendar is marked as Thanksgiving Day. Other important holidays, such as Christmas and the Fourth of July, are marked on calendars too.

Seven of the months of the year have thirty-one days, and four of the months—April, June, September, and November—have thirty days. One month, February, only has 28 days, except in a **leap year**, when it has 29. Leap years happen every fourth year (with very few exceptions). The years 2000 and 2004 were leap years, and 2008 is also a leap year. Normal years have 365 days in them, but leap years have 366. Leap years were implemented because the amount of time it takes the Earth to go around the sun is actually $365\frac{1}{4}$ days, so we have to make every fourth year 366 days long to make up for the extra one-fourth in each regular year. The length of a day is actually based on the Earth too. A day is 24 hours, and that's the time it takes the Earth to spin around once.

There are units of time that are even longer than years. One is called a **decade**, which is equal to 10 years.

$$1 \text{ decade} = 10 \text{ years}$$

To change decades to years, just multiply by 10. Another long unit of time is the **century**, which is 100 years. Since a decade is 10 years and a century is 100 years, there are 10 decades in 1 century.

$$1 \text{ century} = 10 \text{ decades} = 100 \text{ years}$$

It's pretty easy to figure out the time between the years 1700 and 1800 by just subtracting 1800 minus 1700 in your head. However, if the years are messier, then you have to do the subtraction on paper. Here's an example.

In 1798 the first soft drink was created, and in 1969 Neil Armstrong became the first man to walk on the moon. How many years was it between those two events?

To solve this, just subtract the date 1798 from the date 1969.

$$
\begin{array}{r}
\overset{8\ \ 16}{\cancel{1969}} \\
-\ 1798 \\
\hline
171
\end{array}
$$

Just subtract the dates.

So there were 171 years between the invention of the first soft drink and the first man to walk on the moon.

Practice 81

    a. How many days are in the month of January? _____

Divide each pair of numbers below. Check your work, and write any remainders next to your answer.

    b. $3\overline{)927}$ **c.** $28\overline{)925}$

Solve each word problem below.

    d. Abe bought a beard trimmer for $32.39. If he gave the cashier $50, how much did he receive in change? _____

    e. In 1804 the first successful locomotive was invented, and in 1981 the first laptop computer became available for purchase. How many years was it between these two events? _____

Problem Set 81

Tell whether each sentence below is True or False.

    1. There are 7 days in a week and 24 hours in a day. _____

    2. A leap year is 365 days long. _____

    3. There are 100 years in a decade. _____

Write each number below using digits.

    4. nine hundred and fifty-two hundredths. _____

    5. seven hundred eighty-one and six hundredths. _____

Answer each question below.

6. How many minutes are in 24 hours? _____

7. Write the time that is 11 hours and 8 minutes after midnight. _____

(a) 8. How many days are in the month of August? _____

9. On this calendar page, which day of the week is February 14th (Valentine's Day)?
_____

February						
S	M	T	W	T	F	S
				1	2	3
4	5	6	7	8	9	10
11	12	13	14	15	16	17
18	19	20	21	22	23	24
25	26	27	28			

Multiply each pair of numbers below.

10.
$$\begin{array}{r} 65 \\ \times\ 27 \\ \hline \end{array}$$

11.
$$\begin{array}{r} 924 \\ \times\ 126 \\ \hline \end{array}$$

Find estimates for each problem below by rounding each of the numbers to the nearest ten and then multiplying in your head.

12. 81×72 _____

13. 59×41 _____

Divide each pair of numbers below in your head.

14. $60 \div 20$ _____

15. $9,000 \div 300$ _____

16. $4,000 \div 2$ _____

Divide each pair of numbers below. Check your work, and write any remainders next to your answer.

17. $3\overline{)649}$

18. $5\overline{)400}$

(b) 19. $4\overline{)832}$

(c) 20. $27\overline{)871}$

Solve each word problem below.

(d) 21.   Rizzo bought a new antenna for $26.95. If he gave the cashier $40, how much did he receive in change? _____

(e) 22.   In 1776 the Declaration of Independence was signed, and in 1903 the Wright brothers had their first successful flight. How many years was it between these two events? _____

Lesson 82—More Division Word Problems

Some division word problems have bigger numbers. Luckily, these problems can be done in the same way as before; they just take a little longer. Here's an example.

Each pitcher of lemonade can fill 4 cups. How many pitchers of lemonade would be needed to fill 92 cups?

Here we have to divide 92 by 4 using long division. So we need to put 92 inside the division box and 4 on the outside. Then we just divide.

the answer ➡
$$
\begin{array}{r}
2\,3 \\
4\,\overline{\smash{)}\,9\,2} \\
-8 \\
\hline
1\,2 \\
-1\,2 \\
\hline
\end{array}
$$
no remainder ➡ 0

Using the four steps of long division on $92 \div 4$.

The answer is 23 pitchers. Here's another division problem.

Each section in the new stadium has 162 seats arranged in 9 equal rows. How many seats are in each row?

This is asking us to break 162 into 9 equal groups and then count how many are in each group. So we just need to divide 162 by 9, and we'll have to do it on paper again.

the answer ➡
$$
\begin{array}{r}
1\,8 \\
9\,\overline{\smash{)}\,1\,6\,2} \\
-9 \\
\hline
7\,2 \\
-7\,2 \\
\hline
\end{array}
$$
no remainder ➡ 0

Using the four steps of long division on $162 \div 9$.

Since 9 wouldn't go into 1, we divided 9 into 16, wrote the answer on top, multiplied, and subtracted. We then brought down the next number, which gave us 72. Nine went into 72 8 times, and after multiplying and subtracting, we found that there was no remainder. So each row has 18 seats in it.

Practice 82

Divide each pair of numbers below. Check your work, and write any remainders next to your answer.

    a. $9\overline{)450}$ **b.** $7\overline{)758}$

    c. $8\overline{)819}$

Solve each word problem below.

    d. Each section of Claire's border paper is 3 feet long. How many sections will Claire need to cover a space that's 42 feet long? _____

    e. Farmer Brown planted 125 strawberry plants in 5 equal rows. How many strawberry plants are in each row? _____

Problem Set 82

Answer each question below.

    1. Write $\dfrac{23}{1,000}$ as a decimal. _____

    2. Write 0.101 as a fraction. _____

3. If it takes 4 quarters to make $1, how many quarters does it take to make $5?
    _____

4. What is the diameter of circle *M*?

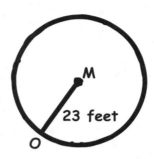

Write each of the amounts below using a dollar sign and a decimal point.

5. ninety-two dollars and three cents _____

6. fifty-seven cents _____

Answer each question below.

7. How many seconds are in 22 minutes? _____

8. How many decades are there in 5 centuries? _____

9. On this calendar page, which day of the week is March 17th (St. Patrick's Day)?
    _____

☘M A R C H☘						
S	M	T	W	T	F	S
		1	2	3	4	5
6	7	8	9	10	11	12
13	14	15	16	17	18	19
20	21	22	23	24	25	26
27	28	29	30	31		

Multiply each pair of numbers below.

10.
$$\begin{array}{r} 72 \\ \times\, 28 \\ \hline \end{array}$$

11.
$$\begin{array}{r} 413 \\ \times\, 127 \\ \hline \end{array}$$

Find estimates for each problem below by rounding each of the numbers to the nearest ten and then multiplying in your head.

12. 37×18 _____

13. 82×24 _____

Divide each pair of numbers below in your head.

14. $90 \div 3$ _____

15. $800 \div 40$ _____

16. $6,000 \div 3$ _____

Divide each pair of numbers below. Check your work, and write any remainders next to your answer.

17. $4\overline{)593}$

(a) 18. $5\overline{)350}$

(b) 19. $5\overline{)519}$ **(c) 20.** $9\overline{)928}$

Solve each word problem below.

(d) 21. Kyle is stacking 4-inch tall playing cards on top of each other. How many levels of cards will he need to create a structure that is 56 inches high? _____

(e) 22. The coin collector has laid out 144 ancient coins in 8 equal rows. How many coins are in each row? _____

Lesson 83—Averages

If somebody were to play a game three separate times and got scores of 37, 39, and 47, one way to tell how well he played overall would be to calculate the average of his scores. Calculating an average is a two-step process. First, we have to add up all the numbers we've been given.

$$
\begin{array}{r}
{}^{2} \\
37 \\
39 \\
+47 \\
\hline
123
\end{array}
$$

First add
up all of
the numbers.

The second step is to divide the total by the number of numbers that were added, which in this case was 3.

the answer ➡

$$
\begin{array}{r}
4\ 1 \\
3\overline{)1\ 2\ 3} \\
-1\ 2 \\
\hline
0\ 3 \\
-\ \ 3 \\
\hline
\end{array}
$$

no remainder ➡ 0

Then divide the
total by the
number of numbers
that were added.

After dividing, we found that the average of the three scores was 41, and that's a pretty good way to describe how well someone does at something. Here's another example.

The first shipment weighed 77 pounds. The second weighed 103 pounds. And the third weighed 96 pounds. What was the average weight of all 3 shipments?

Once again, the first step is to add all of the numbers.

$$
\begin{array}{r}
1\ 1 \\
103 \\
77 \\
+\ 96 \\
\hline
276
\end{array}
$$

First add
up all of
the numbers.

The second step is to divide the sum by the number of numbers that were added, so we have to divide 276 by 3, which appears on the next page.

the answer ➡️
$$3\overline{)276}$$
$$-27$$
$$06$$
$$-6$$
no remainder ➡️ 0

Then divide the total by the number of numbers that were added.

After dividing, we found out that the average of the three packages was 92 pounds.

Here are the steps for finding an average once again.

How to Find an Average

1.	Add up all of the numbers being averaged.
2.	Divide the sum by however many numbers were added.

Practice 83

Divide each pair of numbers below. Check your work, and write any remainders next to your answer.

a. $6\overline{)300}$

b. $2\overline{)215}$

c. $6\overline{)613}$

Solve each word problem below.

    d. Conrad needs to memorize 342 words for the spelling bee. If he wants to memorize all the words in 9 weeks, and he plans to memorize the same number of words each week, how many words should he memorize each week? _____

    e. Iris scored a 79 on her first exam, an 81 on her second exam, and an 86 on her third exam. What was her average score for all 3 exams? _____

Problem Set 83

Tell whether each sentence below is True or False.

    1. To find an average, you first need to multiply all the numbers in the problem. _____

    2. To find an average score, you always end up dividing the total by the largest of the scores. _____

Answer each question below.

    3. If one penny is $\frac{1}{100}$ of a dollar, 71 pennies are what fraction of a dollar? _____

    4. What is the radius of circle P?

5. Tell whether the quadrilateral below is a plain quadrilateral, trapezoid, parallelogram, rhombus, rectangle, or a square. _____

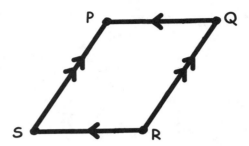

Subtract each pair of numbers below.

6.
$$8,164$$
$$-4,295$$

7.
$$48.52$$
$$-11.53$$

Answer each question below.

8. How many minutes are in 29 hours? _____

9. How many days are in the month of June? _____

10. On this calendar page, which day of the week is October 13th (Columbus Day)?

    _____

OCTOBER

S	M	T	W	T	F	S
			1	2	3	4
5	6	7	8	9	10	11
12	13	14	15	16	17	18
19	20	21	22	23	24	25
26	27	28	29	30	31	

Multiply each pair of numbers below.

11.
$$\begin{array}{r} 87 \\ \times\,31 \\ \hline \end{array}$$

12.
$$\begin{array}{r} 623 \\ \times\,412 \\ \hline \end{array}$$

Find estimates for each problem below by rounding each of the numbers to the nearest ten and then multiplying in your head.

13. 61×88 _____

14. 32×17 _____

Divide each pair of numbers below in your head.

15. $400 \div 40$ _____

16. $8,000 \div 2$ _____

Divide each pair of numbers below. Check your work, and write any remainders next to your answer.

17. $3\overline{)866}$

(a) 18. $3\overline{)150}$

(b) 19. $4\overline{)438}$

(c) 20. $5\overline{)546}$

Solve each word problem below.

(d) 21. Thelma is about to begin a 252-page novel. If she wants to finish the book in 7 days, and she plans to read the same number of pages each day, how many pages should she read each day? _____

(e) 22. Lennox scored an 84 on his first exam, an 89 on his second exam, and a 94 on his third exam. What was his average score for all 3 exams? _____

Lesson 84—What's a Percent?

A **percent** is just another way to show a part of a whole, just like fractions and decimals. However, percents are unique because the whole is made of 100 pieces. Here's an example.

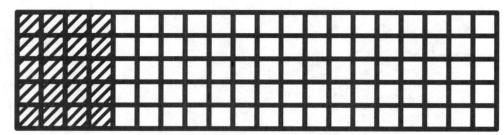

20 out of 100, or 20%, is shaded.

This rectangle is divided into 100 squares and 20 of those are shaded. That means that 20 percent of the rectangle is shaded because the word percent just means "out of one hundred." And since percents are actually written using the percent symbol (%), we can write 20 percent as 20%. Here's another example.

If a cookie shop made 100 peanut butter cookies but sold only 90 of them, what percent did they sell?

Since the problem says they sold 90 out of 100, that's 90%. Here's another example.

If there are 100 cell phone faceplates on display and 52 of them are pink, what percent are pink?

Fifty-two out of 100 is 52%, so 52% are pink. Percents are used all the time in real life, so it's really important to know about them.

Practice 84

a. In a recent survey of 100 snakes, 98 of them said they wished they were taller. What percent wished they were taller? _____.

Divide each pair of numbers below. Check your work, and write any remainders next to your answer.

b. $8\overline{)825}$

c. $7\overline{)708}$

Solve each word problem below.

d. In 1849 the California Gold Rush was in full swing, and in 1945 World War II came to a close. How many years was it between these two events? _____

e. There are 3 jars of gumballs. The first jar has 63 gumballs, the second has 57, and the third has 45. What is the average number of gumballs? _____

Problem Set 84

Tell whether each sentence below is True or False.

1. A percent is just another way to show a part of a whole. _____

2. Percent means "out of one hundred." _____

Answer each question below.

3. Write $\dfrac{709}{1,000}$ as a decimal. _____

4. Write 0.57 as a fraction. _____

5. Tell whether the quadrilateral below is a plain quadrilateral, trapezoid, parallelogram, rhombus, rectangle, or a square. _____

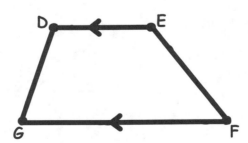

Add or subtract (as required) each pair of numbers below.

6. $56 + 23.75$

7. $\begin{array}{r} 5,095 \\ -\ 3,158 \end{array}$

$+\ \underline{\hspace{3cm}}$

Answer each question below.

8. How many decades are there in 4 centuries? _____

9. How many seconds are in 45 minutes? _____

10. On this calendar page, which day of the week is May 14th (Mother's Day)? _____

S	M	T	W	T	F	S
	1	2	3	4	5	6
7	8	9	10	11	12	13
14	15	16	17	18	19	20
21	22	23	24	25	26	27
25	26	27	28	29	30	31

MAY

Multiply each pair of numbers below.

11. $\begin{array}{r} 223 \\ \times\ 32 \end{array}$

12. $\begin{array}{r} 924 \\ \times\ 721 \end{array}$

Answer each question below.

(a) 13. In a recent survey of 100 bats, only 2 said they prefer daytime over night. What percent prefer daytime? _____

14. In a recent survey of 100 spoons, 93 said they would rather be dipped in ice cream than cough medicine. What percent would rather be dipped in ice cream? _____

15. In a recent survey of 100 princesses, 97 of them said that kissing frogs was hard work. What percent said that kissing frogs was hard work? _____

Divide each pair of numbers below in your head.

16. $600 \div 3$ _____   **17.** $5,000 \div 500$ _____

Divide each pair of numbers below. Check your work, and write any remainders next to your answer.

18. $6\overline{)934}$ **(b) 19.** $7\overline{)738}$

(c) 20. $2\overline{)205}$

413

Solve each word problem below.

(d) 21. In 1891 the game of basketball was invented, and in 1967 the first Super Bowl was played. How many years was it between those two events? _____

(e) 22. Mrs. Lawrence baked 3 batches of cookies. The first batch contained 48 cookies, the second contained 54, and the third contained 36. What was the average number of cookies in a batch? _____

Quiz 12

Tell whether each sentence below is True or False.

1. With some two-digit divisor problems, it's faster to round and estimate when trying to figure out how many times one number will go into another. _____

2. To find an average score, you first need to add all the scores. _____

Answer each question below.

3. Write $\dfrac{163}{1,000}$ as a decimal. _____

4. Write 0.011 as a fraction. _____

5. What is the diameter of circle J? _____

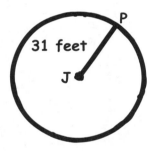

Write each of the amounts below using a dollar sign and a decimal point.

6. twenty-one dollars and eight cents _____

7. sixty-five cents _____

Answer each question below.

8. How many seconds are in 47 minutes? _____

9. How many days are in the month of May? _____

10. On this calendar page, which day of the week is June 18th (Father's Day)? _____

	JUNE					
S	M	T	W	T	F	S
				1	2	3
4	5	6	7	8	9	10
11	12	13	14	15	16	17
18	19	20	21	22	23	24
25	26	27	28	29	30	

Multiply each pair of numbers below.

11.
$$\begin{array}{r} 79 \\ \times\, 62 \\ \hline \end{array}$$

12.
$$\begin{array}{r} 833 \\ \times\, 125 \\ \hline \end{array}$$

Answer each question below.

13. In a recent survey of 100 kids, only 3 said that Brussels sprouts were delicious. What percent said Brussels spouts were delicious? _____

14. In a recent survey of 100 people, 73 said they couldn't imagine eating pancakes without syrup. What percent couldn't imagine eating pancakes without syrup? _____

15. In a recent survey of 100 monsters, 99 said that beauty was only skin deep. What percent said beauty was only skin deep? _____

Divide each pair of numbers below in your head.

16. $90 \div 3$ _____

17. $8,000 \div 20$ _____

18. $6,000 \div 600$ _____

Divide each pair of numbers below. Check your work, and write any remainders next to your answer.

19. $3\overline{)473}$

20. $8\overline{)841}$

21. $5\overline{)457}$

Solve each word problem below.

22. In 1685 the first camera was invented, and in 1981 the first space shuttle was launched. How many years was it between these two events? _____

23. Katie wants to buy her little dog, Demetrius, a matching umbrella. The price tag says $10.95, but that doesn't include the tax. If the tax is 71¢, what will Katie have to pay in dollars? _____

24. There were 3 jets on the runway. The first jet had 32 passengers, the second had 49, and the third had 42. What was the average number of passengers? _____

Lesson 85—Thinking of Fractions as Percents

Fractions can be turned into percents since both represent parts of a whole. Remember, with percents, the whole is 100, and the percent is some part of that. However, people also use the word percent even when the whole is divided into fewer than 100 pieces. Here's an example.

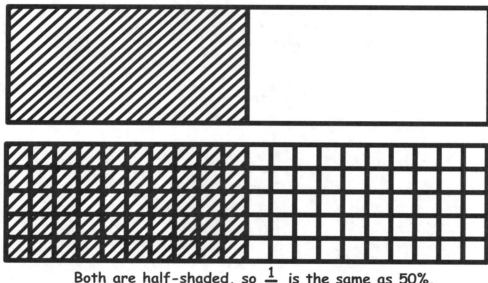

Both are half-shaded, so $\frac{1}{2}$ is the same as 50%.

The top rectangle is half-shaded. If we wanted to know what percent is shaded, we just need to realize that since half of the rectangle is shaded and half of 100 is 50, 50% must be shaded. This can be proven by actually dividing the same rectangle into 100 pieces, as we did above. So the fraction $\frac{1}{2}$ is the same as 50%. Here's another example.

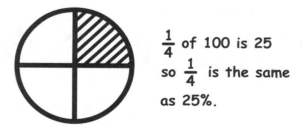

$\frac{1}{4}$ of 100 is 25
so $\frac{1}{4}$ is the same
as 25%.

One-fourth of the circle is shaded, and since $\frac{1}{4}$ of 100 is 25, 25% of the circle must be shaded. So the fraction $\frac{1}{4}$ is the same as 25%. Here's one more important fraction to know as a percent.

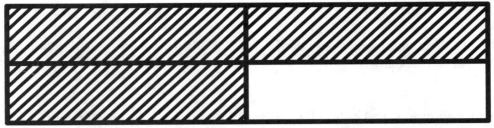

$\frac{1}{4}$ is the same as 25%, so $\frac{3}{4}$ is the same as 75%

Since $\frac{1}{4}$ is the same as 25%, $\frac{3}{4}$ has to be three times that. So $\frac{3}{4}$ is equal to $25 + 25 + 25$, or 75%.

Practice 85

a. In a recent survey of 100 octopuses, 52 said they'd like to learn how to play the drums. What percent said they'd like to learn how to play the drums? _____

b. Write a percent for the part of the whole that is shaded in the picture below.
_____

c. Divide $9\overline{)421}$. Check your work, and write any remainders next to your answer.

Solve each word problem below.

d. Emerald bought a new skateboard for $35.23. If he gave the cashier $40, how much did he receive in change? _____

e. Super entrepreneur Freddie Fandango sold a total of 112 of his hover lawnmowers to 8 stores. If each store bought the same number of hover lawnmowers, how many did each buy? _____

Problem Set 85

Tell whether each sentence below is True or False.

1. Fractions can also be shown as percents. _____

2. Percents can be used even when a whole is divided into fewer than 100 pieces. _____

3. Three-fourths of something is the same as 75%. _____

Answer each question below.

4. Write 95¢ using a dollar sign and decimal point. _____

5. Write ten dollars and forty-two cents using a dollar sign and decimal point. _____

6. If it takes 4 quarters to make $1, how many quarters does it take to make $17? _____

Add or subtract (as required) each pair of numbers below.

7.
$$59.83$$
$$-19.82$$

8. $65 + 48.37$

$$+ \underline{\hspace{3cm}}$$

Answer each question below.

    9. How many decades are there in 6 centuries? _____

  10. How many minutes are in 37 hours? _____

Multiply each pair of numbers below.

  11.
$$\begin{array}{r} 348 \\ \times\ 51 \\ \hline \end{array}$$

  12.
$$\begin{array}{r} 522 \\ \times\ 142 \\ \hline \end{array}$$

Answer each question below.

(a) 13. In a recent survey of 100 hot dogs, 87 said they hated being smothered in onions. What percent said they hated being smothered in onions? _____

  14. In a recent survey of 100 mad scientists, only 2 had normal hairdos. What percent had normal hairdos? _____

Write a percent for the part of the whole that is shaded in each picture below.

  15. _____   **16.** _____

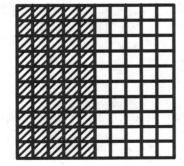 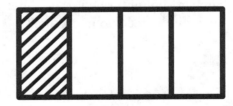

(b) 17. _____

Divide each pair of numbers below. Check your work, and write any remainders next to your answer.

18. $3\overline{)328}$ **19.** $5\overline{)935}$

(c) 20. $8\overline{)419}$

Solve each word problem below.

(d) 21. Mr. Shepherd bought a new flea collar necktie for $13.42. If he gave the cashier $20, how much did he receive in change? _____

(e) 22. Anita sold a total of 135 picture frames to 9 stores. If each store bought the same number of frames, how many did each buy? _____

Lesson 86—More on Percents and Fractions

Any percent can actually be turned into a fraction. Here's an example.

$$9\% \longrightarrow 9 \longrightarrow \frac{9}{100}$$

Changing 9% into a fraction.

To change 9% into a fraction, we first got rid of the percent symbol. Then we put 9 over 100 because the word percent means "out of 100,", so 9% means 9 out of 100. Here's another example.

$$41\% \longrightarrow 41 \longrightarrow \frac{41}{100}$$

Changing 41% into a fraction.

Once again, we just dropped the percent sign and then put the number over 100. So 41% is the same as $\frac{41}{100}$.

It's also easy to take a fraction with 100 in the bottom and turn it into a percent.

$$\frac{7}{100} \longrightarrow 7 \longrightarrow 7\%$$

Changing $\frac{7}{100}$ into a percent.

To turn $\frac{7}{100}$ into a percent, all we had to do was get rid of the fraction bar and the 100 and then add a percent symbol. That means that $\frac{7}{100}$ is the same as 7%.

The main point of the lesson is that it's pretty easy to convert a percent into a fraction. You just drop the percent symbol and write the remaining number over 100. You can even reverse that process to change a fraction with 100 in the bottom into a percent.

Practice 86

   a. Write 9% as a fraction. _____

   b. Write $\dfrac{67}{100}$ as a percent. _____

   c. Divide $2\overline{)413}$. Check your work, and write any remainders next to your answer.

$$\overline{)}$$

Solve each word problem below.

   d. Violet wants to put her 136 family photos in an album. If she can only fit 8 photos on a page, how many pages will she be able to fill? _____

   e. Mikey played 3 games. He scored a 57 in the first game, a 59 in the second game, and a 52 in the third game. What was his average score? _____

Problem Set 86

Tell whether each sentence below is True or False.

   1. It is impossible to change a percent into a fraction. _____

   2. To change a fraction with 100 in its bottom into a percent, just get rid of the 100 and add a percent symbol to the number in the top. _____

Answer each question below.

3. What is the radius of circle A? _____

28 yards

4. Tell which definition best describes the quadrilateral below: plain quadrilateral, trapezoid, parallelogram, rhombus, rectangle, or a square. _____

Add or subtract (as required) each pair of numbers below.

5. $56 + 38.07$

$$\begin{array}{r} 3{,}502 \\ -\ 1{,}914 \\ \hline \end{array}$$ **6.**

$+$ _____

Answer each question below.

7. How many seconds are in 29 minutes? _____

8. How many days are in the month of April? _____

9. In a recent survey of 100 ice cubes, only 18 of them said they sometimes get the chills. What percent of the ice cubes sometimes get the chills? _____

Write a percent for the part of the whole that is shaded in each picture below.

10. _____

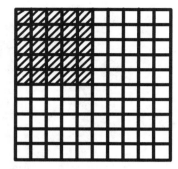

11. _____

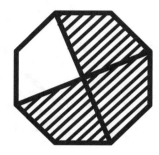

Write each percent below as a fraction.

12. 37% _____

(a) 13. 3% _____

Write each fraction below as a percent.

14. $\dfrac{19}{100}$ _____

(b) 15. $\dfrac{51}{100}$ _____

Multiply each pair of numbers below.

16.
$$\begin{array}{r} 732 \\ \times\, 21 \\ \hline \end{array}$$

17.
$$\begin{array}{r} 831 \\ \times\, 218 \\ \hline \end{array}$$

Divide each pair of numbers below. Check your work, and write any remainders next to your answer.

18. $4\overline{)852}$

19. $5\overline{)546}$

(c) 20. $3\overline{)614}$

Solve each word problem below.

(d) 21. Salvador needs to ship 125 of his paper mache masks to stores. If he can only fit 5 masks in a box, how many boxes will he need? _____

(e) 22. Max spent 3 days shooting arrows. He hit the bullseye 63 times the first day, 72 times the second day, and 48 times the third day. What was his average number of bullseyes? _____

Lesson 87—Units for Length

Units of length are used to measure how long something is. An **inch** is a short unit of length, which is why inches are used to measure smaller things. Inches can be abbreviated as in. (with a period) or just in (without a period).

Inches aren't used to measure larger items though. For those we use **feet**. Feet can be abbreviated as ft. (with a period) or just feet (without a period).

Sometimes it's necessary to change a measurement from feet to inches, which can be done by multiplying the number of feet by 12, since there are 12 inches in 1 foot.

12 inches = 1 foot

So an object that is 3 feet long would be 36 inches long because 3×12 is 36.

A **yard** is even larger than a foot. It takes 3 feet to equal 1 yard.

3 feet = 1 yard

Yards are used to measure even longer things, such as a roll of fabric. The short way to write yards is yd., or you can leave off the period. Here's a problem involving yards.

Wayne has a little fishing boat that's 6 yards long. How many feet long is it?

Since there are 3 feet in each yard, we can convert 6 yards to feet by multiplying 6×3. That means the boat is 18 feet long.

Miles are used to measure really long distances, such as the distance from New York to London. Miles are a lot longer than yards. In fact, 1 mile is 1,760 yards. Miles can be written the short way as mi. (with a period) or mi (without a period). You can convert miles to yards by multiplying by 1,760, but you'll probably want to multiply it out on paper.

1,760 yards = 1 mile

The main things to remember from this lesson are that we use different units to measure things of different sizes and when we want to change a measurement from a longer unit like yards to a shorter unit like feet, we multiply.

Practice 87

a. If the sidewalk is 5 feet wide, how many inches is that? _____

b. If the dolphin is 3 yards long, how many feet is that? _____

c. Divide $7\overline{)789}$. Check your work, and write any remainders next to your answer.

$\overline{)}$

Solve each word problem below.

d. Lilly bought a pink telephone for $12.25, but that doesn't include the tax. If the tax is 77¢, what will she have to pay in dollars? _____

e. Ace has bowled 117 rounds in the last 9 months. If he bowled the same number of rounds each month, how many rounds did he bowl each month? _____

Problem Set 87

Tell whether each sentence below is True or False.

1. There are 10 inches in 1 foot. _____

2. To change a measurement from yards to feet we divide by 3. _____

Answer each question below.

3. Tell whether the quadrilateral below is a plain quadrilateral, trapezoid, parallelogram, rhombus, rectangle, or a square. _____

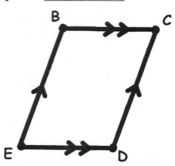

4. If it takes 20 nickels to make $1, how many nickels does it take to make $19? _____

Write each of the amounts below using a dollar sign and a decimal point.

5. seventy dollars and fourteen cents _____

6. nine cents _____

Answer each question below.

7. How many decades are there in 7 centuries? _____

8. How many minutes are in 32 hours? _____

9. In a recent survey of 100 pirates, 58 of them said they didn't really need a patch, but they wore one just to look tougher. What percent didn't really need a patch but wore one just to look tougher? _____

10. Write a percent for the part of the whole that is shaded in the picture below _____

Write each percent below as a fraction.

11. 77% _____

12. 11% _____

Write each fraction below as a percent.

13. $\dfrac{27}{100}$ _____

14. $\dfrac{41}{100}$ _____

Answer each question below.

(a) 15. If the bicycle is 4 feet long, how many inches is that? _____

(b) 16. If the flag pole is 9 yards tall, how many feet is that? _____

Multiply each pair of numbers below.

17. 643
    ×71

18. 943
    × 221

Divide each pair of numbers below. Check your work, and write any remainders next to your answer.

19. 4)426

(c) 20. 8)891

Solve each word problem below.

(d) 21. Jimmy bought a remote-controlled monster truck for $14.75, but that doesn't include the tax. If the tax is 81¢, what will Jimmy have to pay in dollars? _____

(e) 22. Dot baked a total of 126 marshmallow treats for 6 of her friends. If she decided to give each friend the same amount, how many marshmallow treats did each friend get? _____

Lesson 88—Units for Liquid

There are units for measuring liquids, and one of these units is the **ounce**. Ounces are used to measure small amounts of liquid. The short way to write ounce is oz., which may seem strange since there aren't any z's in the word ounce.

Liquids can also be measured in **pints**, which are larger than ounces. Pint is abbreviated as pt. There are 16 ounces in 1 pint, so to convert pints to ounces, we can multiply by 16.

16 ounces = 1 pint

The next unit after the pint is the **quart**, which can be written as qt. There are 2 pints in 1 quart. That means to convert from quarts to pints, we just multiply by 2.

2 pints = 1 quart

The last important unit for measuring liquids in this lesson is the **gallon**. There are 4 quarts in 1 gallon.

4 quarts = 1 gallon

Here's an example of a gallons problem.

If Coach Tiberius usually supplies 3 gallons of water to his players after practice, how many quarts is that?

Since there are 4 quarts in 1 gallon, we can multiply 3×4 to get 12. So 3 gallons is the same as 12 quarts.

It's important to remember the facts about how many of one kind of unit it takes to make another. It's also important to remember to multiply when changing a larger unit like gallons to a smaller unit like quarts.

Practice 88

a. If there are 7 pints of buttermilk in the grocery freezer, how many ounces is that?

_____

b. If there are 12 gallons of orange juice in the cafeteria, how many quarts is that?

_____

c. Divide $8\overline{)621}$. Check your work, and write any remainders next to your answer.

$\overline{)\qquad}$

Solve each word problem below.

d. In 1879 Thomas Edison invented the first practical light bulb, and in 1927 Charles Lindberg flew across the Atlantic. How many years was it between those two events? _____

e. Pepper took 3 tests. She scored an 81 on her first test, a 79 on her second test, and a 92 on her third test. What was her average score? _____

Problem Set 88

Tell whether each sentence below is True or False.

1. There are 14 ounces in a pint. _____

2. It takes two pints to make 1 quart. _____

3. One gallon is equal to 4 quarts. _____

Answer each question below.

4. How many minutes are in 47 hours? _____

5. How many days are in the month of March? _____

6. In a recent survey of 100 firecrackers, 74 of them said they had a short fuse. What percent said they had a short fuse? _____

7. Write a percent for the part of the whole that is shaded in the picture below.
    _____

Write each percent below as a fraction.

8. 91% _____

9. 23% _____

Write each fraction below as a percent.

10. $\dfrac{83}{100}$ _____

11. $\dfrac{59}{100}$ _____

Answer each question below.

12. Garth had to take his bass guitar that was 3 feet long on the airplane, how many inches is the guitar? _____

13. If a canoe is 6 yards long, how many feet is that? _____

(a) 14. If there are 2 pints of ice cream in the freezer, how many ounces is that? _____

15. If you have 8 quarts of oil, how many pints is that? _____

(b) 16. If there are 13 gallons of toxic ooze in the laboratory, how many quarts is that?

_____

Multiply each pair of numbers below.

17.
$$\begin{array}{r} 432 \\ \times\ 13 \\ \hline \end{array}$$

18.
$$\begin{array}{r} 732 \\ \times\ 231 \\ \hline \end{array}$$

Divide each pair of numbers below. Check your work, and write any remainders next to your answer.

19. $3\overline{)235}$

(c) 20. $6\overline{)563}$

Solve each word problem below.

(d) 21. In 1814 the Star Spangled Banner was written, and in 1524 the first pocket watch was invented. How many years was it between those two events? _____

(e) 22. Salt took 3 quizzes. She scored a 71 on her first quiz, a 98 on her second quiz, and an 86 on her third quiz. What was her average score? _____

Lesson 89—Units for Weight

In addition to units for length and liquids, there are also units for showing how much something weighs. One of those units is the **ounce**, and remember, the ounce is also a unit for measuring liquids. Actually, the ounce that is used to measure liquids is also called a fluid ounce, which is abbreviated as fl oz. The two kinds of ounces are different, but both are used to measure small amounts.

After the ounce is the **pound**, which is the unit that people use to measure their weight. It takes 16 ounces to make 1 pound, and the short way to write pound is lb. To convert pounds to ounces, just multiply by 16.

16 ounces = 1 pound

Another unit for measuring weight is the **ton**, and tons are a lot bigger than pounds. In fact, it takes 2,000 pounds to make 1 ton. A car weighs about 1 ton.

2,000 pounds = 1 ton

The main point of this lesson is that there are lots of different units for weight to go with all the different-sized objects in our world.

Practice 89

a. If there are 6 gallons of water in the tank, how many quarts are there? _____

b. Ned barbecued 5 pounds of ribs. How many ounces is that? _____

c. Divide $5\overline{)532}$. Check your work, and write any remainders next to your answer.

$$\overline{)}$$

Solve each word problem below.

d. Wilbur bought some new hedge clippers for $34.52. If he gave the cashier $40, how much did he receive in change? _____

e. The volunteers made a total of 145 sandwiches for 5 food shelters. If each shelter received same number of sandwiches, how many did each receive? _____

Problem Set 89

Tell whether each sentence below is True or False.

1. There are 12 ounces in 1 pound. _____

2. One ton is equal to 2,000 ounces. _____

Answer each question below.

3. If it takes 4 quarters to make $1, how many quarters does it take to make $25? _____.

4. Write 52¢ using a dollar sign and decimal point. _____

5. How many seconds are in 59 minutes? _____

6. Write a percent for the part of the whole that is shaded in the picture below. _____

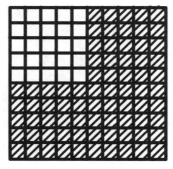

7. In a recent survey of 100 Chihuahuas, 91 of them said they wish they had a scarier bark. What percent do not want wish they had a scarier bark? _____

Write each fraction below as a percent.

8. $\dfrac{49}{100}$ _____

9. $\dfrac{11}{100}$ _____

Write each percent below as a fraction.

10. 81% _____

11. 33% _____

Answer each question below.

12. If the basketball player is 7 feet tall, how many inches tall is he? _____

13. If Itty Bitty bought 4 pints of ice cream, how many ounces did she buy? _____

14. If the hot dog stand used 6 quarts of relish last month, how many pints did they use?
_____

(a) 15. If there are 14 gallons of chocolate in the chocolate fountain, how many quarts is that?
_____

(b) 16. The Extra Cheesy Pizza Parlor made a pizza that weighed 8 pounds. How many ounces is that? _____

Multiply each pair of numbers below.

17. $\begin{array}{r} 831 \\ \times\ 17 \\ \hline \end{array}$

18. $\begin{array}{r} 712 \\ \times\ 129 \\ \hline \end{array}$

Divide each pair of numbers below. Check your work, and write any remainders next to your answer.

19. $2\overline{)613}$ (c) 20. $4\overline{)421}$

Solve each word problem below.

(d) 21. Winston bought a new cane for $18.24. If he gave the cashier $20, how much did he receive in change? _____

(e) 22. The scientist put 126 samples in 3 different notebooks. If he has the same number of samples in each notebook, how many are in each notebook? _____

Lesson 90—Measuring Length with Metric Units

The problem with units like inches, feet, yards, and miles is that it's easy to forget how many of one kind will fit inside another. To fix this, scientists created a simpler system for measuring lengths called the **metric system**, which doesn't require memorizing so many different numbers. In the metric system, the main unit for measuring length is called the **meter**. In fact, all units for length in the metric system have names that end with the word *meter*. A meter is a little bit bigger than a yard.

The next unit that's bigger than the meter is the **decameter**, and it takes 10 meters to make 1 decameter.

10 meters = 1 decameter

After the decameter is the **hectometer**, and it takes 10 decameters to make 1 hectometer.

10 decameters = 1 hectometer

Finally, after the hectometer is the **kilometer**, and it takes 10 hectometers to make 1 kilometer.

10 hectometers = 1 kilometer

Notice that in the metric system, each unit is 10 times bigger than the last one, so the only number you need to remember is 10. That means if you want to change from a larger metric unit to the next smaller unit, you can just multiply by 10, which is why the metric system is far easier than the one that uses inches, feet, and miles.

There are actually even metric units for lengths that are smaller than a meter, and those are also separated by the number 10. Here's a table that shows all of the units for length and how they are connected.

Metric Length Measurements

10 millimeters (mm) = 1 centimeter (cm)
10 centimeters (cm) = 1 decimeter (dm)
10 decimeters (dm) = 1 meter (m)
10 meters (m) = 1 decameter (dam)
10 decameters (dam) = 1 hectometer (hm)
10 hectometers (hm) = 1 kilometer (km)

441

The ones that are smaller than a meter are the ones we didn't discuss in detail. The letters in parentheses are the abbreviations for each unit, so meter can be written just as m, and kilometer can be shorted to km. Here's an example of a problem using metric units.

> If the length of a swimming pool used for competitions is 5 decameters long, how many meters long is it?

Since there are 10 meters is 1 decameter, we just have to multiply 5×10, which means that the swimming pool is 50 meters long. Here's another problem.

> If a diving board is 3 meters long, how many decimeters is it?

The table says that there are 10 decimeters in 1 meter, so we can find the answer by multiplying. Since 3×10 is 30, the diving board must be 30 decimeters long.

Practice 90

    a. If the microphone stand is 7 decimeters long, how many centimeters is that?
    _____

    b. If the trophy case is 6 meters long, how many decimeters is that? _____

    c. Divide $2\overline{)625}$. Check your work, and write any remainders next to your answer.

$$\overline{)}$$

Solve each word problem below.

    d. Julius bought a new baseball cap for $15.25, but that doesn't include the tax. If the tax is 92¢, what will he have to pay in dollars? _____

    e. There were 3 jigsaw puzzles. The first had 54 pieces, the second had 62 pieces, and the third had 58 pieces. What was the average number of pieces? _____

Problem Set 90

Tell whether each sentence below is True or False.

1. The meter is the main metric unit for measuring lengths. _____

2. A meter is a little bit less than a yard. _____

3. The short way to write kilometer is km. _____

Answer each question below.

4. How many decades are there in 8 centuries?_____

5. Write a percent for the part of the whole that is shaded in the picture below _____

6. In a recent survey of 100 pickles, 96 said they were green but not with envy. What percent said they were green but not with envy? _____

7. Write $\dfrac{77}{100}$ as a percent. _____

8. Write 3% as a fraction_____

Add or subtract (as required) each pair of numbers below.

9.
$$\begin{array}{r} 7,421 \\ -\ 2,174 \\ \hline \end{array}$$

10. $45 + 17.63$

$$\begin{array}{r} + \\ \hline \end{array}$$

Answer each question below.

11. If the bench in the dugout is 8 yards long, how many feet is that? _____

12. If the sandcastle is 6 feet tall, how many inches is that? _____

13. If there are 15 gallons of gobbledegoo, how many quarts is that? _____

14. If the box of books weighs 9 pounds, how many ounces is it? _____

(a) 15. If a window is 5 decimeters long, how many centimeters is that? _____

(b) 16. If the cozy sofa is 2 meters long, how many decimeters is that? _____

Multiply each pair of numbers below.

17.
$$534$$
$$\times\, 21$$

18.
$$765$$
$$\times\, 141$$

Divide each pair of numbers below. Check your work, and write any remainders next to your answer.

19. $6\overline{)729}$ **(c) 20.** $3\overline{)938}$

Solve each word problem below.

(d) 21. Alvin bought a pogo stick for $19.95, but that doesn't include the tax. If the tax is 88¢, what will Alvin have to pay in dollars? _____

(e) 22. Holly made three bean bags. The first had 48 beans in it, the second had 37 beans in it, and the third had 47 beans in it. What was the average number of beans? _____

Lesson 91—Other Metric Units

There are also metric units to measure things such as liquids. The most common metric unit for measuring liquids is the **liter**. A giant soft drink cup is about 1 liter. The abbreviation for liter is a capital L. There are other metric units for liquids besides the liter. Some are bigger while others are smaller, but they all end with the word *liter*. For example, there is the centiliter. *Centi* is a prefix that comes from the Latin word for "hundred," so there are 100 centiliters in a liter.

100 centiliters = 1 liter

There is also the kiloliter. *Kilo* stands for "thousand", and there are 1,000 liters in a kiloliter.

1,000 liters = 1 kiloliter

Just as with the metric units for length, all metric units for liquids are separated by the number 10, so changing from one unit to another is really simple.

There are also metric units for measuring weight, but technically they're called units of mass. On Earth, weight and mass are pretty much the same, so you don't need to worry much about the difference. The main metric unit for mass is the **gram**, which can be abbreviated g. The cap on a ballpoint pen, a paper clip, and a dollar bill all weigh about a gram. All other metric units for mass end with the word *gram*, and each one is 10 times bigger than the one before. One really small unit of mass is the milligram. It takes 1,000 milligrams to make just 1 gram.

1,000 milligrams = 1 gram

There are also decagrams, and it takes 10 grams to make 1 decagram.

10 grams = 1 decagram

The main point of this lesson is that the metric units for mass and liquids follow the same pattern as the metric units for length. Each unit is 10 times bigger than the one before.

Practice 91

For each problem below, circle the best answer.

a. Which of these would best describe the amount of water in a swimming pool: 15 centiliters or 15 kiloliters? _____

b. Which do you think best describes the weight of a pencil: 25 milligrams or 25 grams? _____

c. Divide $4\overline{)581}$. Check your work, and write any remainders next to your answer.

$\overline{)}$

Solve each word problem below.

d. At present, there are 152 galaxy bots stationed on the 4 battleships. If each battleship has the same number of galaxy bots, how many are on each battleship? _____

e. Milo took 3 quizzes. He scored an 85 on his first quiz, a 95 on his second quiz, and a 99 on his third quiz. What was his average score? _____

Problem Set 91

Tell whether each sentence below is True or False.

1. The liter is the most common metric unit for measuring liquids. _____

2. The prefix "kilo" stands for hundred. _____

3. The gram is the main metric unit for mass. _____

Answer each question below.

4. What is the diameter of circle K? _____

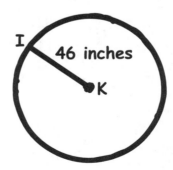

5. Tell whether the quadrilateral below is a plain quadrilateral, trapezoid, parallelogram, rhombus, rectangle, or a square. _____

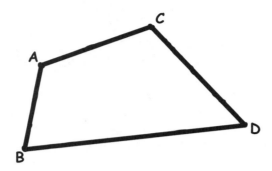

Write each of the amounts below using a dollar sign and a decimal point.

6. ninety dollars and sixty-two cents _____

7. five cents _____

Answer each question below.

8. How many minutes are in 35 hours? _____

9. Write $\dfrac{7}{100}$ as a percent. _____

10. Write 49% as a fraction _____

11. In a recent survey of 100 baby ducks, 62 of them said they would rather paddle than waddle. What percent would rather paddle than waddle? _____

Multiply each pair of numbers below.

12.
$$\begin{array}{r} 625 \\ \times\ 41 \\ \hline \end{array}$$

13.
$$\begin{array}{r} 921 \\ \times\ 134 \\ \hline \end{array}$$

Answer each question below.

14. If there are 15 pints of apple cider in the bowl, how many ounces is that? _____

15. If Sally bought a 4-pound chicken, how many ounces is it? _____

16. If the pole-vaulter's pole is 4 meters long, how many decimeters is that? _____

For each problem below, circle the best answer.

(a) 17. Which of these would best describe the amount of water in a shark tank: 8 centiliters or 8 kiloliters? _____

(b) 18. Which do you think best describes the weight of a granola bar: 45 milligrams or 45 grams? _____

Divide each pair of numbers below. Check your work, and write any remainders next to your answer.

19. $8\overline{)874}$ **(c) 20.** $5\overline{)761}$

Solve each word problem below.

(d) 21. Curly-Q kept her collection of 174 thimbles on 6 separate shelves. If each shelf has the same number of thimbles, how many are on each shelf? _____

(e) 22. Jethro took 3 quizzes. He scored a 78 on his first quiz, an 83 on his second quiz, and a 91 on his third quiz. What was his average score? _____

Quiz 13

Tell whether each sentence below is True or False.

1. One fourth is the same as 25%. _____

2. There are 10 ounces in a pint. _____

Answer each question below.

3. If it takes 20 nickels to make $1, how many nickels does it take to make $24? _____

4. Write 44¢ using a dollar sign and decimal point. _____

5. How many days are in the month of October? _____

6. How many seconds are in 49 minutes? _____

7. In a recent survey of 100 cereal fanatics, 94 of them said that breakfast was the most important meal of the day. What percent said breakfast was the most important meal of the day? _____

Write each percent below as a fraction.

8. 49% _____   9. 87% _____

Write each fraction below as a percent.

10. $\dfrac{9}{100}$ _____   11. $\dfrac{21}{100}$ _____

Multiply each pair of numbers below.

12. $\begin{array}{r} 712 \\ \times\, 81 \\ \hline \end{array}$ 13. $\begin{array}{r} 521 \\ \times\, 142 \\ \hline \end{array}$

Answer each question below.

14. If Jeremy and his teammates have to go 6 yards to get a first down, how many feet is that? _____

15. If the chef cooked some soup in a 9 quart pot, how many pints could the pot hold? _____

16. If the Castle Bot's mace weighs 7 pounds, how many ounces is that? _____

17. If the Asteroid Hunter's mobile rocket launcher is 8 meters long, how many decimeters is that? _____

For each problem below, circle the best answer.

18. Which of these would best describe the amount of butter in the measuring cup: 15 centiliters or 15 kiloliters? _____

19. Which do you think best describes the weight of a house key: 30 milligrams or 30 grams? _____

Divide each pair of numbers below. Check your work, and write any remainders next to your answer.

20. $4\overline{)862}$

21. $5\overline{)546}$

22. $7\overline{)654}$

Solve each word problem below.

23. Francesca bought a new scarf for $43.68. If she gave the cashier $50, how much did she receive in change? _____

24. There were a total of 161 game tokens for the 7 winners. If each winner received the same number of tokens, how many did each receive? _____

Lesson 92—Adding and Subtracting Fractions with the Same Denominators

Sometimes it's necessary to add or subtract two fractions. Here's an example.

Notice that both pies are the same size and both have been cut into 3 equal pieces. Both pies also have 1 shaded piece, so $\frac{1}{3}$ of each pie is shaded. If we added the two shaded pieces, we would end up with $\frac{2}{3}$ of a whole pie.

We can do the same problem without pictures by just adding the tops of the fractions and keeping the bottoms the same.

$$\frac{1}{3} + \frac{1}{3} = \frac{2}{3}$$
Just add the tops and keep the bottoms the same.

The tops are both 1, and $1+1$ is 2. That means the answer is $\frac{2}{3}$, which is the same as we got when we used pictures. This approach will work every time the bottoms of two fractions are the same.

Subtracting fractions works the same way as adding. The only difference is that you subtract the tops instead of adding them. The bottoms still say the same.

$$\frac{7}{9} - \frac{5}{9} = \frac{2}{9}$$
Subtract the tops and keep the bottoms the same.

We just subtracted the tops and kept the bottoms the same. Since $7-5$ is 2, the answer is $\frac{2}{9}$.

The main point of this lesson is that when two fractions have the same bottom, we can add or subtract them just by adding or subtracting the tops.

Practice 92

    a.   If it is 5 miles from Tinyville to Pleasant Valley, how many yards is it? _____

Add or subtract (as required) each pair of fractions below.

    b. $\dfrac{1}{9}+\dfrac{4}{9}$ _____   **c.** $\dfrac{9}{11}-\dfrac{8}{11}$ _____

Solve each word problem below.

    d. Ramone has played in 3 games. He ran for 68 yards in the first game, 81 yards in the second game, and 76 yards in the third game. What was his average number of yards? _____

    e. Thelma sold 144 of her silly oven mitts to 6 different stores. If each store bought the same number of oven mitts, how many did each buy? _____

Problem Set 92

Tell whether each sentence below is True or False.

    1. You can add two fractions by adding their tops and bottoms. _____

    2. When two fractions have the same bottom, you can subtract them by subtracting their tops and keeping the bottom the same. _____

Answer each question below.

    3. What is the radius of circle *M*? _____

4. How many minutes are in 45 hours? _____

5. In a recent survey of 100 little piggies, only 7 of them said they actually ate roast beef. What percent actually ate roast beef? _____

6. Write 93% as a fraction. _____

7. Write $\frac{57}{100}$ as a percent. _____

Multiply each pair of numbers below.

8. 642
   × 24

9. 423
   × 331

Divide each pair of numbers below. Check your work, and write any remainders next to your answer.

10. 6)941

11. 9)983

Answer each question below.

12. If it is 4 miles from Rogersville to Thumbsville, how many yards is it? _____

13. Olivia made 8 pints of chile salsa, how many ounces is that? _____

14. If Hoss has 3 gallons of ice cream in his freezer, how many quarts is that? _____

15. If the bowling ball weighs 6 pounds, how many ounces is that? _____

16. If the princess canopy bed is 2 meters long, how many decimeters is that? _____

Add each pair of fractions below.

(b) 17. $\dfrac{2}{7} + \dfrac{2}{7}$ _____

18. $\dfrac{4}{15} + \dfrac{7}{15}$ _____

Subtract each pair of fractions below.

(c) 19. $\dfrac{4}{5} - \dfrac{2}{5}$ _____

20. $\dfrac{8}{13} - \dfrac{5}{13}$ _____

Solve each word problem below.

(d) 21. Herschel solved 3 puzzles. It took him 46 seconds to figure out the first one, 37 seconds to figure out the second one, and 58 seconds to figure out the third one. What was his average time? _____

(e) 22. Nadia sold 192 of her new purses to 8 different stores. If each store bought the same number of purses, how many did each buy? _____

Lesson 93—Improper Fractions and Mixed Numbers

Sometimes the tops of two fractions that have the same denominator add to a sum that is larger than the denominator. Here's an example.

$$\frac{5}{7} + \frac{3}{7} = \frac{8}{7}$$

The 8 on top is bigger than the 7 on bottom.

Notice that the answer is 8 over 7, and 8 is bigger than 7. Here's what the problem looks like in pictures.

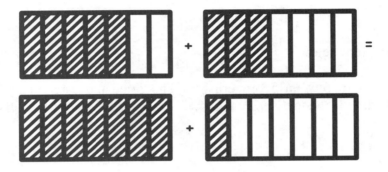

When we combined the two shaded parts, we ended up with a whole rectangle shaded plus $\frac{1}{7}$ of a rectangle shaded. That means that $\frac{8}{7}$ is the same as $1 + \frac{1}{7}$, which most people just write as $1\frac{1}{7}$. This is called a **mixed number**, and the word *mixed* just means that a whole has been mixed with a fraction. Fractions like $\frac{8}{7}$ are called **improper fractions**. An improper fraction is a fraction where the top number is equal to or greater than the bottom number. Improper fractions are always equal to or greater than 1. If a fraction has the same number on top and bottom, it's equal to 1.

$$\frac{9}{9} = 1$$

A fraction with the same number on top and bottom is equal to 1.

If the top is greater than the bottom, then the fraction is greater than 1.

The main point of the lesson is that some fractions stand for more than a whole and these fractions can also be written as mixed numbers.

Practice 93

a. Tell whether $\dfrac{7}{7}$ is a proper or improper fraction. _____

b. Tell whether a <, >, or = should go between $\dfrac{3}{3}$ ____ 1.

c. Add $\dfrac{7}{11} + \dfrac{3}{11}$ _____

Solve each word problem below.

d. Happy wants to buy an acorn crusher. The price tag says $12.35, but that doesn't include the tax. If the tax is 93¢, what will Happy have to pay in dollars? _____

e. The castle bots fired 3 waves of flaming arrows. There were 43 flaming arrows in the first wave, 38 in the second wave, and 51 in the third wave. What was the average number of flaming arrows in each wave? _____

Problem Set 93

Tell whether each sentence below is True or False.

1. A mixed number is part whole number and part fraction. _____

2. An improper fraction is a fraction where the top number is equal to or greater than the bottom number. _____

3. If a fraction has the same number in the top and bottom it's equal to 1. _____

4. If the top of a fraction is bigger than the bottom, the fraction is greater than 1. _____

Answer each question below.

5. If the aquarium is 4 yards long, how many feet is it? _____

6. If a book is 6 decimeters long, how many centimeters is that? _____

Match each improper fraction or mixed number to the correct picture below.

7. $\dfrac{5}{3}$ _____

A.

8. $\dfrac{9}{8}$ _____

B.

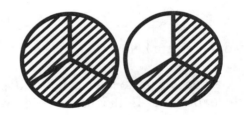

9. $1\dfrac{1}{4}$ _____

C.

Tell whether each fraction below is proper or improper.

10. $\dfrac{1}{7}$ _____   **(a) 11.** $\dfrac{6}{6}$ _____

12. $\dfrac{7}{5}$ _____

Tell whether a <, >, or = should go between each pair of numbers below.

13. $1\dfrac{1}{6}$ ____ 1   **(b) 14.** 1 ____ $\dfrac{5}{5}$

Multiply or divide (as required) each pair of numbers below.

15.
$$\begin{array}{r} 721 \\ \times\,314 \\ \hline \end{array}$$

16. $3\overline{)172}$

Add each pair of fractions below.

(c) 17. $\dfrac{2}{9} + \dfrac{5}{9}$ _____

18. $\dfrac{7}{17} + \dfrac{2}{17}$ _____

Subtract each pair of fractions below.

19. $\dfrac{3}{7} - \dfrac{1}{7}$ _____

20. $\dfrac{9}{19} - \dfrac{4}{19}$ _____

Solve each word problem below.

(d) 21. Peek-a-boo wants to buy a hula hoop. The price tag says $10.55, but that doesn't include the tax. If the tax is 87¢, what will Peek-a-boo have to pay in dollars? _____

(e) 22. The galaxy bots spent 3 days installing motion detectors. They installed 24 on the first day, 32 on the second day, and 37 on the third day. What was the average number of installations made each day? _____

Lesson 94—Converting an Improper Fraction to a Mixed Number

It's not necessary to always draw pictures to show what a mixed number an improper fraction is equal to. Here's an example.

Convert $\frac{8}{7}$ into a mixed number.

We can change the improper fraction into a mixed number just by dividing the bottom of the fraction into the top.

$$7\overline{)8} \quad 1\frac{1}{7} \qquad \frac{8}{7} \text{ converted}$$
$$\underline{-7}$$
$$1 \qquad\qquad\qquad \text{into } 1\frac{1}{7}.$$

We just divided 7 into 8. Since 7 will go into 8 only once, we wrote a 1 on top, multiplied and subtracted. The remainder was 1, and normally we would write 1 R1; however, notice that in this case, the remainder was written as a fraction by putting it over the divisor. That's perfectly legal, which means $1\frac{1}{7}$ is the same as $\frac{8}{7}$. So to convert an improper fraction into a mixed number, just divide the bottom into the top and turn the remainder into a fraction. Here's another example.

Convert $\frac{12}{5}$ into a mixed number.

Once again we can just divide the bottom into the top and turn the remainder into a fraction.

$$5\overline{)12} \quad 2\frac{2}{5} \qquad \frac{12}{5} \text{ converted}$$
$$\underline{-10}$$
$$2 \qquad\qquad\qquad \text{into } 2\frac{2}{5}.$$

Since 5 goes into 12 twice, we wrote a 2 on top, multiplied, and subtracted. We ended up with a remainder of 2, which we put over the divisor, 5. That means that $\frac{12}{5}$ is the same as $2\frac{2}{5}$.

The main point is that to convert an improper fraction into a mixed number, you just need to divide the bottom into the top and write the remainder as a fraction.

Practice 94

    a.   Write a mixed number to tell what this picture represents. _____

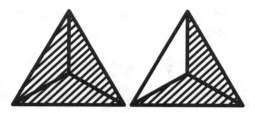

    b.   Add $\dfrac{6}{25} + \dfrac{7}{25}$ _____

    c.   Convert $\dfrac{6}{5}$ into a mixed number. _____

Solve each word problem below.

    d.   In 1814 the first photograph was taken. In 1946 the microwave oven was invented. How many years was it between these events? _____

    e.   The Little Prince Toy Company sold a total of 126 of its remote-controlled helicopters to 9 stores. If each store bought the same number of helicopters, how many did each buy? _____

Problem Set 94

Tell whether each sentence below is True or False.

    1.   You cannot change an improper fraction to a mixed number. _____

    2.   You can write the remainder to a division problem as a fraction just by putting the remainder over the divisor. _____

Answer each question below.

3. Martha is making a dish that calls for 4 pounds of sausage. How many ounces is that?
    _____

4. If a ladder is 8 feet tall, how many inches tall is it? _____

Write a mixed number to tell what each picture below represents.

(a) 5. _____

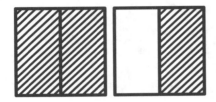

6. _____

Tell whether each fraction below is proper or improper.

7. $\dfrac{19}{15}$ _____   8. $\dfrac{10}{10}$ _____

9. $\dfrac{5}{12}$ _____

Tell whether a <, >, or = should go between each pair of numbers below.

10. 1 ____ $\dfrac{3}{8}$ 11. $\dfrac{14}{14}$ ____ 1

Multiply or divide (as required) each pair of numbers below.

12.
$$\begin{array}{r} 423 \\ \times\ 32 \\ \hline \end{array}$$

13. $4\overline{)823}$

Add each pair of fractions below.

14. $\dfrac{2}{13}+\dfrac{6}{13}$ _____

(b) 15. $\dfrac{8}{21}+\dfrac{2}{21}$ _____

Subtract each pair of fractions below.

16. $\dfrac{5}{15}-\dfrac{1}{15}$ _____

17. $\dfrac{9}{23}-\dfrac{3}{23}$ _____

Convert each improper fraction below into a mixed number.

(c) 18. $\dfrac{9}{8}$ _____

19. $\dfrac{7}{3}$ _____

20. $\dfrac{13}{2}$ _____

Solve each word problem below.

(d) 21.   In 1709 the piano was invented. In 1861 the bicycle was invented. How many years was it between these events? _____

(e) 22.   Gwen sold a total of 105 of her gingerbread houses to 7 catalog companies. If each catalog company bought the same number of gingerbread houses, how many did each buy? _____

Lesson 95—Division Word Problems with a Remainder

Some division word problems have remainders, and it's sometimes difficult to know what the remainder means. Here's an example.

Melanie stores all of her CDs in clear plastic sleeves that she keeps in a big notebook. If Melanie can fit 8 CDs in every sleeve and she has a total of 57 CDs, how many sleeves will she need to store all her CDs?

This problem is asking how many groups of 8 it takes to make 57, which means it's a division problem. Here it is worked out.

$$\begin{array}{r} 7 \\ 8\overline{)57} \\ -56 \\ \hline 1 \end{array}$$

The remainder tells how many CDs are left over.

All we did was follow the four steps of long division to get 7 with a remainder of 1. However, the question asks how many sleeves she needs to store all of her CDs. Since Melanie will fill 7 sleeves completely and then have 1 CD left over, she'll need 7 plus an 8th sleeve to put the extra CD in. Notice that this means the answer to the problem is different than the answer to the division. Here's another example.

Stanley works at a lumber yard, and he needs to cut a 38-foot board into 7-foot long pieces. How many pieces will he end up with? Write your answer as a mixed number.

Once again we have to set up a long-division problem.

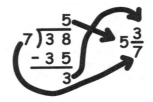

Writing the answer as a mixed number.

After dividing, we got an answer of 5 with a remainder of 3, but a remainder of 3 doesn't mean there are 3 extra pieces. Remember, though, that the instructions said to write the answer as a mixed number, which is why we wrote $5\frac{3}{7}$. The mixed number answer makes sense because it means that Stanley will end up with 5 boards and $\frac{3}{7}$ of another. With some division word problems, it's always best to write the answer as a mixed number.

Practice 95

a. Write a mixed number to tell what the picture below represents. _____

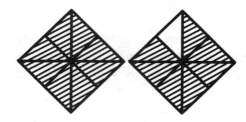

b. Convert $\frac{19}{6}$ into a mixed number. _____

c. Subtract $\frac{14}{31} - \frac{8}{31}$ _____

Solve each word problem below.

d. Curtis works at the Sugar Sweet Donut House, and he just made 74 rainbow-sprinkled donut holes. Now he needs to put them in plastic cups that can hold 9 holes each. How many cups will Curtis need? _____

e. Sally needs to cut a 59-foot long piece of fabric into 8-foot long pieces. How many pieces will she end up with? Write your answer as a mixed number. _____

Problem Set 95

Tell whether each sentence below is True or False.

1. Some division word problems have a remainder. _____

2. It's better to write the answer to some division word problems as a mixed number. _____

Answer each question below.

3. If Jill lost 3 pounds last week, how many ounces did she lose? _____

4. The orange juice dispenser at the cafeteria has 11 quarts in it. How many pints is that? _____

5. The storage silo is 22 meters tall. How many decimeters is that? _____

Write a mixed number to tell what each picture below represents.

(a) 6. _____

7. _____

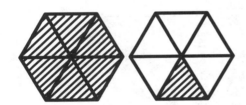

Tell whether a <, >, or = should go between each pair of numbers below.

8. $\dfrac{4}{4}$ ____ 1   **9.** 1 ____ $\dfrac{12}{11}$

Tell whether each fraction below is proper or improper.

10. $\dfrac{18}{18}$ _____   **11.** $\dfrac{14}{17}$ _____

12. $\dfrac{14}{5}$ _____

Multiply or divide (as required) each pair of numbers below.

13. $7\overline{)921}$

14. $\begin{array}{r} 932 \\ \times\ 124 \\ \hline \end{array}$

Convert each improper fraction below into a mixed number.

(b) 15. $\dfrac{17}{4}$ _____

16. $\dfrac{21}{8}$ _____

Subtract each pair of fractions below.

(c) 17. $\dfrac{4}{5} - \dfrac{3}{5}$ _____

18. $\dfrac{17}{27} - \dfrac{7}{27}$ _____

Add each pair of fractions below.

19. $\dfrac{1}{9} + \dfrac{7}{9}$ _____

20. $\dfrac{14}{29} + \dfrac{11}{29}$ _____

Solve each word problem below.

(d) 21. Heart Panda just baked 43 cupcakes. Now she plans to put them in sacks that can hold 6 cupcakes each. How many sacks will Heart Panda need? _____

(e) 22. Rochelle needs to cut a 48-inch piece of ribbon into 5-inch long pieces. How many pieces will she end up with? Write your answer as a mixed number. _____

Lesson 96—Adding Mixed Numbers with the Same Denominator

Adding two mixed numbers that have the same denominator is pretty simple. Here's an example.

$$3\frac{1}{5} + 6\frac{2}{5} = 9\frac{3}{5}$$

$$3 + 6 = 9$$

$$\frac{1}{5} + \frac{2}{5} = \frac{3}{5}$$

Add the whole number and fraction parts separately.

The best way to do problems like this is to add the whole number parts and the fraction parts separately. Since the whole number parts are 3 and 6, the whole number part of the answer is $3+6$, which is 9. Then, to add the fraction parts, we just added the tops since the bottoms were the same. The last step was to put the two parts together, which gave us an answer of $9\frac{3}{5}$.

Sometimes the sum of the fraction parts is an improper fraction. Here's an example.

$$2\frac{1}{3} + 4\frac{2}{3} = 6 + 1 = 7$$

$$2 + 4 = 6$$

$$\frac{1}{3} + \frac{2}{3} = \frac{3}{3} = 1$$

The fraction part is equal to 1.

Notice that when we added the fraction parts we got $\frac{3}{3}$, which is equal to 1 since any number divided by itself is 1[1]. The last step was just to add the two parts back together, and since the sum of 6 and 1 is 7, the answer is 7. So sometimes the fraction parts of two mixed numbers will add to a whole number. In cases like that, just add the new whole number to the rest of the whole numbers to get the final answer.

---

[1] This is true for all numbers other than zero.

Practice 96

a. Convert $\dfrac{19}{3}$ into a mixed number. _____

Add each pair of mixed numbers below

b. $1\dfrac{2}{11} + 4\dfrac{5}{11}$ _____

c. $5\dfrac{1}{6} + 3\dfrac{5}{6}$ _____

Solve each word problem below.

d. The castle bots launched their siege pods in 3 waves. There were 21 pods in the first wave, 36 in the second wave, and 39 in the third wave. What was the average number of pods in each wave? _____

e. The bakery has 26 cakes on display on shelves. If each shelf can only hold 7 cakes, how many shelves are being used? _____

Problem Set 96

Tell whether each sentence below is True or False.

1. It's impossible to add two mixed numbers. _____

2. Any number (except 0) divided by itself is equal to 1. _____

Write each percent below as a fraction.

3. 9% _____

4. 71% _____

Answer each question below.

5. If it's 3 miles from Crab Town to Turtle Junction, how many yards is that? _____

6. Believe it or not, Brad's extreme truck is 9 feet tall. How many inches tall is it? _____

7. The average American eats 22 quarts of ice cream each year. How many pints is that?
    _____

8. The giant telescope had a diameter of 3 decameters. How many meters is that?
    _____

Tell whether a <, >, or = should go between each pair of numbers below.

9. 1 ____ $\dfrac{7}{6}$

10. $\dfrac{13}{14}$ ____ 1

Tell whether each fraction below is proper or improper.

11. $\dfrac{5}{6}$ _____

12. $\dfrac{7}{2}$ _____

Multiply or divide (as required) each pair of numbers below.

13. $\begin{array}{r} 394 \\ \times\ 18 \\ \hline \end{array}$

14. $3\overline{)629}$

Convert each improper fraction below into a mixed number.

(a) 15. $\dfrac{36}{7}$ _____

16. $\dfrac{27}{4}$ _____

Add or subtract (as required) each pair of fractions below.

17. $\dfrac{15}{33}+\dfrac{4}{33}$ _____

18. $\dfrac{26}{35}-\dfrac{13}{35}$ _____

Add each pair of mixed numbers below.

(b) 19. $2\frac{1}{7} + 4\frac{3}{7}$ _____

(c) 20. $5\frac{1}{8} + 2\frac{7}{8}$ _____

Solve each word problem below.

(d) 21. Nathaniel pitched for 3 seasons. He had 54 strikeouts in his first season, 61 in his second season, and 74 in his third season. What was his average number of strikeouts? _____

(e) 22. Alexandra is putting 37 bars of lemon soap into little wicker baskets. If each basket can only hold 5 bars, how many baskets will she have to use? _____

Lesson 97—Subtracting Mixed Numbers with the Same Denominator

Subtracting mixed numbers works basically the same as adding them. Just subtract the whole number parts and fraction parts separately, and then combine those results to get the final answer. Here's an example.

$$4\frac{2}{3} - 3\frac{1}{3} = 1\frac{1}{3}$$

$$4 - 3 = \boxed{1}$$

$$\frac{2}{3} - \frac{1}{3} = \boxed{\frac{1}{3}}$$

Subtract the whole number and fraction parts separately.

The first step was to calculate 4 minus 3, which is 1. Then, we just subtracted the tops of the fraction parts and kept the bottoms the same. Finally, we combined the 1 and the $\frac{1}{3}$ to get $1\frac{1}{3}$.

Sometimes the difference between two fraction parts is zero. Here's an example.

$$9\frac{5}{8} - 2\frac{5}{8} = 7 + 0 = 7$$

$$9 - 2 = \boxed{7}$$

$$\frac{5}{8} - \frac{5}{8} = \frac{0}{8} = \boxed{0}$$

The fraction part is equal to 0.

First, we subtracted 9 minus 2 to get 7. Then, since the fraction parts had the same denominators, we just subtracted the tops and kept the bottom the same. Five minus 5 is 0, and zero divided by any number, except 0, is 0, so the fraction part was equal to 0. The last step was to combine the 7 and the 0, which is just 7.

The main point of the lesson is that subtracting mixed numbers is pretty much the same as adding them, but when the fractions that are being subtracted are the same, they'll end up equaling 0.

Practice 97

a. Add $7\frac{11}{15} + 4\frac{2}{15}$ _____

Subtract each pair of mixed numbers below.

b. $9\frac{5}{9} - 6\frac{1}{9}$ _____   c. $7\frac{5}{6} - 2\frac{5}{6}$ _____

Solve each word problem below.

d. Maximus bought a new speed bag for $27.38. If he gave the cashier $40, how much did he receive in change? _____

e. Veronica sent out a total of 144 of her ladybug backpacks to 6 stores. If each store bought the same number of backpacks, how many did each buy? _____

Problem Set 97

Tell whether each sentence below is True or False.

1. You can subtract two mixed numbers by subtracting their whole number parts and fraction parts separately, then combining the results. _____

2. Zero divided by any number, except 0, is 0. _____

Write each fraction below as a decimal.

3. $\frac{23}{1,000}$ _____

4. $\frac{493}{1,000}$ _____

Answer each question below.

5. The chef cooked 2 pounds of barbecue shrimp for the party. How many ounces is that?

_____

6. If a small refrigerator has a capacity of 32 quarts, how many pints can it hold?

_____

Write a mixed number to tell what each picture below represents.

7. _____

8. _____

Tell whether each fraction below is proper or improper.

9. $\dfrac{9}{9}$ _____   10. $\dfrac{11}{3}$ _____

Multiply or divide (as required) each pair of numbers below.

11. $8\overline{)427}$

12. $\begin{array}{r} 812 \\ \times\,124 \\ \hline \end{array}$

Convert each improper fraction below into a mixed number.

13. $\dfrac{25}{4}$ _____

14. $\dfrac{29}{7}$ _____

Add or subtract (as required) each pair of fractions below.

15. $\dfrac{11}{23}+\dfrac{2}{23}$ _____

16. $\dfrac{21}{25}-\dfrac{3}{25}$ _____

Add each pair of mixed numbers below.

(a) 17. $3\dfrac{1}{9}+5\dfrac{4}{9}$ _____

18. $6\dfrac{5}{13}+4\dfrac{4}{13}$ _____

Subtract each pair of mixed numbers below.

(b) 19. $8\dfrac{6}{7}-4\dfrac{2}{7}$ _____

(c) 20. $5\dfrac{1}{2}-1\dfrac{1}{2}$ _____

Solve each word problem below.

(d) 21. Darren bought a model race car for \$31.67. If he gave the cashier \$40, how much did he receive in change? _____

(e) 22. Jasmine sent out a total of 126 of her painted hairbrushes to 7 stores. If each store bought the same number of hairbrushes, how many did each buy? _____

Lesson 98—Equivalent Fractions – Part 1

Two fractions can actually be equal even if the numbers on top and bottom aren't the same. Here's an example.

Notice that the pan on the left is cut into 4 equal pieces and 1 of those is shaded, while the one on right is cut into 8 equal pieces and 2 of those are shaded. However, the shaded amounts are actually equal, which means that $\frac{2}{8}$ must be equal to $\frac{1}{4}$. Here's another example.

The left-hand cheesecake has been divided into 2 equal pieces with 1 of them shaded, and the right-hand cheesecake has been divided into 10 equal pieces with 5 of them shaded. Once again though, the shaded parts are equal, which means that $\frac{5}{10}$ is equal to $\frac{1}{2}$.

To turn a fraction into one that looks different but has the same value, we just have to multiply the top and bottom by the same number. Here's an example.

$$\frac{1}{2} = \frac{1 \times 5}{2 \times 5} = \frac{5}{10}$$

Multiplying the top and bottom of $\frac{1}{2}$ by 5.

This works for any number as long as we use the same number on top and bottom[1]. Two fractions that look different but have the same value are actually called **equivalent fractions**. So technically, $\frac{1}{2}$ and $\frac{5}{10}$ are equivalent fractions.

The main point of this lesson is that you can create an equivalent fraction by multiplying the top and bottom of a fraction by the same number.

---

[1] Remember, zero won't work because that would make the fraction have a zero on bottom.

Practice 98

a. Subtract $6\frac{14}{15} - 5\frac{13}{15}$ _____

b. How many pieces of the rectangle on the right must be shaded to create a fraction that's equal to $\frac{1}{2}$? _____

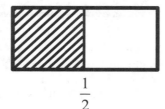

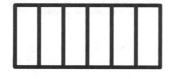

$\frac{1}{2}$

c. Which two equivalent fractions do these pies represent? _____

Solve each word problem below.

d. Gizmo needs to buy a replacement circuit. The price tag says $9.25, but that doesn't include the tax. If the tax is 69¢, what will Gizmo have to pay in dollars? _____

e. Allen took 3 tests. He made an 82 on the first, an 86 on the second, and a 99 on the third. What was his average score? _____

Problem Set 98

Tell whether each sentence below is True or False.

1. To turn a fraction into one that looks different but has the same value, you should multiply the top and bottom by the same number. _____

2. Equivalent fractions are fractions that look different but stand for the same thing. _____

Answer each question below.

3. If it takes 4 quarters to make $1, how many quarters does it take to make $28? _____

4. Write seventy-three dollars and fourteen cents using a dollar sign and decimal point. _____

5. Write 39% as a fraction. _____

6. Write $\dfrac{63}{100}$ as a percent. _____

Write a mixed number to tell what each picture below represents.

7. _____

8. _____

Answer each question below.

    9. The Siberian tiger is 13 feet long. How many inches is that? _____

   10. The chef made 5 pints of spaghetti sauce. How many ounces is that?
_____

Multiply or divide (as required) each pair of numbers below.

   11. $\begin{array}{r} 184 \\ \times\, 91 \\ \hline \end{array}$
               12. $7\overline{)717}$

Convert each improper fraction below into a mixed number.

   13. $\dfrac{14}{3}$ _____
               14. $\dfrac{31}{5}$ _____

Add or subtract (as required) each pair of fractions below.

   15. $\dfrac{10}{17}+\dfrac{6}{17}$ _____
        16. $\dfrac{8}{19}-\dfrac{6}{19}$ _____

Add or subtract (as required) each pair of mixed numbers below.

   17. $7\dfrac{3}{11}+6\dfrac{7}{11}$ _____
       (a) 18. $9\dfrac{8}{13}-2\dfrac{5}{13}$ _____

Answer each question below.

(b) 19. How many pieces of the pie on the right must be shaded to create a fraction that's equal to $\frac{2}{3}$? _____

$\frac{2}{3}$

(c) 20. Which two equivalent fractions do these rectangles represent? _____

Solve each word problem below.

(d) 21. Julius wants to buy a boomerang. The price tag says $11.75, but that doesn't include the tax. If the tax is 97¢, what will Julius have to pay in dollars? _____

(e) 22. Melanie took 3 tests. She made a 77 on her first test, an 81 on her second test, and a 97 on her third test. What was her average score? _____

Quiz 14

Tell whether each sentence below is True or False.

1. You can write the remainder to a division problem as a fraction just by putting the remainder over the divisor. _____

2. You can subtract two mixed numbers by subtracting their whole number parts and fraction parts separately, then combining the results. _____

Answer each question below.

3. Write 0.609 as a fraction. _____

4. Write $\dfrac{59}{1,000}$ as a decimal. _____

Tell whether each fraction below is proper or improper.

5. $\dfrac{5}{8}$ _____

6. $\dfrac{12}{12}$ _____

Tell whether a <, >, or = should go between each pair of numbers below.

7. $\dfrac{5}{5}$ ____ 1

8. $\dfrac{7}{9}$ ____ 1

Write a mixed number to tell what each picture below represents.

9. _____

10. _____

Answer each question below.

11. The tallest free standing statue in the world is called The Golden Driller. If the statue is 76 feet tall, how many inches is that? _____

12. Timothy is competing to become a lifeguard. In one stage of the competition, he had to sprint 5 decameters. How many meters is that? _____

Multiply or divide (as required) each pair of numbers below.

13. $9\overline{)809}$

14. $\begin{array}{r} 721 \\ \times\ 147 \\ \hline \end{array}$

Convert each improper fraction below into a mixed number.

15. $\dfrac{19}{5}$ _____

16. $\dfrac{28}{9}$ _____

Add or subtract (as required) each pair of fractions below.

17. $\dfrac{4}{25} + \dfrac{7}{25}$ _____

18. $\dfrac{10}{17} - \dfrac{8}{17}$ _____

Add or subtract (as required) each pair of mixed numbers below.

19. $5\dfrac{8}{21}+1\dfrac{2}{21}$ _____

20. $7\dfrac{6}{23}-4\dfrac{4}{23}$ _____

Answer each question below.

21. How many pieces of the square on the right must be shaded to create a fraction that's equal to $\dfrac{1}{2}$? _____

$\dfrac{1}{2}$

22. Which two equivalent fractions do these circles represent? _____

Solve each word problem below.

23. Darren has played in 3 games. He threw for 85 yards in the first, 96 yards in the second, and 83 yards in the third. What was his average? _____

24. Curly-Q just made 66 coconut drops. Now she plans to put them in little pouches that can only hold 7 drops each. How many pouches will Curly-Q need? _____

Lesson 99—Equivalent Fractions – Part 2

In addition to multiplying the top and bottom by the same number to get an equivalent fraction, we can also divide the top and bottom by the same number to get an equivalent fraction. Here's an example.

$$\frac{2}{8} = \frac{2 \div 2}{8 \div 2} = \frac{1}{4}$$

Dividing the top and bottom by 2 to get an equivalent fraction.

We just divided the 2 and 8 in $\frac{2}{8}$ by 2 to get $\frac{1}{4}$, and we already know that $\frac{1}{4} = \frac{2}{8}$. Here's what the division looks like in pictures.

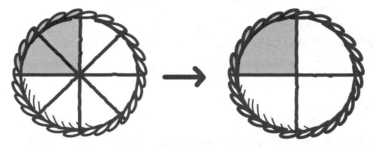

Dividing is like gluing some of the pieces back together.

The pie on the left is divided into 8 pieces and two of them are shaded. Dividing the top and bottom of $\frac{2}{8}$ by 2 is like gluing some of the pieces of the pie back together again. That leaves us with 4 pieces altogether and 1 shaded piece, so now the shaded piece is $\frac{1}{4}$, but it's the same amount of pie that we had before. Dividing the top and bottom of a fraction by the same number will always create an equivalent fraction[1].

The rule from last lesson and the rule from this lesson together say that you can multiply the top and bottom of a fraction by the same number to get an equivalent fraction or divide the top and bottom of a fraction by the same number to get an equivalent fraction. Both of these rules together are called the **Law of Equivalent Fractions**.

The Law of Equivalent Fractions

> **You can multiply or divide the top and bottom of a fraction by the same number to get another equal fraction.**

---

[1] Remember, dividing the top and bottom by 0 doesn't work because you can't divide by 0.

Practice 99

a. Add $8\frac{3}{5}+3\frac{1}{5}$ _____

b. Which two equivalent fractions do these pentagons represent? _____

c. If we divided the top and bottom of $\frac{12}{18}$ by 6, what would we get? _____

Solve each word problem below.

d. In 1783 the hot air balloon was invented, and in 1958 lasers were invented. How many years was it between these events? _____

e. Helen has made 58 pieces of homemade fudge and now she's putting those pieces into Christmas tins. If each tin can only hold 9 pieces of fudge, how many tins will she need? _____

Problem Set 99

Tell whether each sentence below is True or False.

1. Dividing the top and bottom of a fraction by the same number will always create an equivalent fraction. _____

2. The Law of Equivalent Fractions says that you can multiply or divide the top and bottom of any fraction by the same number, except 0, without changing the fraction's value. _____

Answer each question below

3.   What is the radius of circle *P*? _____

4.   Tell whether the quadrilateral below is a plain quadrilateral, trapezoid, parallelogram, rhombus, rectangle, or a square. _____

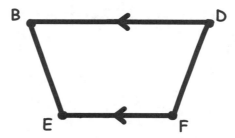

Write a mixed number to tell what each picture below represents.

5.   _____

6.   _____

Answer each question below.

7. If it is 7 miles from Doolittle to Perfect City, how many yards is it? _____

8. In 2007, a 16-pound baby was born in northeastern Brazil. How many ounces did the baby weigh? _____

Convert each improper fraction below into a mixed number.

9. $\dfrac{14}{9}$ _____   **10.** $\dfrac{35}{8}$ _____

Multiply or divide (as required) each pair of numbers below.

11. $5\overline{)625}$ **12.** $\begin{array}{r} 521 \\ \times\, 431 \\ \hline \end{array}$

Add or subtract (as required) each pair of fractions below.

13. $\dfrac{2}{11} + \dfrac{7}{11}$ _____   **14.** $\dfrac{8}{9} - \dfrac{4}{9}$ _____

Add or subtract (as required) each pair of mixed numbers below.

(a) 15. $8\dfrac{6}{17} + 4\dfrac{5}{17}$ _____   **16.** $7\dfrac{9}{13} - 4\dfrac{2}{13}$ _____

Answer each question below.

17. How many pieces of the rectangle on the right must be shaded to create a fraction that's equal to $\frac{3}{4}$? _____

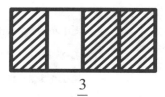 

$\frac{3}{4}$

(b) 18. Which two equivalent fractions do these pies represent? _____

(c) 19. If we divided the top and bottom of $\frac{6}{8}$ by 2, what would we get? _____

20. If we divided the top and bottom of $\frac{12}{15}$ by 3, what would we get? _____

Solve each word problem below.

(d) 21. In 1841 the stapler was invented. In 1969 the staple remover was invented. How many years was it between these events? _____

(e) 22. Darla needs to put a total of 77 coupons into plastic bags. If she plans to put 3 coupons into every bag, how many bags will she need? _____

Lesson 100—Reducing Fractions

Dividing the top and bottom of a fraction by the same number to get an equivalent fraction is actually called **reducing** the fraction, and reducing is useful because smaller numbers are easier to work with. Here's an example.

$$\frac{6}{8} = \frac{6 \div 2}{8 \div 2} = \frac{3}{4}$$

Dividing the top and bottom by the same number is called reducing.

Since we divided the top and bottom by the same number, we know that $\frac{6}{8}$ and $\frac{3}{4}$ are equivalent fractions. Here's another example of reducing.

$$\frac{10}{15} = \frac{10 \div 5}{15 \div 5} = \frac{2}{3}$$

Reducing $\frac{10}{15}$ to $\frac{2}{3}$.

To reduce this, we just asked ourselves, "What number will divide both 10 and 15 with no remainder?" Since 5 divides both 10 and 15 evenly, we divided the top and bottom by 5 to get $\frac{2}{3}$. Here's one more example.

Try to reduce $\frac{8}{13}$.

We start by looking for the number that will divide both 8 and 13 with no remainder, but as it turns out, no number will work besides 1. Dividing by 1 won't make the top or bottom smaller, so this fraction can't be reduced.

The main point of the lesson is that we can use the Law of Equivalent Fractions to make the top and bottom of fractions smaller, and that makes them easier to work with.

Practice 100

a. If we divided the top and bottom of $\frac{8}{16}$ by 8, what would we get? _____

Reduce each fraction below if possible.

b. $\frac{10}{12}$ _____   **c.** $\frac{9}{14}$ _____

Solve each word problem below.

d. Terry just baked 5 pizzas. If each pizza is cut into 14 slices, how many slices are there in all? _____

e. Jules bought a mini trampoline for $23.74. If she gave the cashier $30, how much did she receive in change? _____

Problem Set 100

Tell whether each sentence below is True or False.

1. When you change a fraction by dividing its top and bottom by the same number, it's called reducing the fraction. _____

2. When you make the top and bottom of a fraction smaller, it makes the fraction easier to work with. _____

Answer each question below.

3. If the desert cactus is 11 feet tall, how many inches tall is it? _____

4. If the mural painter bought 19 gallons of paint, how many quarts is that? _____

5. If the ant marathon is 5 meters long, how many decimeters is that? _____

Convert each improper fraction below into a mixed number.

6. $\dfrac{23}{5}$ _____

7. $\dfrac{41}{9}$ _____

Multiply or divide (as required) each pair of numbers below.

8. $\begin{array}{r} 612 \\ \times\, 17 \\ \hline \end{array}$

9. $4\overline{)165}$

10. $8\overline{)873}$

Add or subtract (as required) each pair of fractions below.

11. $\dfrac{7}{15}+\dfrac{1}{15}$ _____

12. $\dfrac{10}{17}-\dfrac{6}{17}$ _____

Add or subtract (as required) each pair of mixed numbers below.

13. $7\dfrac{3}{23}+2\dfrac{1}{23}$ _____

14. $8\dfrac{6}{13}-5\dfrac{4}{13}$ _____

Answer each question below.

15. Write a mixed number to tell what the picture below represents. _____

16. How many pieces of the pie on the right must be shaded to create a fraction that's equal to $\frac{1}{4}$? _____

$\frac{1}{4}$

(a) 17. If we divided the top and bottom of $\frac{7}{21}$ by 7, what would we get? _____

Reduce each fraction below if possible.

(b) 18. $\frac{8}{10}$ _____   **19.** $\frac{6}{9}$ _____

(c) 20. $\frac{7}{11}$ _____

Solve each word problem below.

(d) 21. Valerie put 6 candy canes in each gift basket. If there were 17 gift baskets, how many candy canes were there in all? _____

(e) 22. Happy bought a balancing pole for $21.58. If he gave the cashier $30, how much did he receive in change? _____

Lesson 101—Comparing Fractions

Sometimes it's necessary to compare two fractions to see which is greater. Here's an example.

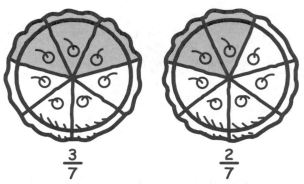

$$\frac{3}{7} \qquad \frac{2}{7}$$

Which fraction is greater?

In this problem, the pictures give it away because you can see that the pie on the left has more pieces shaded than the pie on the right. However, if we don't have a picture, we can still compare the fractions really easily because the bottoms of both fractions are the same. When the bottoms are the same, we just have to compare the tops, so $\frac{3}{7} > \frac{2}{7}$.

Sometimes there are no pictures to look at and the two fractions don't have the same number on bottom either, which means we can't just compare their tops. Fortunately, in a case like that, there's still a way to tell which fraction is bigger. Here's an example.

$$\frac{3}{9} \;\; ? \;\; \frac{2}{3}$$

$$\frac{3 \div 3}{9 \div 3} = \frac{1}{3} \;\; < \;\; \frac{2}{3}$$

Make the bottoms the same, then just compare the tops.

All we did was make the bottoms the same by dividing the top and bottom of three ninths by three, which gave us $\frac{1}{3}$. Then, since the bottoms were the same, we could compare the tops.

The main point of the lesson is that we can compare two fractions even when we don't have pictures to look at or the bottoms of the fractions are different. All we have to do is make the bottoms the same using the Law of Equivalent Fractions.

Practice 101

a. Reduce $\dfrac{6}{18}$ if possible. _____

Tell whether a <, >, or = should go between each pair of fractions below.

b. $\dfrac{1}{6}$ ___ $\dfrac{5}{6}$

c. $\dfrac{3}{7}$ ___ $\dfrac{4}{14}$

Solve each word problem below.

d. Mindy wants to buy a volleyball. The price tag says $13.25, but that doesn't include the tax. If the tax is 89¢, what will Mindy have to pay in dollars? _____

e. Alicia sent out a total of 144 of her floppy hats to 4 stores. If each store bought the same number of hats, how many did each buy? _____

Problem Set 101

Tell whether each sentence below is True or False.

1. When the bottoms of two fractions are the same, you just need to look at their tops to tell which is bigger. _____

2. When the bottoms of two fractions are different, you have to make the bottoms the same before you can tell which is bigger. _____

Answer each question below.

3. Kendra's hotel was 8 miles from the airport. How many yards was it from the airport? _____

4. By the time he reaches adulthood, a Chihuahua could weigh 8 pounds. How many ounces is that? _____

5. Moose, the all-star defensive lineman, ate 11 quarts of triple chocolate fudge ice cream in one weekend. How many pints is that? _____

Convert each improper fraction below into a mixed number.

6. $\dfrac{31}{6}$ _____

7. $\dfrac{25}{8}$ _____

Multiply or divide (as required) each pair of numbers below.

8. $3\overline{)314}$

9. $\begin{array}{r} 732 \\ \times\,613 \\ \hline \end{array}$

Add or subtract (as required) each pair of fractions below.

10. $\dfrac{3}{7}+\dfrac{2}{7}$ _____

11. $\dfrac{9}{11}-\dfrac{3}{11}$ _____

Add or subtract (as required) each pair of mixed numbers below.

12. $6\dfrac{4}{21}+1\dfrac{13}{21}$ _____

13. $4\dfrac{7}{19}-2\dfrac{2}{19}$ _____

Answer each question below.

14. How many pieces of the pie on the right must be shaded to create a fraction that's equal to $\dfrac{1}{4}$? _____

$\dfrac{1}{4}$

15. If we divided the top and bottom of $\dfrac{10}{12}$ by 2, what would we get? _____

Reduce each fraction below if possible.

(a) 16. $\dfrac{5}{15}$ _____

17. $\dfrac{5}{8}$ _____

Tell whether a <, >, or = should go between each pair of fractions below.

(b) 18. $\dfrac{4}{5}$ ___ $\dfrac{2}{5}$

(c) 19. $\dfrac{3}{12}$ ___ $\dfrac{3}{4}$

20. $\dfrac{2}{3}$ ___ $\dfrac{4}{6}$

Solve each word problem below.

(d) 21.   Garrett wants to buy a model hot rod kit. The price tag says $14.75, but that doesn't include the tax. If the tax is 74¢, what will Garrett have to pay in dollars? _____

(e) 22.   Adrianna sent out a total of 196 of her butterfly capes to 7 stores. If each store bought the same number of capes, how many did each buy? _____

Lesson 102—More on Reducing Fractions

Sometimes after adding or subtracting two fractions, the answer will need to be reduced. Here's an example.

$$\frac{1}{9} + \frac{2}{9} = \frac{3}{9}$$

$$\frac{3}{9} = \frac{3 \div 3}{9 \div 3} = \frac{1}{3}$$

Reducing $\frac{3}{9}$ to get a final answer of $\frac{1}{3}$.

After we added the fractions, we got $\frac{3}{9}$. However, we knew from before that $\frac{3}{9}$ could be reduced by dividing the top and bottom by 3 to get $\frac{1}{3}$. Remember, it's always better to reduce fractions if possible because it's easier to work with smaller numbers. Here's another example.

$$\frac{3}{8} - \frac{1}{8} = \frac{2}{8}$$

$$\frac{2}{8} = \frac{2 \div 2}{8 \div 2} = \frac{1}{4}$$

Reducing $\frac{2}{8}$ to get a final answer of $\frac{1}{4}$.

Since the bottoms were the same, we just subtracted the tops and kept the same bottom. However, the answer of $\frac{2}{8}$ could be reduced by dividing the top and bottom by 2. After reducing, the final answer is $\frac{1}{4}$.

There are even times when we need to reduce an answer after adding or subtracting mixed numbers. Here's an example.

$$5\frac{3}{4} - 2\frac{1}{4} = 3\frac{1}{2}$$

$$5 - 2 = \boxed{3}$$

$$\frac{3}{4} - \frac{1}{4} = \boxed{\frac{2}{4}} = \frac{2 \div 2}{4 \div 2} = \boxed{\frac{1}{2}}$$

Subtract the whole number and fraction parts separately, then reduce the fraction part.

After subtracting the fraction part, we ended up with $\frac{2}{4}$, which can be reduced. The final answer, then, was $3\frac{1}{2}$.

The main point of the lesson is that whenever there's a fraction in your answer, check to see whether there's a number (besides 1) that will divide the top and bottom without a remainder. If there is, the answer needs to be reduced.

Practice 102

a. Tell whether a <, >, or = should go between these two fractions $\dfrac{6}{10}$ ___ $\dfrac{4}{5}$.

b. Subtract $\dfrac{7}{12} - \dfrac{5}{12}$, and make sure your answer is reduced. _____

c. Add $4\dfrac{1}{10} + 3\dfrac{1}{10}$, and make sure the fraction part of your answer is reduced. _____

Solve each word problem below.

d. Phillip needs to memorize 288 words for his French test. If he wants to memorize all the words in 6 days, and he plans to memorize the same number of words each day, how many words should he memorize each day? _____

e. The iron-jawed lizard has been helping to destroy the enemy's power supply for the last 3 weeks. He ate 42 fuse boxes in the first week, 39 in the second week, and 54 in the third week. What was the average number of fuse boxes eaten each week? _____

Problem Set 102

Tell whether each sentence below is True or False.

1. Sometimes after you add or subtract two fractions the answer will need to be reduced.
    _____

2. When you add or subtract two mixed numbers the answer never needs to be reduced.
    _____

Answer each question below.

3. Write 89% as a fraction. _____

4. Write $\frac{13}{100}$ as a percent. _____

Multiply or divide (as required) each pair of numbers below.

5. $\begin{array}{r} 321 \\ \times\,41 \\ \hline \end{array}$

6. $5\overline{)627}$

Answer each question below.

7. Johnny bought a remote-controlled tank that was 2 feet long. How many inches long was it? _____

8. The soccer player made a goal from a distance of 7 decameters. How many meters is that? _____

Convert each improper fraction below into a mixed number.

9. $\frac{17}{2}$ _____

10. $\frac{33}{7}$ _____

11. If we divided the top and bottom of $\frac{9}{15}$ by 3, what would we get? _____

Reduce each fraction below if possible.

12. $\dfrac{3}{18}$ _____

13. $\dfrac{7}{12}$ _____

Tell whether a <, >, or = should go between each pair of fractions below.

14. $\dfrac{5}{7}$ ___ $\dfrac{6}{7}$

(a) 15. $\dfrac{6}{16}$ ___ $\dfrac{1}{8}$

Add or subtract (as required) each pair of fractions below, and make sure your final answer is reduced.

16. $\dfrac{5}{17}+\dfrac{1}{17}$ _____

(b) 17. $\dfrac{5}{6}-\dfrac{1}{6}$ _____

18. $\dfrac{1}{4}+\dfrac{1}{4}$ _____

Add or subtract (as required) each pair of mixed numbers below, and make sure the fraction part of your answer is reduced.

19. $7\dfrac{5}{9}-2\dfrac{4}{9}$ _____

(c) 20. $3\dfrac{1}{8}+2\dfrac{5}{8}$ _____

Solve each word problem below.

(d) 21. Danielle needs to memorize 252 words for her Spanish test. If she wants to memorize all the words in 7 days, and she plans to memorize the same number of words each day, how many words should she memorize each day? _____

(e) 22. The castle bot has been practicing his jousting skills for the last 3 days. On the first day, he made 59 jousting runs. On the second day, he made 51 jousting runs, and on the third day he made 61 jousting runs. What was the average number of runs each day? _____

Lesson 103—Adding and Subtracting Fractions with Different Denominators

It's actually possible to add two fractions that don't have the same bottoms by making the denominators the same. Here's an example.

$$\frac{1}{8} + \frac{1}{4} = \frac{1}{8} + \frac{2}{8} = \frac{3}{8}$$

$$\frac{1}{4} = \frac{1 \times 2}{4 \times 2} = \frac{2}{8}$$

Make the bottoms the same, then just add the tops.

The bottoms of the two fractions were different, but we made them the same by multiplying the top and bottom of $\frac{1}{4}$ by 2. We couldn't change $\frac{1}{8}$ because there is no number besides 1 that will divide both the top and bottom evenly. After we multiplied the top and bottom of $\frac{1}{4}$ by 2, we were left with $\frac{1}{8} + \frac{2}{8}$. So the final answer was $\frac{3}{8}$, but the main point is that whenever we add two fractions with different denominators, we first have to make both denominators the same.

Here's an example using subtraction.

$$\frac{2}{5} - \frac{3}{10} = \frac{4}{10} - \frac{3}{10} = \frac{1}{10}$$

$$\frac{2}{5} = \frac{2 \times 2}{5 \times 2} = \frac{4}{10}$$

Make the bottoms the same, then just subtract the tops.

Once again, we had to multiply the top and bottom of one of the fractions to make the bottoms the same. First, we thought of the number that can be multiplied by 5 to get 10, which was 2. We then multiplied the top and bottom of $\frac{2}{5}$ by 2 to get $\frac{4}{10}$, which made the problem $\frac{4}{10} - \frac{3}{10}$. The last step was to just subtract the tops since the bottoms were the same. The main point of this example is that subtracting fractions with different denominators works basically the same as adding with different denominators. Just remember to multiply both the top and bottom of the fraction that's being changed. Otherwise, the new fraction won't be equivalent to the original one.

Practice 103

Add or subtract (as required) each pair of fractions below.

a. $\dfrac{5}{12}+\dfrac{1}{6}$ _____

b. $\dfrac{4}{5}-\dfrac{4}{15}$ _____

c. Add $4\dfrac{3}{8}+3\dfrac{1}{8}$, and make sure the fraction part of your answer is reduced. _____

Solve each word problem below.

d. Everyday, Digger delivers mail to 54 different houses. How many houses will he deliver mail to after 6 days? _____

e. Ursula bought a new costume for $24.35. If she gave the cashier $40, how much did she receive in change? _____

Problem Set 103

Tell whether each sentence below is True or False.

1. To add two fractions with different denominators, you first have to make both denominators the same. _____

2. Subtracting fractions with different denominators works basically the same as adding fractions with different denominators. _____

Multiply or divide (as required) each pair of numbers below.

3. $6\overline{)503}$

4. $\begin{array}{r} 165 \\ \times\, 12 \\ \hline \end{array}$

5. $4\overline{)435}$

Answer each question below.

6. If the playground is 26 yards wide, how many feet is that? _____

7. If the bowling ball weighs 14 pounds, how many ounces is that? _____

8. For lunch, Baby Gargantua ate some nachos that had 6 gallons of melted cheese on them. How many quarts of cheese is that? _____

Convert each improper fraction below into a mixed number.

9. $\dfrac{29}{5}$ _____

10. $\dfrac{43}{7}$ _____

Reduce each fraction below if possible.

11. $\dfrac{5}{13}$ _____

12. $\dfrac{12}{15}$ _____

Tell whether a <, >, or = should go between each pair of fractions below.

13. $\dfrac{8}{9}$ ____ $\dfrac{7}{9}$

14. $\dfrac{2}{14}$ ____ $\dfrac{1}{7}$

Add or subtract (as required) each pair of fractions below, and make sure your final answer is reduced.

15. $\dfrac{6}{19}+\dfrac{2}{19}$ _____

16. $\dfrac{7}{10}-\dfrac{1}{10}$ _____

(a) 17. $\dfrac{1}{6}+\dfrac{2}{3}$ _____

(b) 18. $\dfrac{4}{7}-\dfrac{3}{14}$ _____

Add or subtract (as required) each pair of mixed numbers below, and make sure the fraction part of your answer is reduced.

19. $5\dfrac{4}{13}-4\dfrac{2}{13}$ _____

(c) 20. $3\dfrac{1}{4}+2\dfrac{1}{4}$ _____

Solve each word problem below.

(d) 21.   Everyday, Sven does 95 push-ups. How many push-ups will he do after 7 days?

   _____

(e) 22.   Clarisse bought a new tea set for $35.65. If she gave the cashier $50, how much did she receive in change?   _____

Lesson 104—Adding and Subtracting More than Two Fractions

Adding or subtracting more than two fractions works basically the same as adding two. Here's an example.

$$\frac{1}{9} + \frac{2}{9} + \frac{4}{9} = \frac{7}{9}$$

Just add the tops and keep the bottoms the same.

Notice that all three denominators were the same, so we were able to just add the tops while keeping the bottoms the same, which gave us an answer of $\frac{7}{9}$. Here's a subtraction example.

$$\frac{5}{7} - \frac{2}{7} - \frac{1}{7} = \frac{2}{7}$$

Just subtract the tops and keep the bottoms the same.

Again, we first looked at the denominators and noticed that they were all the same, so we just subtracted the tops and put the result over 7. The final answer, then, was $\frac{2}{7}$. Here's an example that includes both addition and subtraction.

$$\frac{7}{10} + \frac{1}{10} - \frac{3}{10} = \frac{5}{10}$$

The bottoms are the same, so add and subtract the tops.

After adding and subtracting the tops, we got an answer of $\frac{5}{10}$, but that can be reduced by dividing the top and bottom by 5.

$$\frac{5}{10} = \frac{5 \div 5}{10 \div 5} = \frac{1}{2}$$

Make sure the answer is fully reduced.

Once we reduced, we found the answer to the problem was $\frac{1}{2}$. The key thing to remember, though, is that adding three fractions with the same denominators is basically the same as adding two, but don't forget to check to see if the answer can be reduced.

Practice 104

Add or subtract (as required) each group of fractions below, and make sure your final answer is reduced.

a. $\dfrac{5}{9}+\dfrac{1}{18}$ _____

b. $\dfrac{3}{7}+\dfrac{2}{7}+\dfrac{1}{7}$ _____

c. $\dfrac{5}{12}+\dfrac{5}{12}-\dfrac{1}{12}$ _____

Solve each word problem below.

d. Malcolm put 7 cans in each box for the food drive. If there were 22 boxes, how many cans were there in all? _____

e. Rex needs to cut a 59-inch piece of tubing into 8-inch long pieces. How many pieces will he end up with? Write your answer as a mixed number. _____

Problem Set 104

Tell whether each sentence below is True or False.

1. To add three fractions with the same denominators, just add the tops and keep the bottom the same. _____

2. It's impossible to subtract three fractions with the same denominator. _____

Multiply or divide (as required) each pair of numbers below.

3. $7\overline{)764}$

4. $\begin{array}{r}41\\ \times\,24\\ \hline\end{array}$

Answer each question below.

5. If there are 17 pints of orange juice left in the cafeteria, how many ounces is that? _____

6. If it is 6 miles from Gridiron to Hoopsville, how many yards is that? _____

7. If the water slide is 36 meters high, how many decimeters is that? _____

Convert each improper fraction below into a mixed number.

8. $\dfrac{19}{4}$ _____

9. $\dfrac{35}{6}$ _____

Tell whether a <, >, or = should go between each pair of fractions below.

10. $\dfrac{5}{11}$ ___ $\dfrac{6}{11}$

11. $\dfrac{5}{12}$ ___ $\dfrac{5}{6}$

Add or subtract (as required) each pair of fractions below, and make sure your final answer is reduced.

12. $\dfrac{8}{13}+\dfrac{4}{13}$ _____

13. $\dfrac{7}{9}-\dfrac{4}{9}$ _____

(a) 14. $\dfrac{1}{10}+\dfrac{4}{5}$ _____

15. $\dfrac{3}{8}-\dfrac{1}{16}$ _____

Add or subtract (as required) each pair of mixed numbers below, and make sure the fraction part of your answer is reduced.

16. $6\dfrac{2}{5}+1\dfrac{1}{5}$ _____

17. $7\dfrac{8}{9}-6\dfrac{2}{9}$ _____

Add or subtract (as required) each group of fractions below, and make sure your final answer is reduced.

(b) 18. $\dfrac{4}{9} + \dfrac{2}{9} + \dfrac{1}{9}$ _____

19. $\dfrac{9}{11} - \dfrac{5}{11} - \dfrac{2}{11}$ _____

(c) 20. $\dfrac{5}{14} + \dfrac{3}{14} - \dfrac{1}{14}$ _____

Solve each word problem below.

(d) 21. Marilu put 8 mini candy bars in each of the kids' baskets. If there were 29 baskets, how many mini candy bars were there in all? _____

(e) 22. Hoss needs to cut a 53-inch strip of leather into 7-inch long pieces. How many pieces will he end up with? Write your answer as a mixed number. _____

Lesson 105—Multiplication and Decimals

Sometimes it's necessary to multiply two decimals. Here's an example.

$$5.46 \times 2.3$$

We start off by putting 5.46 on top of 2.3, but when multiplying decimals, the decimal points don't actually have to be lined up. Instead, we put the bottom number all the way over to the right. This is different from adding and subtracting decimals where the decimal points *do* have to be lined up. The next step is to multiply the numbers without paying any attention to the decimal points.

$$
\begin{array}{r}
\overset{1}{5}.\overset{1}{4}6 \\
\times \quad 2.3 \\
\hline
1638 \\
+\ 10920 \\
\hline
12558
\end{array}
$$

Ignore the decimal points and multiply like they're whole numbers.

Notice that we just ignored the decimal points and multiplied as though both numbers were whole numbers. After we multiplied and added the columns, we ended up with 12558, and now we'll put in the decimal point. To place the decimal point, we just have to count the number of digits to the right of the point in each of the numbers we multiplied. That tells us where to put the decimal point in the answer.

5.46   2.3

two places to the right   one place to the right

2 + 1 = 3, so move decimal point three places from the right in the answer.

Since there are two places to the right in 5.46 and one place to the right in 2.3, the answer needs to have three places to the right of the decimal point.

12558.

12.558

Moving the decimal point over three places.

So the final answer is 12.558. Here's one more example.

$$
\begin{array}{r}
\overset{1}{6}.23 \\
\times \quad 4 \\
\hline
2492
\end{array}
$$

Ignore the decimal points and multiply.

Again, we just multiplied, ignoring the decimal points, to get 2492. Now we just need to place the decimal point in the answer by counting the number of digits to the right point in each of the numbers that were multiplied.

$$6.23 \qquad\qquad 4$$

two places to the right   no places to the right

2 + 0 = 2, so move decimal point two places from the right in the answer.

Since there are two places to the right of the point in 6.23 and no places to the right in 4 (because it's a whole number), the answer should have only two places to the right.

2492.   **Moving the decimal**

24.92   **point over two places.**

Practice 105

a. Calculate $\dfrac{8}{15} + \dfrac{4}{15} - \dfrac{2}{15}$, and make sure your final answer is reduced. _____

Multiply each pair of numbers below.

b.
$$\begin{array}{r} 7.45 \\ \times\, 1.3 \\ \hline \end{array}$$

c.
$$\begin{array}{r} 2.87 \\ \times\, 3 \\ \hline \end{array}$$

Solve each word problem below.

d. Chester wants to buy a kaleidoscope for his friend. The price tag says $7.25, but that doesn't include the tax. If the tax is 54¢, what will Chester have to pay in dollars? _____

e. Sergio has been reading a book about pirates for the last 3 days. He read 24 pages the first day, 36 pages the second day, and 27 pages the third day. How many pages did he read on average each day? _____

Problem Set 105

Tell whether each sentence below is True or False.

1. When multiplying two decimals, the decimal points need to be lined up. _____

2. To multiply a whole number and a decimal, you must first change the whole number into a decimal. _____

Write each number below as a decimal.

3. eighty-five and thirty-six hundredths _____

4. twenty-three and forty-one thousandths _____

Add or subtract (as required) each pair of decimals below.

5. $\begin{array}{r} 34.92 \\ + \ 2.17 \\ \hline \end{array}$

6. $\begin{array}{r} 59.84 \\ - \ 42.72 \\ \hline \end{array}$

Answer each question below.

7. If the butler has 13 quarts of window cleaner in the closet, how many pints is that? _____

8. If the computer monitor weighs 15 pounds, how many ounces is that? _____

Reduce each fraction below if possible.

9. $\dfrac{3}{21}$ _____

10. $\dfrac{2}{9}$ _____

Add or subtract (as required) each pair of numbers below, and make sure your final answer is reduced.

11. $\dfrac{7}{12} - \dfrac{5}{12}$ _____

12. $\dfrac{1}{20} + \dfrac{7}{10}$ _____

13. $\dfrac{9}{14} - \dfrac{1}{7}$ _____

14. $8\dfrac{4}{9} + 4\dfrac{1}{9}$ _____

Add or subtract (as required) each group of fractions below, and make sure your final answer is reduced.

15. $\dfrac{5}{13} + \dfrac{3}{13} + \dfrac{2}{13}$ _____

16. $\dfrac{11}{14} - \dfrac{5}{14} - \dfrac{1}{14}$ _____

(a) 17. $\dfrac{3}{6} + \dfrac{2}{6} - \dfrac{1}{6}$ _____

Multiply each pair of numbers below.

(b) 18.
$\begin{array}{r} 4.13 \\ \times\, 1.5 \\ \hline \end{array}$

19.
$\begin{array}{r} 6.47 \\ \times\, 1.2 \\ \hline \end{array}$

(c) 20.
$\begin{array}{r} 5.43 \\ \times\, 4 \\ \hline \end{array}$

Solve each word problem below.

(d) 21. Franklin wants to buy a frozen pizza at the store. The price tag says $5.85, but that doesn't include the tax. If the tax is 38¢, what will Millie have to pay in dollars?

_____

(e) 22. The skyscraper window washer has worked only part-time for each of the last 3 weeks. The first week, he worked 39 hours. The second week, he worked 31 hours, and the third week he worked 38 hours. How many hours did he work on average each week?

_____

Lesson 106—Multiplying Whole Numbers and Decimals by 10, 100, and 1,000

It's actually possible to multiply decimal numbers by 10 without multiplying the numbers on paper. Here's an example.

$$7.89 \times 10$$

To solve this problem, all we have to do is move the decimal point one place to the right.

$$7.89 \rightarrow 78.9$$

To multiply a decimal by 10, move the decimal point one place to the right.

To multiply a decimal by 100, just move the decimal *two* places to the right.

$$2.534 \times 100$$
$$2.534 \rightarrow 253.4$$

To multiply a decimal by 100, move the decimal point two places to the right.

Multiplying a decimal by 1,000 is also easy; you just move the decimal point *three* places to the right.

$$0.567 \times 1,000$$
$$0.567 \rightarrow 567$$

To multiply a decimal by 1,000, move the decimal point three places to the right.

So the pattern here is that every time we multiply a decimal by 10 or a multiple of 10, like 100 or 1,000, all we have to do is move the decimal point to the right. And we always move it as many places to the right as there are zeros in the number we're multiplying by.

This rule for multiplying by moving the decimal point will work on whole numbers as well as decimals. You've already learned that you can multiply numbers by 10 in your head by adding a zero to the number being multiplied. Well, we could also multiply by 10 by moving the decimal point to the right. Here's an example.

$$1,986 \times 10$$
$$1,986.0 \rightarrow 19,860$$

Multiplying by 10 by moving the decimal point.

Notice that we got the same answer that we would have gotten had we just added a zero.

Practice 106

a. Multiply $\begin{array}{r} 8.17 \\ \times\ 2 \\ \hline \end{array}$

Multiply each pair of numbers below in your head.

b. 16.73×10 _____

c. $0.052 \times 1,000$ _____

Solve each word problem below.

d. In 1915 the first tank was invented, and in 1783 the first successful hot air balloon was launched. How many years was it between these two events? _____

e. Mr. Davidson picked 132 apples. If he put the apples into 6 sacks with the same number in each sack, how many apples are in each sack? _____

Problem Set 106

Tell whether each sentence below is True or False.

1. To multiply a decimal by 10, just move the decimal point one place to the right. _____

2. To multiply a decimal by 100, move the decimal point three places to the right. _____

Answer each question below.

3. If the seamstress has 21 yards of silk, how many feet is that? _____

4. If there are 11 gallons of sweet tea at the grocery store, how many quarts is that? _____

Divide each pair of numbers below.

5. $4\overline{)429}$

6. $5\overline{)624}$

Convert each improper fraction below into a mixed number.

7. $\dfrac{20}{9}$ _____

8. $\dfrac{32}{7}$ _____

Add or subtract (as required) each pair of numbers below, and make sure your final answer is reduced.

9. $\dfrac{1}{15}+\dfrac{4}{5}$ _____

10. $\dfrac{7}{18}-\dfrac{5}{18}$ _____

11. $6\dfrac{4}{5}-2\dfrac{3}{5}$ _____

12. $\dfrac{5}{12}-\dfrac{1}{4}$ _____

Add or subtract (as required) each group of fractions below, and make sure your final answer is reduced.

13. $\dfrac{11}{17}-\dfrac{5}{17}-\dfrac{1}{17}$ _____

14. $\dfrac{7}{16}+\dfrac{5}{16}-\dfrac{3}{16}$ _____

Multiply each pair of numbers below.

15. $\begin{array}{r} 8.32 \\ \times\ 2.4 \\ \hline \end{array}$

(a) 16. $\begin{array}{r} 3.72 \\ \times\ 6 \\ \hline \end{array}$

Multiply each pair of numbers below in your head.

(b) 17. 24.51×10 _____

18. 3.425×100 _____

(c) 19. $0.074 \times 1,000$ _____

20. $2,367 \times 100$ _____

Solve each word problem below.

(d) 21.   In 1623 the first automatic calculator was invented, and in 1284 the first pair of wearable eyeglasses was invented. How many years was it between these two events?

_____

(e) 22.   The goldsmith has a total of 115 medallions. If he separated the medallions into 5 groups with the same number in each group, how many medallions are in each group?

_____

Lesson 107—Multiplying with Decimals in the Real World

Multiplying decimals comes up quite often in real-life situations. Here's an example

The art teacher bought each of her 8 students a watercolor set. If each set cost $4.32, how much did she spend in all?

This problem is asking us to add 4.32 to itself 8 times, which is the same as 4.32×8.

$$
\begin{array}{r}
\overset{2}{}\overset{1}{} \\
4.32 \\
\times 8 \\
\hline
3456
\end{array}
$$

Multiplying but ignoring the decimal points at first.

After multiplying, we have to place the decimal point by counting the number of digits to the right of the point in each of the numbers that we multiplied. Then we need to put the dollar sign back.

$$
\begin{array}{r}
3456. \\
\$34.56
\end{array}
$$

Placing the decimal point and dollar sign.

Here's another problem.

Mrs. Adams bought 2.5 gallons of premium French vanilla ice cream. If she paid $5.89 for each gallon, how much did she spend in total?

Once again, we just need to multiply to solve the problem.

$$
\begin{array}{r}
\overset{1}{}\overset{1}{} \\
\overset{4}{}\overset{4}{} \\
5.89 \\
\times 2.5 \\
\hline
{}^{1}2945 \\
+ 11780 \\
\hline
14725
\end{array}
$$

Multiplying but ignoring the decimal points at first.

After multiplying, we just have to put in the decimal point and dollar sign. Since 5.89 has two places after the decimal point and 2.5 has one place, the answer should have three places after the decimal point. That leaves us with an amount that has thousandths in it, but since you can't pay somebody with part of a penny, we have to round.

$$
\begin{array}{r}
14725. \\
\$14.725 \longrightarrow \$14.73
\end{array}
$$

Round the answer to the nearest cent.

Also, notice that we had to round up because the number to the left of the 2 was 5.

The main point of this example is that sometimes with money problems, we end up with a digit in the thousandths place. When that happens, just round to the nearest hundredth—the nearest penny—the same way we round with whole numbers.

Practice 107

a. Calculate $\dfrac{7}{12} + \dfrac{1}{12} - \dfrac{5}{12}$, and make sure your final answer is reduced. _____

b. Multiply $0.092 \times 1,000$ in your head. _____

c. Multiply $\begin{array}{r} 9.17 \\ \times\ 6 \\ \hline \end{array}$

Solve each word problem below.

d. Kayla bought 7 deep dish pizzas. If each pizza costs $8.25, how much did she spend in all? _____

e. Mrs. Honeycutt bought 4.5 pints of syrup. If she paid $1.85 for each pint, how much did she spend in total? Round your answer to the nearest penny. _____

Problem Set 107

Tell whether each sentence below is True or False.

1. Whenever you're multiplying with decimals, it's better to ignore the decimal points until the end of the problem. _____

2. Sometimes when you multiply two dollar amounts, you have to round your answer to the nearest penny. _____

Add or subtract (as required) each pair of decimals below.

3. $\begin{array}{r} 82.73 \\ -\ 31.52 \\ \hline \end{array}$

4. $\begin{array}{r} 25.19 \\ +\ 17.46 \\ \hline \end{array}$

Divide each pair of numbers below.

5. $2\overline{)503}$

6. $3\overline{)625}$

Answer each question below.

7. If Tootsie has 14 feet of yarn, how many inches is that? _____

8. If the stage is 9 decameters wide, how many meters is that? _____

Reduce each fraction below if possible.

9. $\dfrac{3}{24}$ _____

10. $\dfrac{5}{20}$ _____

Add or subtract (as required) each pair of numbers below, and make sure your final answer is reduced.

11. $\dfrac{1}{9} + \dfrac{2}{3}$ _____

12. $\dfrac{7}{8} - \dfrac{1}{8}$ _____

13. $7\frac{6}{7} - 4\frac{1}{7}$ _____

14. $\frac{8}{21} - \frac{1}{7}$ _____

Add or subtract (as required) each group of fractions below, and make sure your final answer is reduced.

15. $\frac{4}{19} + \frac{2}{19} + \frac{3}{19}$ _____

(a) 16. $\frac{3}{10} + \frac{3}{10} - \frac{1}{10}$ _____

Multiply each pair of numbers below in your head.

17. 8.412×100 _____

(b) 18. $0.081 \times 1,000$ _____

Multiply each pair of numbers below.

19.
$$\begin{array}{r} 2.81 \\ \times\ 3.1 \\ \hline \end{array}$$

(c) 20.
$$\begin{array}{r} 7.93 \\ \times\ 8 \\ \hline \end{array}$$

Solve each word problem below.

(d) 21. Sammy bought 9 packages of baseball cards. If each package costs $3.15, how much did he spend in all? _____

(e) 22. Mr. Wrigley bought 3.5 quarts of potato salad. If he paid $2.95 for each quart, how much did he spend in total? Round your answer to the nearest penny. _____

Lesson 108—Zeros We Don't Need

There are some special situations that come up when multiplying decimals. Here's an example.

$$
\begin{array}{r}
\overset{1}{\overset{}{}}\ \overset{1}{\overset{}{}} \\
4.08 \\
\times\ \ \ 1.5 \\
\hline
2040 \\
+4080 \\
\hline
6120
\end{array}
$$

Multiplying but ignoring the decimal points at first.

After multiplying, we just have to put in the decimal point. Since there are a total of three digits to the right of the decimal points in the numbers being multiplied, the answer should have three digits to the right of the decimal point. That leaves us with 6.120, but we can get rid of the zero to make the answer look simpler.

6120

6.120 → 6.12

Eliminate the zero at the end.

So whenever you end up with an answer that has a 0 on the very end of it, you should get rid of the 0 unless the answer involves dollars and cents and the 0 is in the hundredths place.

You *can't* get rid of a zero if your answer is a number like 3.06.

3.06

You can't get rid of the zero here.

Notice that in this case, the 0 isn't on the far right. The 6 in 3.06 stands for 6 hundredths, so 3.06 means 3 and 6 hundredths. If we were to change the number to 3.6, we'd be making it bigger since 3.6 is the same as 3.60 and that stands for 3 and *60* hundredths. So again, remember that you can get rid of zeros on the end of an answer unless the 0 is in the hundredths place of a money problem, and the reason for getting rid of zeros is that it makes the answer look a little simpler without actually changing it.

Practice 108

a. Simplify 65.800 (without changing the value of the number). _____

Multiply each pair of numbers below, and if there are any extra 0s, be sure to eliminate them.

b.
```
  7.29
×    4
─────
```

c.
```
  9.85
× 6.4
─────
```

Solve each word problem below.

d. Carmen took 3 quizzes. She made an 85 on her first quiz, a 78 on her second quiz, and a 92 on her third quiz. What was her average score? _____

e. Sherman bought 4 model cars with his birthday money. If each model car cost $6.75, how much did he spend in all? _____

Problem Set 108

Tell whether each sentence below is True or False.

1. When you are multiplying decimals, a lot of times you'll get extra zeros to the right, after figuring out where the decimal point goes. _____

2. If you end up with an answer like 8.07, it's okay to just get rid of the 0 and make the answer 8.7. _____

Add or subtract (as required) each pair of decimals below.

3.
```
  49.21
+ 23.84
──────
```

4.
```
  64.15
− 32.92
──────
```

Tell whether a <, >, or = should go between each pair of fractions below.

5. $1 \underline{\quad\quad} \dfrac{7}{6}$

6. $\dfrac{2}{9} \underline{\quad\quad} \dfrac{2}{18}$

Answer each question below.

7. If the race is 2 miles long, how many yards is that? _____

8. If a pitcher contains 2 pints, how many ounces is that? _____

9. Simplify 23.400 (without changing the value of the number). _____

Reduce each fraction below if possible.

10. $\dfrac{2}{9}$ _____

11. $\dfrac{7}{28}$ _____

Add or subtract (as required) each pair of numbers below, and make sure your final answer is reduced.

12. $\dfrac{1}{12} - \dfrac{1}{24}$ _____

13. $5\dfrac{1}{8} + 2\dfrac{3}{8}$ _____

Add or subtract (as required) each group of fractions below, and make sure your final answer is reduced.

14. $\dfrac{6}{7} - \dfrac{3}{7} - \dfrac{1}{7}$ _____

15. $\dfrac{7}{11} + \dfrac{3}{11} - \dfrac{2}{11}$ _____

Multiply each pair of numbers below in your head.

16. 16.253×10 _____

17. 0.068×100 _____

Multiply each pair of numbers below, and if there are any extra 0s, be sure to eliminate them.

18.
$$\begin{array}{r} 6.37 \\ \times\ 2.6 \\ \hline \end{array}$$

(b) 19.
$$\begin{array}{r} 8.35 \\ \times\ 5 \\ \hline \end{array}$$

(c) 20.
$$\begin{array}{r} 7.94 \\ \times\ 4.5 \\ \hline \end{array}$$

Solve each word problem below.

(d) 21. Eugene took 3 tests. He made a 95 on his first test, an 88 on his second test, and a 93 on his third test. What was his average score? _____

(e) 22. Happy bought 6 jumbo candy bars with his allowance. If each candy bar cost $1.25, how much did he spend in all? _____

Quiz 15

Tell whether each sentence below is True or False.

1. When multiplying two decimals, the decimal points need to be lined up. _____

2. To multiply a decimal by 100, move the decimal point three places to the right. _____

Tell whether a <, >, or = should go between each pair of fractions below.

3. $\frac{2}{5}$ ___ 1

4. $\frac{5}{15}$ ___ $\frac{2}{3}$

Add or subtract (as required) each pair of decimals below.

5. 62.47
   + 57.64

6. 83.52
   − 48.27

Answer each question below.

7. If a moon rock weighs 5 pounds, how many ounces is that? _____

8. If a cooking pot can hold up to 2 quarts, how many pints is that? _____

Convert each improper fraction below into a mixed number.

9. $\frac{13}{4}$ _____

10. $\frac{16}{5}$ _____

Add or subtract (as required) each pair of numbers below. Make sure your final answer is reduced.

11. $\dfrac{9}{10} - \dfrac{7}{10}$ _____

12. $8\dfrac{1}{3} + 5\dfrac{1}{3}$ _____

13. $\dfrac{7}{15} + \dfrac{5}{15}$ _____

Add or subtract (as required) each group of fractions below. Make sure your final answer is reduced.

14. $\dfrac{9}{14} - \dfrac{5}{14} - \dfrac{1}{14}$ _____

15. $\dfrac{7}{19} + \dfrac{4}{19} + \dfrac{3}{19}$ _____

Multiply each pair of numbers below in your head.

16. 7.852×100 _____

17. $0.109 \times 1,000$ _____

Answer each question below.

18. Simplify 42.900 (without changing the value of the number). _____

19. Simplify 30.610 (without changing the value of the number). _____

Multiply each pair of numbers below.

20. $\begin{array}{r} 634 \\ \times\ 12 \\ \hline \end{array}$

21. $\begin{array}{r} 6.27 \\ \times\ 3.1 \\ \hline \end{array}$

22.
$$
\begin{array}{r}
8.36 \\
\times\ 8 \\
\hline
\end{array}
$$

Solve each word problem below.

23. Each member of the golf team hit a total of 45 balls at the driving range. If there are 5 members on the team, how many balls did they hit altogether? _____

24. Mr. Patterson bought 6.5 gallons of gasoline. If he paid $2.65 for each gallon, how much did he spend in total? Round your answer to the nearest penny. _____

Lesson 109—Adding a Zero to the Answer

Sometimes it's necessary to actually put a 0 in an answer when dealing with decimals. Here's an example.

$$0.12 \times 0.3$$

First, we need to put the number with more digits on top, and remember that the decimal points don't need to be lined up since we're multiplying. Also, we can erase the 0s to the left of each decimal point. Those are just there to show that there are no whole number parts in the numbers, and if we take them out it will help us do the problem faster. Next we can multiply, ignoring the decimal points at first.

$$\begin{array}{r} .12 \\ \times \ .3 \\ \hline 36 \end{array}$$

Multiplying but ignoring the decimal points at first.

Multiplying leaves us with 36, but to put the decimal point in the answer, we need to have three places to the right of the point, because .12 has two places after the decimal point and .3 has one place after the decimal point. Since there are only two digits in our answer, we can't count three spaces over from the right, so we have to put an extra zero to the left of the 3.

$$36 \longrightarrow 0.036$$

Fill in the hole with a zero.

After we filled in the zero and placed the decimal point, we also put a 0 to the left of the point just to make the point easier to see. That gave us a final answer of 0.036.

The main idea in this lesson is that there are times when we have to insert a 0 in order to place the decimal point in our answer. Otherwise, we wouldn't be able to count over enough spaces.

Practice 109

a. Subtract $\dfrac{14}{15} - \dfrac{7}{15} - \dfrac{2}{15}$, and make sure your final answer is reduced. _____

Multiply each pair of numbers below.

b.
$$\begin{array}{r} 2.74 \\ \times\ 8 \\ \hline \end{array}$$

c.
$$\begin{array}{r} 0.13 \\ \times 0.6 \\ \hline \end{array}$$

Solve each word problem below.

d. Wanda sold a total of 147 of her creature cookie jars to 7 stores. If each store bought the same number of cookie jars, how many did each buy? _____

e. Reese bought some new batting gloves for $27.65. If he gave the cashier $40, how much should he receive in change? _____

Problem Set 109

Tell whether each sentence below is True or False.

1. There are times when we have to put in an extra 0 in order to place the decimal point in our answer. _____

2. When multiplying $\begin{array}{r} 0.85 \\ \times\ 0.7 \\ \hline \end{array}$, you don't need the 0s to the left of the decimal point.

_____

Divide each pair of numbers below.

3. $7\overline{)638}$

4. $4\overline{)831}$

Convert each improper fraction below into a mixed number.

5. $\dfrac{57}{8}$ _____

6. $\dfrac{37}{4}$ _____

Answer each question below.

7. If you must be 5 feet tall to ride the roller coaster, how many inches tall do you need to be? _____

8. If the tree is 12 meters tall, how many decimeters is that? _____

(a) 9. If Brennan's dog weighs 15 pounds, how many ounces is that? _____

Reduce each fraction below if possible.

10. $\dfrac{3}{6}$ _____

11. $\dfrac{9}{10}$ _____

Add or subtract (as required) each pair of numbers below, and make sure your final answer is reduced.

12. $\dfrac{1}{2}-\dfrac{5}{14}$ _____

13. $3\dfrac{4}{9}+1\dfrac{1}{9}$ _____

Add or subtract (as required) each group of fractions below, and make sure your final answer is reduced.

14. $\dfrac{6}{13}+\dfrac{2}{13}+\dfrac{1}{13}$ _____

(a) 15. $\dfrac{11}{12}-\dfrac{7}{12}-\dfrac{1}{12}$ _____

Multiply each pair of numbers below in your head.

16. 14.375×100 _____

17. $0.847 \times 1,000$ _____

Multiply each pair of numbers below.

18.
$$\begin{array}{r} 5.41 \\ \times\ 6.3 \\ \hline \end{array}$$

(b) 19.
$$\begin{array}{r} 1.82 \\ \times\ 9 \\ \hline \end{array}$$

(c) 20.
$$\begin{array}{r} 0.21 \\ \times 0.4 \\ \hline \end{array}$$

Solve each word problem below.

(d) 21. Melinda sent out a total of 155 beaded necklaces to 5 stores. If each store bought the same number of necklaces, how many did each buy? _____

(e) 22. Victor bought some new bike reflectors for $12.35. If he gave the cashier $20, how much should he receive in change? _____

Lesson 110—Dividing a Decimal by a Whole Number

It's sometimes necessary to do division with decimals. Here's an example.

$$387.2 \div 4$$

In this case, we're dividing a decimal by a whole number, and the first step is to put the dividend inside the division box and the divisor outside. Next, we place the decimal point where it should go in the answer, which is always right above the decimal point in the dividend.

$$4\overline{)3\ 8\ 7.2}$$

Put the decimal point directly above the decimal point in the box.

After the decimal point is placed, we don't have to worry about it anymore. We can just pretend that we're dividing the whole number 3,872 by 4.

```
      9 6.8
 4 )3 8 7.2
   -3 6
      2 7
    -2 4
        3 2
      -3 2
          0
```

Just ignore the decimal point and divide normally.

Notice that we followed the four steps of normal long division, and after we brought down the last number, divided, multiplied, and subtracted, we got an answer of 96.8 with no remainder. The most important thing to remember is that dividing a decimal by a whole number is basically just like dividing two whole numbers. The only difference is that at the beginning, we have to put the decimal point where it belongs in the answer, and that's right above the decimal point in the dividend.

Practice 110

    a. Multiply $\begin{array}{r} 0.17 \\ \times\, 0.2 \\ \hline \end{array}$

Divide each pair of numbers below.

    b. $6\overline{)152.4}$ **c.** $7\overline{)834.4}$

Solve each word problem below.

    d. The Gamma force fired 27 missiles in the first battle, 36 missiles in the second battle, and 39 missiles in the third battle. What was the average number of missiles fired in each battle? _____

    e. Lizzie bought 5 fun bracelets at the mall. If each bracelet cost $2.85, how much did she spend in all? _____

Problem Set 110

Tell whether each sentence below is True or False.

    1. Dividing a decimal by a whole number is similar to dividing two whole numbers, except at the beginning, we have to put the decimal point where it belongs in the answer. _____

    2. When dividing a decimal by a whole number, the decimal point in the answer needs to go right above the decimal point in the number inside the box. _____

Add or subtract (as required) each pair of decimals below.

3. $\begin{array}{r} 29.15 \\ + 16.87 \\ \hline \end{array}$

4. $\begin{array}{r} 72.98 \\ - 35.61 \\ \hline \end{array}$

Answer each question below.

5.   If the bus is 15 yards long, how many feet is that? _____

6.   If Nate made 3 pints of snow ice cream, how many ounces is that? _____

Convert each improper fraction below into a mixed number.

7. $\dfrac{44}{5}$ _____

8. $\dfrac{65}{9}$ _____

Add or subtract (as required) each pair of numbers below, and make sure your final answer is reduced.

9. $7\dfrac{1}{6} + 4\dfrac{1}{6}$ _____

10. $\dfrac{9}{17} - \dfrac{4}{17}$ _____

Add or subtract (as required) each group of fractions below, and make sure your final answer is reduced.

11. $\dfrac{8}{19} + \dfrac{5}{19} + \dfrac{3}{19}$ _____

12. $\dfrac{11}{15} - \dfrac{7}{15} - \dfrac{1}{15}$ _____

Multiply each pair of numbers below in your head.

13. 29.846×100 _____

14. $1.269 \times 1,000$ _____

Multiply each pair of decimals below.

15.
$$
\begin{array}{r}
9.75 \\
\times\ 4.1 \\
\hline
\end{array}
$$

(a) 16.
$$
\begin{array}{r}
0.29 \\
\times\ 0.3 \\
\hline
\end{array}
$$

Divide each pair of numbers below.

17. $3\overline{)267}$

18. $8\overline{)819}$

Divide each pair of numbers below.

(b) 19. $2\overline{)133.8}$

(c) 20. $5\overline{)628.5}$

Solve each word problem below.

(d) 21. Monty hit 25 homeruns the first season, 31 homeruns the second season, and 43 homeruns the third season. What was the average number of homeruns for each season? _____

(e) 22. Valerie bought 7 thank you cards at the store. If each card cost $3.15, how much did she spend in all? _____

Lesson 111—Dividing Whole Numbers and Decimals by 10, 100, and 1,000

Dividing whole numbers and decimals by 10, 100, and 1,000 is just as easy as multiplying them. Here's an example.

$$143.7 \div 10$$

We could set this up in a division box and divide on paper, but the quickest way is to do it in your head by moving the decimal point. However, instead of moving the point to the right as we do when multiplying, we have to move it to the left.

$$143.7 \rightarrow 14.37$$

To divide a decimal by 10, move the decimal point one place to the left.

Dividing by 100 is nearly the same, except we have to move the decimal point *two* places to the left.

$$184.6 \div 100$$
$$184.6 \rightarrow 1.846$$

To divide a decimal by 100, move the decimal point two places to the left.

Notice that the number of places we moved the decimal point was always equal to the number of zeros in the number we were dividing by. Since 10 has *one* 0, we moved the point *one* place to the left, and since 100 has *two* 0s, we moved the point *two* places to the left.

Counting the zeros and moving the decimal point will even work with whole numbers. Here's an example.

$$593 \div 1,000$$
$$593 \rightarrow 0.593$$

To divide by 1,000, move the decimal point three places to the left.

Remember, 593 is the same as 593.0, and since there are *three* 0s in 1,000, we had to move the decimal point *three* places to the left. Also, notice that when we wrote the final answer, we made sure to add a 0 to the left of the point.

If you have trouble remembering whether to move the decimal point to the left or to the right, just remember that when you multiply, you're making the number bigger, and moving the point to the right also makes the number bigger. But when you divide, you're making the number smaller, and moving the decimal point to the left will also make the number smaller.

Practice 111

Divide each pair of numbers below in your head.

    a. $812.7 \div 10$ _____

    b. $732 \div 1,000$ _____

    c. Divide $9\overline{)577.8}$

Solve each word problem below.

    d. In 1492 Christopher Columbus set sail across the Atlantic, and in 1602 the colony of Jamestown was founded. How many years was it between these two events? _____

    e. Angelica wants to buy a new doll. The price tag says $11.45, but that doesn't include the tax. If the tax is 78¢, what will Angelica have to pay in dollars? _____

Problem Set 111

Tell whether each sentence below is True or False.

    1. Dividing a decimal by 10 is just like multiplying a decimal by 10 except instead of moving the point one place to the right, we move it one place to the left. _____

    2. We can divide any decimal by 100 just by moving the decimal point two places to the right. _____

    3. When dividing a decimal by 10, 100, or 1,000, the number of places we move the decimal point to the left is always equal to the number of zeros in the number we're dividing by. _____

Answer each question below.

4. If the ice cream store has 17 gallons of strawberry in the freezer, how many quarts is that? _____

5. If Archie has 16 feet of rope, how many inches is that? _____

Tell whether a <, >, or = should go between each pair of fractions below.

6. $\dfrac{8}{11}$ ____ 1

7. $\dfrac{3}{12}$ ____ $\dfrac{1}{4}$

Subtract each pair of numbers below, and make sure your final answer is reduced.

8. $4\dfrac{6}{7} - 2\dfrac{2}{7}$ _____

9. $\dfrac{5}{8} - \dfrac{5}{16}$ _____

Add or subtract (as required) each group of fractions below, and make sure your final answer is reduced.

10. $\dfrac{2}{9} + \dfrac{4}{9} + \dfrac{1}{9}$ _____

11. $\dfrac{7}{18} - \dfrac{5}{18} - \dfrac{1}{18}$ _____

Multiply each pair of numbers below in your head.

12. 51.32×10 _____

13. $0.015 \times 1,000$ _____

Divide each pair of numbers below in your head.

(a) 14. $154.3 \div 10$ _____

15. $1,732.9 \div 100$ _____

(b) 16. $207 \div 1,000$ _____

Multiply each pair of numbers below.

17.
8.27
× 4

18.
0.24
× 0.2

Divide each pair of numbers below.

(c) 19. 8)341.6

20. 3)415.5

Solve each word problem below.

(d) 21. In 1804 Lewis and Clark, began their famous expedition, and in 1926 Max Fleischer created the first animated cartoon. How many years was it between these two events?

_____

(e) 22. Theo wants to buy a new pair of sunglasses. The price tag says $12.65, but that doesn't include the tax. If the tax is 83¢, what will Theo have to pay in dollars? _____

Lesson 112—Dividing with Decimals in the Real World

In real-life, there are lots of situations where you have to divide with decimals. Here's an example.

> Tom bought 4 bags of Galaxy potato chips. If he spent $8.72 altogether, how much did each bag cost?

Since the total was $8.72, we have to break 8.72 down into 4 equal groups to find out how much each bag cost, which means we have to divide. The first step is to set up the division box and put 4 on the outside and 8.72 on the inside. Next, we just have to put the decimal point where it should go in the answer, which is directly above the decimal point inside the box. Then we can use the four steps of long division.

$$
\begin{array}{r}
2.1\ 8 \\
4\,\overline{)8.7\ 2} \\
-8 \\
\hline
0\ 7 \\
-\ 4 \\
\hline
3\ 2 \\
-3\ 2 \\
\hline
0
\end{array}
$$

Place the decimal point, then just divide normally.

After dividing, we found out that Tom must have paid $2.18 for each bag of potato chips. Here's another example.

> The scientist had 9.81 ounces of the special mixture. Then he poured it into 3 separate beakers. If each beaker now contains the same amount of mixture, how many ounces are in each beaker?

Once again, we just need to divide, remembering to put the decimal point in the answer directly above the decimal point in the number inside the box.

$$
\begin{array}{r}
3.2\ 7 \\
3\,\overline{)9.8\ 1} \\
-9 \\
\hline
0\ 8 \\
-\ 6 \\
\hline
2\ 1 \\
-2\ 1 \\
\hline
0
\end{array}
$$

Place the decimal point, then just divide normally.

So each beaker contains 3.27 ounces of the special mixture.

Practice 112

Divide each pair of numbers below in your head.

    a. $507.6 \div 100$ _____

    b. $652 \div 1,000$ _____

    c.   Divide $7\overline{)541.1}$

Solve each word problem below.

    d.   Willie scored a 78 on his first exam, an 81 on his second exam, and a 96 on his third exam. What was his average score? _____

    e.   Madeline bought 4 boxes of saltwater taffy. If she spent \$9.24 altogether, how much did each box cost? _____

Problem Set 112

Add or subtract (as required) each pair of decimals below.

    1.
$$\begin{array}{r} 56.32 \\ -\ 14.29 \\ \hline \end{array}$$

    2.
$$\begin{array}{r} 31.75 \\ +\ 28.94 \\ \hline \end{array}$$

Answer each question below.

    3.   Bruiser went to the gym and lifted 25 pounds. How many ounces is that? _____

    4.   If Chip ran 5 miles, how many yards is that? _____

Reduce each fraction below if possible.

5. $\dfrac{4}{17}$ _____

6. $\dfrac{10}{12}$ _____

Add or subtract (as required) each pair of numbers below, and make sure your final answer is reduced.

7. $\dfrac{1}{7}+\dfrac{8}{21}$ _____

8. $7\dfrac{5}{8}-3\dfrac{3}{8}$ _____

Add or subtract (as required) each group of fractions below, and make sure your final answer is reduced.

9. $\dfrac{5}{11}+\dfrac{2}{11}+\dfrac{3}{11}$ _____

10. $\dfrac{9}{20}-\dfrac{3}{20}-\dfrac{1}{20}$ _____

Multiply each pair of numbers below in your head.

11. 78.24×10 _____

12. $0.428\times1,000$ _____

Divide each pair of numbers below in your head.

13. $361.48\div10$ _____

(a) 14. $804.5\div100$ _____

(b) 15. $136\div1,000$ _____

Multiply each pair of numbers below.

16. $\begin{array}{r} 312 \\ \times\,123 \\ \hline \end{array}$

17. $\begin{array}{r} 4.13 \\ \times\,9 \\ \hline \end{array}$

18. $\begin{array}{r} 0.15 \\ \times\,0.5 \\ \hline \end{array}$

Divide each pair of numbers below.

(c) 19. $4\overline{)278.8}$ **20.** $6\overline{)794.4}$

Solve each word problem below.

(d) 21.   Herbie made a 68 on his first exam, a 74 on his second exam, and an 89 on his third exam. What was his average score? _____

(e) 22.   Jonathan bought 5 packs of super-sized bubble gum. If he spent $6.35 altogether, how much did each pack cost? _____

Lesson 113—The Number Line

There are times in math when it helps to write numbers on a line. Look at this line below.

The arrows show the number line
keeps going on forever.

Notice that we started at the mark with 0 underneath and as we move to the right, each new mark stands for the next whole number. Since the line goes on forever, so can the whole numbers.

Some lines don't even show every whole number.

Some number lines don't show a
mark for every whole number.

This line only shows every 5th whole number, which makes it easier to show larger numbers.

Mixed numbers can also appear on number lines.

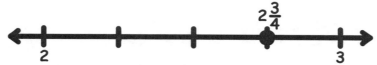

Mixed numbers can also appear
on a number line.

The marks between 2 and 3 create four segments in all, and notice that the segments are the same distance apart. That means that each segment is equal to $\frac{1}{4}$, so the dot stands for $2\frac{3}{4}$. Here's another line.

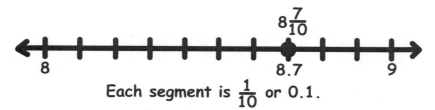

Each segment is $\frac{1}{10}$ or 0.1.

On this line, there are 10 equal segments between 8 and 9, which means that each segment is $\frac{1}{10}$ or 0.1. Since the dot is on the seventh mark, it stands for 8.7 or $8\frac{7}{10}$.

Numbers that aren't marked are still there. For instance, on the line below, 7 isn't marked, but it's there, halfway between the 6 and the 8.

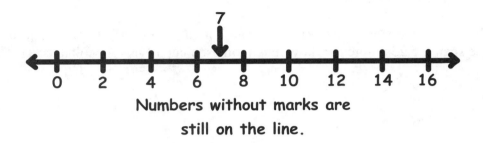

Numbers without marks are
still on the line.

Thinking about where numbers fall on a line can sometimes help you tell which of the two numbers is greater. That's because as we move to the right of 0, the numbers get bigger, and as we move toward 0, the numbers get smaller. The main point of the lesson is that we can use a line to show whole numbers, mixed numbers, fractions, and decimals, and as we move to the right of zero, the numbers get bigger.

Practice 113

a. Divide $2\overline{)315.8}$

b. Tell what number the dot stands for on the number line. _____

c. Tell what number the dot stands for on the number line. Write your answer as a mixed number. _____

Solve each word problem below.

d. When Hannah was at the ski resort, she bought 3 cups of hot chocolate in one day! If she spent $5.25 altogether, how much did each cup of hot chocolate cost? _____

e. Peek-a-Boo bought a new hammock for $32.15. If she gave the cashier $40, how much did she receive in change? _____

Problem Set 113

Tell whether each sentence below is True or False.

1. Some number lines don't show a mark for every whole number. _____

2. As we move to the right of 0 on a number line, the numbers get bigger, and as we move toward 0, the numbers get smaller. _____

Answer each question below.

3. If Junior Bullfrog has a trampoline that is 5 yards wide, how many feet is that? _____

4. If Checkers has 4 pints of juice, how many ounces is that? _____

Add or subtract (as required) each pair of numbers below. Make sure your answers are reduced.

5. $\dfrac{5}{12} - \dfrac{1}{6}$ _____

6. $9\dfrac{1}{6} + 3\dfrac{1}{6}$ _____

Add or subtract (as required) each group of fractions below, and make sure your answers are reduced.

7. $\dfrac{6}{13}+\dfrac{1}{13}+\dfrac{2}{13}$ _____

8. $\dfrac{8}{15}-\dfrac{2}{15}-\dfrac{1}{15}$ _____

Multiply each pair of numbers below in your head.

9. 9.312×100 _____

10. $0.517\times1,000$ _____

Divide each pair of numbers below in your head.

11. $6,221.7\div10$ _____

12. $215.8\div100$ _____

Multiply each pair of decimals below.

13.
$$\begin{array}{r} 3.27 \\ \times\ 5 \\ \hline \end{array}$$

14.
$$\begin{array}{r} 0.23 \\ \times\ 0.4 \\ \hline \end{array}$$

Divide each pair of numbers below.

(a) 15. $4\overline{)183.2}$

16. $3\overline{)742.8}$

For each problem below, tell what number the dot stands for on the number line.

(b) 17. _____

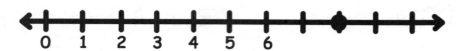

18. _____

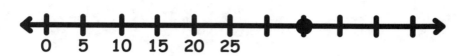

For each problem below, tell what number the dot stands for on the number line. Write your answer as a mixed number.

(c) 19. _____

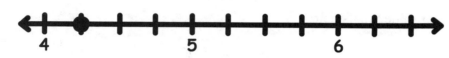

20. _____

Solve each word problem below.

(d) 21. Walter bought 7 hotdogs at the baseball game for his friends. If he spent $9.45 altogether, how much did each hotdog cost? _____

(e) 22. Ginger bought a new necklace for $23.65. If she gave the cashier $30, how much should she have received in change? _____

Lesson 114—Equations

Equations are like other problems we've done, but there are a few important differences. Here's an equation.

$$? + 4 = 9$$

Notice that the problem has an equals sign in it. All equations have equals signs. Second, the problem has a question mark, which stands for a missing number. So this equation actually means, "What number, when added to 4, equals 9?" To find the missing number, we just have to remember that 5 plus 4 equals 9. Here's another example.

$$8 + ? = 17$$

The best way to find the missing number in this equation is to figure out 17 minus 8, so the missing number is 9.

$$8 + ? = 17$$
$$17 - 8 = 9$$
$$? = 9$$

Subtract to find the answer.

Here's an equation involving subtraction. This equation is asking, "What number, when you take 3 away from it, will equal 11?"

$$? - 3 = 11$$
$$11 + 3 = 14$$
$$? = 14$$

Add to find the answer.

The best way to solve this is by adding. Here's another subtraction equation.

$$16 - ? = 9$$
$$16 - 9 = 7$$
$$? = 7$$

Subtract to find the answer.

At first, you might think that because this is a subtraction equation we need to find the missing number by adding, but the best way to find the answer in this case is to *subtract*, not add. This makes sense because the equation is just asking us what the difference between 16 and 9 is.

Here's a multiplication equation, and the question is "What number times 4 is equal to 36?"

$$? \times 4 = 36$$

If you know your multiplication tables, you know the missing number is 9. However, if you can't remember that 9 times 4 is 36, the best way to solve the problem is to use division. Solving multiplication equations with division always works.

$$? \times 4 = 36$$
$$36 \div 4 = 9$$
$$? = 9$$

Divide to find the answer.

The main point of this lesson is that equations are just like regular arithmetic problems, except they have an equals sign, and instead of being able to just add, subtract, and multiply right away, you usually have to stop and think a bit before you can figure out the answer.

Practice 114

Find the missing number in each equation below.

a. $? + 3 = 7$ _____

b. $? - 3 = 9$ _____

c. $? \times 6 = 42$ _____

Solve each word problem below.

d. Pepe wants to buy a new cape. The price tag says $20.25, but that doesn't include the tax. If the tax is 89¢, what will Pepe have to pay in dollars? _____

e. Polly has 3 flower beds in her yard. There are 25 flowers in the first flower bed, 20 in the second bed, and 21 in the third. What is the average number of flowers in each flower bed? _____

Problem Set 114

Tell whether each sentence below is True or False.

1. All equations have an equals sign. _____

2. To find the missing number in $? + 5 = 17$, you should take 5 away from 17. _____

Answer each question below.

3. If Blake has 3 gallons of frozen custard, how many quarts is that? _____

4. If Natalie's backpack weighs 9 pounds, how many ounces is that? _____

Add or subtract (as required) each group of numbers below, and make sure your answers are reduced.

5. $\dfrac{3}{10} + \dfrac{1}{5}$ _____
6. $8\dfrac{5}{7} - 5\dfrac{1}{7}$ _____

7. $\dfrac{1}{8} + \dfrac{3}{8} + \dfrac{1}{8}$ _____

Multiply each pair of numbers below in your head.

8. 58.51×10 _____
9. 1.426×100 _____

Divide each pair of numbers below in your head.

10. $319.5 \div 100$ _____

11. $425 \div 1,000$ _____

Multiply each pair of decimals below.

12. $\begin{array}{r} 6.75 \\ \times\ 9 \\ \hline \end{array}$
13. $\begin{array}{r} 0.17 \\ \times\ 0.5 \\ \hline \end{array}$

Divide each pair of numbers below.

14. $5\overline{)329.5}$ **15.** $7\overline{)415.8}$

Answer each question below.

16. Tell what number the dot stands for on the number line. _____

17. Tell what number the dot stands for on the number line. Write you answer as a mixed number. _____

Find the missing number in each equation below.

(a) 18. $? + 5 = 8$ _____   **(b) 19.** $? - 6 = 10$ _____

(c) 20. $? \times 3 = 24$ _____

Solve each word problem below.

(d) 21. Happy wants to buy an electric toothbrush. The price tag says $15.75, but that doesn't include the tax. If the tax is 82¢, what will Happy have to pay in dollars? _____

(e) 22. Phillip has 3 stacks of sports magazines. There are 26 magazines in the first stack, 28 magazines in the second stack, and 33 magazines in the third stack. What is the average number of magazines in each stack? _____

Quiz 16

Tell whether each sentence below is True or False.

1. When dividing a decimal by a whole number, the decimal point in the answer needs to go right above the decimal point in the number inside the box. _____

2. We can divide a whole number by 1,000 just by moving the decimal point three places to the right. _____

Answer each question below.

3. If Dexter has 7 quarts of the secret recipe, how many pints is that? _____

4. If Gizmo has 15 yards of duct tape, how many feet is that? _____

Add or subtract (as required) each group of numbers below. Make sure your answers are reduced.

5. $\dfrac{11}{12} - \dfrac{5}{12}$ _____

6. $\dfrac{4}{9} + \dfrac{2}{9}$ _____

7. $4\dfrac{4}{11} + 3\dfrac{3}{11}$ _____

8. $\dfrac{3}{14} + \dfrac{1}{14} + \dfrac{5}{14}$ _____

Multiply each pair of numbers below in your head.

9. 46.732×100 _____

10. 137.296×10 _____

Divide each pair of numbers below in your head.

11. $2,576.1 \div 10$ _____

12. $812.4 \div 100$ _____

Multiply each pair of decimals below.

13. $\begin{array}{r} 12.43 \\ \times\ 3 \\ \hline \end{array}$

14. $\begin{array}{r} 0.21 \\ \times\ 0.4 \\ \hline \end{array}$

Divide each pair of numbers below.

15. $8\overline{)427.2}$

16. $4\overline{)295.6}$

For each problem below, tell what number the dot stands for on the number line.

17. _____

18. _____

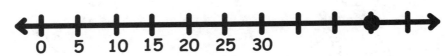

Find the missing number in each equation below.

19. $?+10=15$ _____

20. $6+?=18$ _____

21. $?-6=4$ _____

22. $?\times 7=35$ _____

Solve each word problem below.

23. Margo sold a total of 225 of her denim aprons to 5 stores. If each store bought the same number of denim aprons, how many did each buy? _____

24. Nancy bought 4 boxes of holiday cookies. If each box costs $5.96, how much did she spend in all? _____

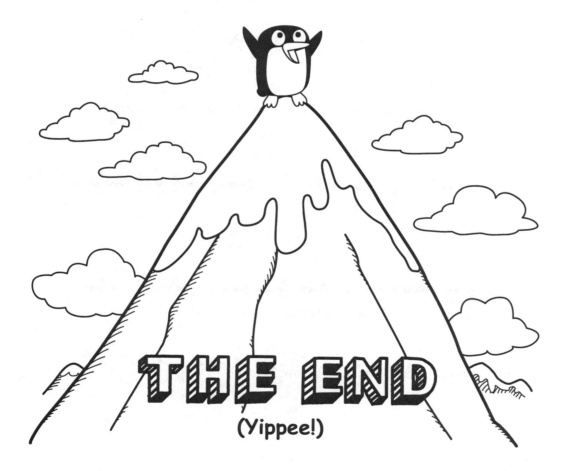

THE END
(Yippee!)